THE ANTIQUITIES OF EGYPT

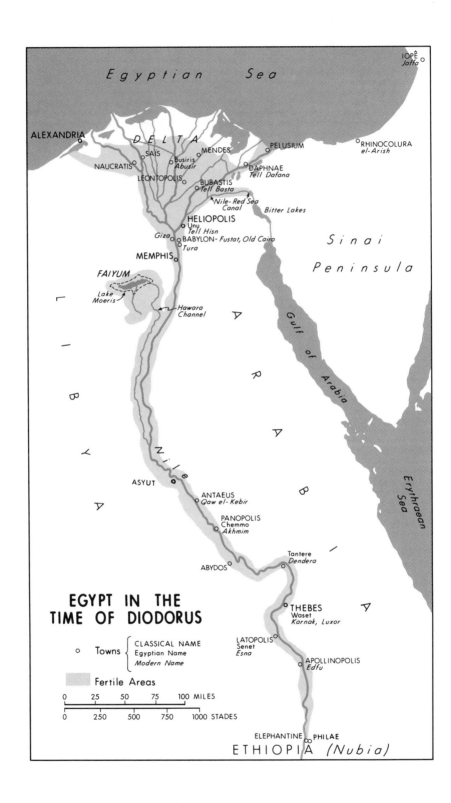

IOPÊ
Jaffa

Egyptian   Sea

ALEXANDRIA

D E L T A

MENDES

PELUSIUM

RHINOCOLURA
el-Arish

SAIS

NAUCRATIS

Busiris
Abusir

DAPHNAE
Tell Dafana

LEONTOPOLIS

BUBASTIS
Tell Basta

Nile-Red Sea
Canal

Bitter Lakes

Sinai

HELIOPOLIS
Unu
Tell Hisn

Giza

BABYLON- *Fustat, Old Cairo*
Tura

Peninsula

MEMPHIS

FAIYUM

Lake
Moeris

Hawara
Channel

Gulf

of

Arabia

A

R

A

Nile

ASYUT

ANTAEUS
Qaw el-Kebir

B

A

PANOPOLIS
Chemmo
Akhmim

Erythraean
Sea

Tantere
Dendera

ABYDOS

I

EGYPT IN THE
TIME OF DIODORUS

THEBES
Waset
Karnak, Luxor

A

LATOPOLIS
Senet
Esna

o Towns { CLASSICAL NAME
           Egyptian Name
           Modern Name

APOLLINOPOLIS
Edfu

Fertile Areas

0   25   50   75   100 MILES

0   250   500   750   1000 STADES

ELEPHANTINE   PHILAE

ETHIOPIA *(Nubia)*

THE ANTIQUITIES OF EGYPT

A Translation with Notes of Book I of the
Library of History of Diodorus Siculus

Revised and Expanded,
with Bibliography and Illustrations

Edwin Murphy

Transaction Publishers
New Brunswick (U.S.A.) and London (U.K.)

Library of Congress Catalog Number: 89-20373
ISBN: 0-88738-303-3
Printed in the United States of America

Library of Congress Cataloging-in-Publication Data

Diodorus, Siculus.
    [Bibliotheca historica. Book 1. English] The antiquities of Egypt: a translation with notes of book I of the Library of history, of Diodorus Siculus/Edwin Murphy.
        p.   cm.
    Translation of: Bibliotheca historica, book 1.
    Rev. ed. of: Diodorus "On Egypt." 1985.
    Includes bibliographical references.
    ISBN 0-88738-303-3
    1. Egypt–Civilization–To 332 B.C. 2. Egypt–Antiquities.
I. Murphy, Edwin. II. Diodorus, Siculus. Diodorus "On Egypt."
III. Title.
PA3965.D4E5   1990
932–dc20
                                                89-20373
                                                CIP

To my family

Contents

Translator's Preface

Diodorus Siculus lived in the first century before Christ, in what we now call "ancient" times. But even in his day the world was old, and many civilizations had come and gone. The oldest civilization was that of Egypt, whose past stretched back into eras so remote that they were far more ancient to Diodorus than he is to us. Diodorus wrote a history of ancient Egypt for the literate Greeks of his day. It covered the entire period from the emergence of civilization along the Nile, up to the conquest of Egypt by the Persians in 525 B.C. He also wrote of the culture, religion, laws, customs, geography, flora and fauna of Egypt in olden times, although his observations may often apply more to the Ptolemaic than to earlier eras.

Diodorus' work on Egypt was the opening book of his enormous history of the world called the *Library of History*. This veritable encyclopedia of all the known world's history consumed thirty years of Diodorus' life. Much of it survives today, but it is little known except among specialists, and often unappreciated even by them. In point of information about ancient history, Diodorus has preserved more than any other author. Why then is he so neglected?

The once fashionable view holds that Diodorus is somewhat of a bungler as an historian; that his work abounds in errors, omissions, repetitions, and contradictions. Then too, he has been charged with unoriginality, with being an uncritical compiler and plagiarizer of earlier works to which he added nothing of his own, no new insights or grand unifying themes. In fact, it is often said that there is little in Diodorus which is not covered in other writers' extant works, with the implication that the labors of the indefatigable Sicilian Greek are superfluous to the study of ancient history. Diodorus is also accused of having an uneven but generally uninspiring style of writing, and (in most cases) of adhering unwisely to an annalistic arrangement which makes it hard to follow the continuity of events as he jumps from topic to topic within a given year.

But in addition to the above criticisms, I suspect that there is just too much of Diodorus to tempt most scholars or translators. While it is true that Polybius is more accurate than Diodorus, Herodotus more interesting, Thucydides more insightful, Sallust more eloquent, and Caesar more original, the fact remains that these authors are also easier to contend with than Diodorus because their works are much shorter.

Many historians who pass critical judgment on Diodorus seem never to have read him, or at most to have read only selections. His work is just not very available in English, and few people nowadays can read

Greek well enough to attempt it in the original (which is hardly available either). The layman or student, consequently, has practically no chance of reading anything that Diodorus wrote, because Diodorus has been ignored by the scholarly community.

Yet scholarship should do more than pass judgment for the benefit of the masses. A legitimate role of scholarship is to present in usable form the raw materials from which judgments are made. Scholarship also seeks truth. If Diodorus does not measure up to the canons of accuracy demanded by modern historical research, it is far better to study him, analyse him, annotate him, comment on him, and determine where he is reliable and where he is not, than to relegate him through neglect to the dustbin of literature. For while it is true that Diodorus contains much that is mistaken, contradictory, and misleading, the same can be said of every ancient writer: it is simply a matter of degree. Like other ancient historians, Diodorus also has much that is accurate, useful, and enjoyable.

Diodorus preserves much that is valuable for the student of ancient society and history. He is often our only source for certain periods of antiquity. My aim in translating Book I of Diodorus is to make available for the general reader at least a small portion of the *Library of History*, in an English translation which is accurate but easy to read, and with enough critical notes to elucidate the text for the non-specialist and point out where some of the pitfalls lie. I hope my translation will give the reader the intellectual enjoyment of discovering something new: some fact he didn't know, some insight he didn't have, or some well-turned phrase he has never seen before.

Prefaces have a way of running on to unbearable lengths, so to speed the reader's way to the text itself, I will limit my remarks here to a short summary of Diodorus' life. Many more details about Diodorus and his work will be found in the footnotes.

Diodorus Siculus, as his name implies, was from Sicily. He was of Greek descent, although by his day the island had long been under the sway of the Romans. He lived in the first century, B.C. and was contemporary with Julius Caesar. The avowed task to which he devoted thirty years of his life was to collect all the historical knowledge of the world into one comprehensive work, the *Library of History*. Diodorus claims to have known Latin as well as Greek, and to have made use of the Roman archives. He also claims to have traveled extensively, although the only specific visits he mentions are to Egypt and Rome. Of the forty books he wrote, less than half survive. He apparently succeeded in collecting, arranging, and summarizing the historical works of most of the authors who preceded him, and he frequently quotes and credits his sources. In many cases our primary knowledge of an otherwise forgotten writer comes from the extracts, fragments, or mention of him found in the pages of Diodorus.

The opening book, *The Antiquities of Egypt* (a title that does not appear in the manuscripts) is one of the most fascinating and valuable in the whole work. As part of the first five books dealing with events prior to the Trojan war, it is not arranged annalistically like most of the *Library of History*, nor does it contain material from later Greek and Roman times well covered by other authors. Aside from the long sections of Herodotus concerning Egypt, and monographs like Plutarch's *On Isis and Osiris*, not much descriptive and historical literature on Egypt has survived except as incidental portions of works on other subjects. As factual history, *The Antiquities of Egypt* is of limited value. Diodorus shared the ignorance of his time concerning the chronology and events of ancient Egyptian history. But as a source of invaluable observations on Egyptian government, law, society, geography, religion, and natural history, the work of Diodorus deserves a place on the bookshelf of every serious student of the past.

A Note on the Translation

My first aim in translating Book I of Diodorus Siculus was to make this valuable but neglected work easily accessible and useful for nonspecialist scholars and researchers. A secondary objective was to provide a translation that is both enjoyable and profitable for that segment of the general public which still takes an interest in ancient history. I set three standards by which I judged every word, phrase, and passage in the translation. In order of importance, these standards are:

Fidelity of meaning — I strove for complete accuracy in conveying the exact thought and meaning of Diodorus from Greek into English, avoiding unnecessary paraphrase, elaboration, and interpretation in the text;

Readability — I made every effort to render Diodorus' thoughts into the best possible English prose, for I believe history should reclaim its rightful place as a province of literature;

Literalness of expression — Although a rigidly literal translation would have been incompatible with my first two standards, I retained the literal use of vocabulary, phraseology, and sentence structure whenever this did not obscure the meaning or result in barbarous English.

I did not attempt to replicate the uneven quality of Diodorus' own style. No literary purpose is served by translating awkward Greek into awkward English, or by preserving constructions permissible in one language but not in the other. The works of ancient authors too frequently are transmuted from excellent Greek or Latin into mediocre (or worse) English, and no one will object if I have tried to redress the balance a little.

To avoid incongruity, I retained Greek terms of measurement, such as cubit and talent, in the translation. These and other terms are defined in Appendix II: Terminology. Biographical and geographical names are identified in Appendix I: Proper Names, which provides an easy reference for names that appear more than once in the text or footnotes and which may not be readily familiar to some readers. This arrangement seemed preferable to an overabundance of footnotes. The footnotes themselves contain information necessary or useful to understanding passages in the text or important names and terms occurring only once.

I was not consistent in the use of *-os* or *-us* in the English termination of Greek proper nouns. The *-os* is usually more correct, the *-us* more common. Students of ancient history soon grow accustomed to seeing it either way. The same is true of *c* and *k*, *ae* and *ai*, and other diphthongs.

In transliterating Egyptian names, there is even less agreement among specialists than there is with Greek. The orthographic, diacritical, and accentual conventions are varied, and these problems are of legitimate concern to Egyptologists. But since such questions matter little to others, I hope the reader will absolve me for any errors or inconsistencies in this esoteric field of expertise.

My translation of Book II of Diodorus, *The Antiquities of Asia*, which covers the history of Assyria, Media, Arabia, Scythia, and India, is also available from Transaction Publications. Comments on the present volume are welcome. Write to me in care of the publisher.

Edwin Murphy
Arlington, Virginia
Spring 1989

The Antiquities of Egypt

(Book I of the *Library of History*)

Contents of the
First Book of Diodorus
as contained in the manuscripts

THE FOLLOWING IS IN THE FIRST BOOK OF DIODORUS:

Introduction to the whole work (chapters 1-5).

What the Egyptians say about the origin of the universe (chapters 6-7). √

About the gods who established cities in Egypt.[1]

About the first men and their earliest mode of life (chapter 8).

About the honor paid to the gods and the building of their temples.[2] √

About the topography of the land of Egypt and the wonders related of the river Nile — of the causes for its inundation, and the theories of the historians and philosophers (chapters 30ff.). √

About the first kings in Egypt and their deeds, in turn (chapters 44ff.). √

About the building of the pyramids, which are counted as one of the seven works of wonder (chapters 63ff.).

About the laws and the courts of justice (chapters 69ff.).

About the animals held sacred among the Egyptians (chapters 83ff.).

About the customs of the Egyptians concerning the dead (chapters 91ff.). √

---

1. There are no chapters specifically devoted to this topic, but only brief allusions in chapter 12 and elsewhere to cities founded by the gods.

2. There are no chapters devoted to this subject, although chapters 11-27 deal with the gods (see note 3, below).

2   Diodorus Siculus

About the many Greeks, noted for learning, who came to Egypt and brought much of the useful knowledge they acquired back to Greece (chapters 96ff.).[3]

---

3. The table of contents seems to be the work of later editors and is not fully accurate (see notes 1 and 2, above). A more useful grouping of chapters by general subject matter, leaving aside Diodorus' minor inconsistencies, repetitions, and digressions, is as follows:

Chapters 1-5   General Introduction; theory and value of universal history; apologia for the work.

Chapters 6-10   Origin of the universe, of life, of man, and of culture.

Chapters 11-27   Treatment of the gods, especially Isis and Osiris.

Chapters 28-29   Digression on Egyptian colonization.

Chapters 30-41   Geography of Egypt; the sources of the Nile; and theories about the annual inundation.

Chapter 42   Introduction to second half of the book.

Chapters 43-48   Chronological history of the kings of Egypt.

Chapters 69-95   Customs, class structure, laws, sciences, medicine, religion, and lawgivers of the Egyptians.

Chapters 96-98   The cultural debt of Greece to Egypt.

Part One

1   All men owe a just debt of gratitude to the authors of universal histories, for the individual labors of these writers have been of great service to the human race. In the first place, their systematic treatment of world history presents the reader with a trouble-free education in useful knowledge and preserves for his benefit an excellent fund of experiences. Of course, through personal experience alone, one may eventually attain the wisdom of discerning what is useful, but only at the expense of much toil and peril; for this indeed is just what Odysseus did, the most worldly-wise of all our heroes, who after great travail

> Had seen the towns and known the minds of many men.
> [*Odyssey* 1.3]

Yet one may also gain this knowledge, without all the pains, by a thorough acquaintance with history and by studying the successes and failures of others.

Secondly, universal historians, as if they were agents of Divine Providence, attempt to encompass all men in a unified system, since all men indeed share a common ancestry despite being separated by time and space. For just as Divine Providence reduces both the paths of the stars and the destinies of men to a single interconnected system, and operates unceasingly for all eternity, allotting to every person whatever falls to his fate, so also these historians have published their works, recording the affairs of all the world just as if they were the annals of a single city, or a common public register for all that has occurred. And in truth, what a blessing it is to be able to use the mistakes of others as examples for our own guidance and to have no doubt what to do, when confronting the vicissitudes of life, but to imitate past successes. Again, everyone prefers the counsels of the aged, because of their greater length of experience, to the advice of youngsters; yet the experience of the aged is as far surpassed by the lessons of history as we see history excels it also in wealth of examples. Therefore one might say that the study of history is of enormous value in all the circumstances of life: it preserves the wisdom of age for the benefit of the young, and for the elderly themselves it multiplies their fund of experience; it renders commoners fit to command, and inspires commanders to essay deeds of the noblest virtue for the sake of undying fame; besides this, it makes soldiers more willing to face danger in their country's defense, by the prospect of posthumous glory; and finally, it dissuades wicked men from their love of vice through the certainty of everlasting infamy.

2   And often, it is because their noble achievements will be commemorated by history that some men have been prompted to found cities; others to frame laws protecting the security of society; and many avidly to seek new arts and sciences of benefit to the race of men. But since complete happiness comes from all such things, one must accord the highest tribute to the principal motivation behind them, that is, to history, which one may regard as a repository for the virtues of the noble, a witness against the vices of the wicked, and the benefactor of mankind in general. For if in truth the myth (whose substance is false) about those in Hades contributes greatly to piety and justice among men, by how much more must one suppose that history, the prophetess of truth and the metropolis, as it were, of the whole realm of philosophy, is able to influence morals towards goodness and virtue?   Man, in the frailty of his nature, lives but a moment of eternity and is dead forever after; and for those who achieve nothing of note in their lives, all else concerning their existence perishes along with their bodies, and at the same time; but the deeds of those who attain fame through their virtue are remembered for all time, proclaimed by the most holy voice of history.

I find it sublime that noble men may purchase eternal renown by their earthly labors. For instance, it is well known that Heracles, in all the time he spent among men, voluntarily endured great and never-ending toil and danger so that, by conferring benefits on the race of men, he might gain immortality.[4] And of other famous men, some have achieved

---

4. Heracles (or Hercules) performed the legendary twelve labors for king Eurystheus of Tiryns; although ordered by his father, Zeus, to perform all that Eurystheus might command, Heracles had assurances from the Pythoness of Delphi that immortality would be his reward.

the glory of heroes, others the divine honor of gods; and all are held in high esteem because history still perpetuates their virtue. For other memorials last but a short while and are obliterated by many accidents; but the power of history extends over all the inhabited world, and time, which ravages all else, is the guardian of its everlasting transmission to posterity.

History also increases the value of language, than which a more exalted thing may not easily be found. It is in speech that the Greeks excel the barbarians and the learned surpass the ignorant, and, in addition to this, by eloquence alone is it possible for one man to prevail over the multitude; and indeed all subjects of public debate appear but in such a light as the power of the orator may present them. It is thus we call good men "worth speaking about" [*axiologos*], as if in this they have attained the pinnacle of excellence. But dissecting language into its various categories, we find that poetry is more delightful than useful, that the laws correct rather than instruct, and that likewise the other departments of speech either contribute nothing to our happiness, or contain a measure of harm along with their benefits, and in some cases substitute lies for the truth. But history alone, in which words agree with deeds, comprehends in its writing all else that is useful, for we see it encouraging justice, praising the good, arraigning the wicked, and, in short, preserving for its readers the most exemplary experiences.

3   Therefore, seeing the well-deserved praises bestowed upon writers of universal histories, we were moved by a spirit of emulation to follow the same course. Yet turning our mind to the historians who had gone before us, while we fully commended their intentions, we found their works less usefully contrived than they might have been. For whereas the advantage to the reader lies in encountering the greatest number and diversity of situations, yet most writers have described only the isolated wars of one people or a single city. Few begin from ancient times and endeavor to write of worldwide affairs down to their own day; and of those who do, some fail to assign the correct date to each event, some ignore the affairs of the barbarians, yet others reject the ancient myths because the subject is perplexing, and some, their lives cut short by fate, do not complete their attempted design. And of those who have adopted the universal approach, not one has carried his history beyond the Macedonian era, for some close their accounts with the exploits of Philip, some with those of Alexander, and others with the

Diadochi or the Epigoni;[5] yet many and important are the affairs subsequent to these, right down to our own lifetime, which are neglected by the historians, none of whom, because of the extent of the subject matter, has essayed to treat of them in the course of a single work. As a result, since both the dates and events lie scattered through many works and various authors, it is hard to sort them into a larger perspective and difficult to remember them.

Therefore, having studied the systems of each of these writers, we determined to undertake a method of historical research offering both the greatest utility and the least inconvenience to our readers. For if one writes of the affairs handed down to memory over all the world as if they were those of a single city, commencing with the most remote periods and continuing as far as possible until his own time, even though he should endure much hard work, yet he will create a book more useful than any other to those fond of reading. From such a treatise it is possible for anyone to extract with ease whatever is pertinent to his own design, as if drawing water from a copious spring. For in the first place, those attempting to examine in detail the narratives of so many historians find it difficult to get possession of the books they happen to need; then too, the reconstruction of past events is hard to follow or understand perfectly because of the large number of books and their diversity of opinions. But a book having the chronicles of affairs systematized in one outline affords effortless reading and makes the reconstruction of the past perfectly easy to grasp. And in general, you may be sure this approach to history is as much superior to the others as continuity is to discontinuity, or as the whole is more useful than its parts; and in addition to this, events discussed with precise regard for time sequence are preferable to those for which the dates are unknown.

4   Therefore, seeing that this proposed undertaking would be of the greatest utility, yet would require much time and effort, we have labored upon it these thirty years. With great toil and danger we have visited many parts of Asia and Europe, so that we might be eyewitnesses of the most essential and most important places therein; for many historians,

---

5. The Diadochi were the Macedonian kings who first succeeded to the dismembered parts of Alexander the Great's empire after his death in 323 B.C. The final winners after forty years of savage warfare and shifting alliance were Antigonus (posthumously through his grandson) in Macedonia, Seleucus in Asia, and Ptolemy in Egypt. The Epigoni were the second and subsequent generations of kings in these "successor kingdoms."

and not just the commonplace ones but also some of excellent repute, have gone astray through their ignorance of locale.[6]

As mainstays in our attempt we have relied especially on our enthusiasm for the work (by which tasks that seem difficult to all men are brought to completion), and secondly on the wealth of pertinent resource material existing in Rome. Indeed, the hegemony of this city, extending in might to the limits of the known world, supplied us, during our sojourn there, with numerous and convenient sources of information. For we are from Agyrium in Sicily, and through our intercourse with the Romans in that island we attained great familiarity with their language; we thus accurately extracted all the circumstances of the Romans' ascendancy from their own ancient records. But we will begin our history with the mythic stories told among both Greeks and barbarians, having examined minutely, as far as possible, the historical records of every nation concerning ancient times.

My book being now complete, though the volumes are as yet unpublished, I wish as a preface to briefly outline the work as a whole. Our first six books treat of the facts and myths prior to the Trojan War; and of these the first three cover the early history of the barbarians, and the next three mainly that of the Greeks; in the subsequent eleven books we have described world events after the Trojan War down to the death of Alexander; and in the following three and twenty books we have arranged in order all remaining occurrences until the beginning of the war the Romans waged against the Celts, in which the commander Gaius Julius Caesar, who has been deified for his achievements, overcame the most numerous and warlike of the Celtic tribes and extended the dominion of Rome as far as the British Isles. The opening campaign in this war took place during the first year [60/59 B.C.] of the

---

6. There is no reason to doubt that Diodorus worked on his massive compendium for thirty years, as he proudly boasts. In I.44, Diodorus says the Macedonians had ruled Egypt for 276 years, which means this part of his work received its final revision no later than 55 B.C.; in XVI.7 Diodorus mentions the Roman colonization of Tauromenium in Sicily, which probably took place in 36 B.C., the latest datable event mentioned in the surviving portions of the *Library of History*. So it is certain that Diodorus worked on his book for at least nineteen years. His extensive travels and researches undoubtedly took years, although he does not specifically mention visits to any places besides Sicily, Rome, and Egypt, and he himself displays some of the "ignorance of locale" which he deplores in other historians (for instance, he incorrectly places Nineveh on the Euphrates River). His visit to Egypt is certain to have included the year 60/59 B.C.; see chapter 83 below, note 162.

One Hundred and Eightieth Olympiad, when Herodes was archon at Athens.[7]

5   We cannot define with precision the chronology for those periods in our history prior to the War of Troy, since we have found no reliable annals for those times. But after the Trojan War, following Apollodorus the Athenian, we calculate it was eighty years until the return of the Heracleidae, then three hundred and twenty-eight years more until the First Olympiad (reckoning the time by the Lacedaemonian king lists), and finally from the First Olympiad to the commencement of the Celtic War, which we have made the terminus of our history, seven hundred and thirty years. Thus, our entire work in forty books covers eleven hundred and thirty-eight years, not counting the periods comprising events before the Trojan War.[8]

We have given this exact outline in advance for two reasons: first, to afford our readers an idea of the work as a whole; and second, to discourage those, whose practice is to edit books for publication, from ruining the works of another.[9] But throughout our entire history, let no

---

7. Since Caesar was deified in 44 B.C., Diodorus must have completed work on his preface no earlier than this date. The first year of Caesar's Gallic War was 58 B.C., not 60/59 B.C. as Diodorus states. Perhaps Diodorus was confused because the *Lex Vatinia*, which conferred Caesar's command of Cisalpine Gaul, was passed in 59 B.C. For the term Olympiad see Appendix II, Terminology. The archonship at Athens was an annual magistracy sometimes used by Greek writers as a chronological reference, just as the Romans used their annual list of consuls.

8. Diodorus makes an obvious error in arithmetic here. The First Olympiad ended in 780/779 B.C., and the Gallic War began in 58 B.C. (60/59 B.C. according to Diodorus, see note 7, above). But the difference is not 730 years, as Diodorus computes it, but 721 years. Apollodorus the Athenian, whom Diodorus followed, placed the fall of Troy in 1184 B.C., and this date, which was the most widely accepted scholarly estimate in Diodorus' day, agrees remarkably well with the archaeological record. The Heracleidae, or descendants of Heracles, made several unsuccessful attempts to recover the rule of the Peloponnese, which they considered their patrimony. The complex legends surrounding this quest seem to incorporate historical aspects of the Dorian conquest of the Achaeans. The return of the Heracleidae was successfully accomplished at last, in 1104 B.C. according to Apollodorus.

9. Apparently some of Diodorus' work was published in a pirated, possibly abbreviated version before he had completely finished his entire set of forty books. He complains of this in book XL. St. Jerome's *Chronology* refers to a publication date of 49 B.C., and since the existing version includes events as late

one envy what is written well, and let those who are more able correct our ignorance. And having now completed what we intended, we shall attempt to fulfill the promises of this introduction.

6   Albeit those who first instituted divine worship held certain opinions about the gods, in our account we shall forgo a lengthy treatment of their thoughts, and of the myths surrounding each deity, since such an undertaking would exhaust too many words; we shall briefly summarize only as much of this as we deem appropriate to our intended histories, that nothing worth hearing may be left out. Of the entire race of men, on the contrary, and of its exploits in the known parts of the inhabited world from the most ancient times, we shall write as complete an account as possible for times so remote.

Now two different opinions have grown up among the most learned of the natural philosophers and historians concerning the origin of man. On one hand, those who propound a universe without end or beginning reason that mankind too has existed from all eternity, nor had his existence ever a beginning. But conversely, those who view the universe as finite and perishable acknowledge that, in like manner, man had his origin at a specific point in time.[10]

7   For in the chaos at the beginning of the universe, the elements of heaven and earth were thoroughly intermixed and constituted a single entity; but later, when their substances had disengaged from one another, the earth took on the overall permanence that we see, while the air commenced its unceasing motion. Air's fiery element, borne aloft by its extremely buoyant nature, ascended to the highest regions of the atmosphere, which is how the sun and all the multitudes of other stars came to be part of the revolving vault of heaven. But the muddy and turbid element, loaded with moisture, settled down through its weight into one plane where, agitated ceaselessly and condensing, its waters became the seas, and its more solid constituents formed a land mass of uniformly soft and clay-like consistency. First, from the sun's fiery rays beating down upon it, this land acquired solidity; then, its surface in

---

as 44 B.C. and perhaps 36 B.C., it is possible that Jerome refers to an early unauthorized edition.

10.   Aristotle and the early Peripatetic school of philosophers taught that the universe, including the human race, had always existed. The Stoics opposed this view.

ferment from the heat, part of its remaining moisture congealed in numerous places where, encompassed in delicate membranes, it began to incubate. (One can see this occurring yet today in marshes and stagnating swamps, whenever the air over a chilly countryside suddenly becomes hot without a gradual change.) The life forms, generated from the moisture in this manner by the heat, took nourishment directly from the mists descending out of the surrounding atmosphere by night, and gained solidity from the burning heat by day. Finally, the embryos having reached their full gestation, their overheated membranes ruptured, and animals of all kinds were free to grow.[11]   Those which had absorbed the most heat had wings and ascended into the air, while those which kept a more earthlike nature were reckoned among the class of reptiles and other terrestrial creatures; finally, those which had partaken mostly of the watery humour gravitated to the corresponding places and are known as aquatic animals. But the earth, baked ever more solid by winds and the blaze of sun, at last was able no longer to generate a single one of the larger animals; yet each species was perpetuated by sexual intercourse among its members.

And it seems Euripides, a disciple of Anaxagoras the natural philosopher, does not contradict our account of the nature of the universe, for in his *Melanippe* he puts it thus:

> Heaven and earth in form were as one,
> But when they were cleft from each other asunder
> They brought forth all things to the light of the sun:
> The beasts of the sea; the trees, birds, and men.
>
> [Frag. 488, Nauck.]

---

11.   Diodorus alludes to the concept of spontaneous generation, or the propagation of living things from inanimate materials. The idea was widely accepted in classical antiquity. Plutarch, for example, in his biography of Agis and Cleomenes, mentions the generation of bees from the rotting corpses of oxen, wasps from horses, beetles from asses, and serpents from men. Sextus Empiricus (*Outlines of Pyrrhonic Philosophy* I.41) gives a list of creatures spontaneously generated and the substances from which they supposedly issue. Belief in spontaneous generation, especially the creation of animals from the fertile alluvial mud of the Nile, long persisted. In *The Compleat Angler*, A.D. 1653, Isaak Walton marvels at it (chapter XVIII); in other parts of his book he credulously describes weeds which become pike (chapter VIII) and cites Pliny for his authority that insects are congealed from dew through the heat of the sun.

8   The foregoing, then, is what we are told about the first beginning of the universe. As for the first-born men, it is said they endured a precarious and subhuman existence. They roamed about individually in search of food, plucking the most digestible plants and natural fruits from the trees. The attacks of wild beasts taught them the advantage of mutual assistance; and, once thrown together by fear, they gradually came to recognize each other's features. Then, from inarticulate and confused sounds, they little by little refined their power of speech: they agreed with each other on verbal symbols for everything they encountered and made the meaning of all words clear among themselves. But with such conventions arising all over the world, every group spoke a different language, since each one chose its vocabulary at random. In this way all the different varieties of human speech came about, and these first existing societies were the origin of every nation.

With none of the useful things of life as yet discovered, these first men lived but miserably. They were innocent of clothes, unacquainted with houses or fire, and lacking the very notion of cultivated food. In fact, ignorant even of how to store their wild foodstuffs, they made no stockpile of provisions against future needs, wherefore many perished in the winters from cold and lack of food. But in the course of time, taught by experience, they sought the shelter of caves for the winter and put aside for later use those foods capable of being preserved. And, after gaining knowledge of fire and other conveniences, by degrees they discovered the arts and other things of advantage to human existence. For generally speaking, necessity itself served as man's tutor in all things, and she grudged not her lessons on all subjects to a creature naturally adept and having the benefit of hands, speech, and shrewdness of mind in all endeavors.[12]

---

12.   Two opposite traditions coexisted in the Greek world to explain the origin of culture. The mythological apparatus of a divine or heroic culture-bringer such as Prometheus competed with the rational idea, espoused by Diodorus, of a natural development of culture in response to external stimuli. Both traditions agree on humanity's advance from an original state of primitive misery, which is in opposition to the far earlier poetic concept, found in Homer and Hesiod, of a steady descent from a "Golden Age" in remote antiquity. Although dutifully reporting Egyptian mythological explanations of the origins of things (or rather the Hellenized interpretation of these myths), Diodorus consistently favors rational explanations, as in this chapter, for the beginning of speech, discovery of fire, origin of culture, and the like. (See note 26, below.)

But, to observe reasonable proportions in our work, we shall let what has already been said of man's beginnings and earliest way of life suffice us.

9   Now we shall attempt to relate in detail the events that have occurred in the known parts of the world and have been handed down to posterity.

However, we ourselves have nothing to say about who were the first kings, nor do we agree with those historians who profess to know; for it is impossible that the invention of writing was so ancient as to be contemporary with the first kings. Even if one were to concede this possibility, it is plainly evident that the profession of writing history is but a recent addition to human society. Now concerning the antiquity of each race, not only do the Greeks differ, but also many of the barbarians, all declaring themselves to be autochthonous and the first of all mankind to have discovered life's useful inventions; and all consider their own achievements the earliest to be worthy of public record. But we can determine neither the real age of every race, nor which nations antedate the others chronologically or by how many years, so we shall merely cover briefly, keeping reasonable proportions, what each group has to say about its own remote beginnings and ancient history. We shall first discuss the barbarians; not that we hold them more ancient than the Greeks, as Ephorus says, but because we wish to relate most of what pertains to them beforehand; then, when we come to the records of the Greeks, we need not intermix any extraneous matters with their ancient histories. Therefore, since the myths place the origins of the gods in Egypt, and the earliest observations of the stars are said to have been made there; and since, in addition, many remarkable achievements of mighty men are there preserved, we shall begin our history with the affairs of Egypt.

10   Indeed, the Egyptians claim that in the beginning, at the birth of the universe, the first men came into existence in Egypt, thanks to the beneficent climate of the country and to the nature of the Nile. For the marvelous fecundity of this river, with its naturally occurring food supply, lavishly sustains animate life. Both the lotus and the root of the reed, as well as the Egyptian bean and the plant called "corsaeum," and many other plants such as these provide a ready-made source of food for the race of men.[13]   And they would offer this proof that animal life as well first arose in Egypt: that even now the soil of the Thebaid still occasionally engenders so many large mice that those seeing it are dumbfounded; some of these mice have form and movement down to the breast and forepaws, while the rest of their bodies are shapeless, still retaining the nature of lumps of dirt. It is evident from this fact that, at the first formation of the world, men originated in the land of Egypt, whose soil was created of such exceeding fertility.   For even today, though no other land engenders anything of the kind, in Egypt alone can living things be seen miraculously propagated.[14]

During the flood in Deucalion's time,[15] some say, the inhabitants of southern Egypt alone were saved, since their country is almost wholly rainless, while most living things were destroyed; others contend that all animate life perished, that the earth later was replenished anew with animal species, and that the rebirth of life obviously began in Egypt. For when the rain falling among other peoples encounters the blazing heat prevalent among the Egyptians, this mixture not surprisingly renders the climate most congenial to the generation of all kinds of living things.[16] Even in our day, during flood time in Egypt, life forms can plainly be seen taking shape in the last of the flood waters; for, they say, when the sun has thoroughly dried the surface of the mire, animals are spontaneously generated. Some reach their full animate state while others, but half-formed, remain encumbered in the clods of earth.

---

13.   Corsaeum: the tuber of the water lily. The Egyptian bean is the species *Nelumbium speciosum*, which along with the lotus is described more fully in chapter 34. Diodorus also describes the preparation of marsh plants for food in chapter 80.

14.   For spontaneous generation of life, see note 11, above.

15.   There were a number of flood stories in Hellenic myth, such as the Ogygian and others, besides the well-known flood of Deucalion. The son of Prometheus, Deucalion was king of Phthia in Thessaly when Zeus sent a flood to punish mankind for the human sacrifice and cannibalism practiced by Lycaon's sons. Deucalion and his wife survived the deluge. At their request, Zeus repopulated the earth by turning stones into women and men.

16.   ". . . the rain falling among other peoples," i.e., and flowing via the Nile into Egypt. Egypt is practically rainless; the Nile is the main source of water, and Diodorus here assumes correctly that it originates from the rain falling among other peoples and flowing north into Egypt. There, its encounter with the "blazing heat" helps explain the spontaneous generation mentioned in the previous paragraph. Diodorus covers the origin of the Nile more fully in chapter 37.

11   Now when the ancient Egyptians, awestruck and wondering, turned their eyes to the heavens, they concluded that two gods, the sun and the moon, were primeval and eternal; and they called the former Osiris, the latter Isis, assigning each of these names according to some relevant characteristic. For, translating these appellations into the Greek idiom, Osiris is the "many-eyed," and quite properly so; for he spreads everywhere his rays, as if to observe with many eyes all the land and sea.[17] Even the poet expresses his agreement with this conceit:

> The Sun, who sees and hears all things.[18]

Some of the early Greek mythologists call Osiris "Dionysus" and also, changing the word slightly, "Sirius;" of these, Eumolpos in his Bacchanalian verses says:

> Dionysus shining like a star, eyes aflame with rays.[19]

And writes Orpheus;

> For that reason they call him "Bright" and "Dionysus."
> [Frag. 237, Kern.]

---

17.   Diodorus may have been close in his etymology of Osiris = the many-eyed; it is generally thought that the Egyptian name means "seat of the eye." But Diodorus wrongly ascribes to Osiris both his antiquity and his association in olden days with the sun. At first a local deity of the eastern Delta, possibly derived from the Babylonian god Asari (=Marduk), Osiris does not seem to have enjoyed widespread worship before the Fifth Dynasty, c. 2400 B.C. Originally a god of the dead, he grew in importance and only later acquired some of the solar aspects of Ammon-Re', as well as many fertility characteristics.

18.   "The poet" was, of course, Homer. This line appears frequently, such as in *Iliad* 3.277 and *Odyssey* 12.323.

19.   The Greeks of the Hellenistic period made heroic and ingenious attempts to rationalize and reconcile the mass of confusing and complex myths they found in their own and in foreign cultures. This syncretism reached extraordinary lengths and, to modern laymen who have not specialized in the study of mythology, the results are more confusing than ever. Diodorus attempts, wherever possible, to trace familiar Greek gods and heroes back to some Egyptian prototype; sometimes, as with Dionysus and Osiris, their similarity of attributes and stories is so marked that Diodorus uses the two names almost interchangeably. But little of his thinking is original, and he seems to reflect ideas common in his day among the Alexandrian schools.

And some also attribute to him the spotted fawnskin cloak, in token of the splendor of stars surrounding the sun.[20]   Now Isis, in translation, signifies "ancient" — a name bestowed for her ancient and immortal origin.[21]   They depict horns on her head, both from the moon's horned appearance when in its crescent, and because the horned cow is sacred to her among the Egyptians.

The Egyptians believe that these gods regulate the entire universe, all life being nourished and multiplied by their three seasons, whose imperceptible advances complete each yearly round: the spring, summer, and winter times; which, though of completely different natures, together comprise the year in perfect harmony.   Furthermore, most of the elements essential to the propagation of life come from these gods: fire and spirit from the sun, the wet and dry elements from the moon, and the air from both together.   Through these elements all things are begotten and nurtured, and thus all parts of the entire "body" of nature are, through sun and moon, sustained; for, just as on a man we distinguish the head, hand, foot, and other members, so too the "body" of the universe consists of the five components just mentioned, namely the spirit and the fire, the dry and the wet, and lastly the airy element.[22]

12   Each of these things they esteem a god, and the first men of Egypt to use intelligent speech assigned naturally suitable names to

---

20.   The spots on the fawnskin represented the stars and Osiris himself the sun. The Greeks commonly depicted Dionysus wearing a fawnskin cloak.

21.   This etymology has little merit. An Egyptian word *ís* means "old." But in Egyptian, the goddess' name is *As-t*, and her hieroglyph represents a seat or throne.

22.   In this passage, and continuing in chapter 12 which follows, Diodorus has reference to the Aristotelian doctrine of four basic elements of nature, namely fire; earth (the "dry" element); water (the "wet"); and air. To these four elements, whose shifting combinations constitute all physical matter, Diodorus adds a fifth, the spirit, sometimes known as the ethereal element. The elements were thought seldom to exist in a pure state, but always in some degree of intermixture. In general, however, they tended to arrange themselves concentrically in successive spheres, with earth as the heaviest element, cold and dry, at the center; followed by water, air, fire, and ether. Although widely believed in antiquity (and well beyond into the Middle Ages), the theory of the four elements was not universally accepted. Lucretius, a contemporary of Diodorus, disparages it roundly in Book I, lines 705-829 of *De Rerum Natura*. The four elements were not a feature of ancient Egyptian thought, as Diodorus wrongly asserts, but a late Hellenistic import.

every one. Thus the spirit they named "Zeus" (translated from their language), who, being the life-giving principle in all creatures, they considered to be, in a way, the father of all. They assert that even Homer, the most famous of all Greek poets, agrees with them, referring frequently to "The father of men and gods."

Next is the fire, which they call, in our language, "Hephaestos," holding him a great god with pervasive influence on the genesis and development of all that lives. And they conceive of the earth as a sort of womb for all life, denoting it the "mother." Similarly, the Greeks designate the earth as "Demeter." This name evolved as the language developed; for our ancestors called her "ge meter" [earth-mother], even as Orpheus testifies when he says:

> Earth, mother of all; Demeter the font of riches.
>
> [Frag. 302, Kern.]

Now the primitive Egyptians, they say, named the moist element "Oceanê," which translates as "nourishing mother," though some of the Greeks understand it to mean the Oceanus of whom the poet says:

> Oceanus, source of gods, and Tethys too, their mother.
>
> [*Iliad*, 14.302]

For the Egyptians hold Oceanus to be their river Nile, from whence they derive the origins of their gods.[23] For throughout the entire habitable world, only in Egypt are there numerous cities founded by the primeval gods, such as those of Zeus, Helios, Hermes, Apollo, Pan, Eileithyia, and many others.

The air, it is said, they named Athena (translated from their language); and they considered her Zeus' daughter and a virgin, because the air is naturally pure and occupies the highest place in the whole universe; hence the myth arose that Athena was born from the brow of Zeus. And she was styled "Tritogeneia" [thrice-born] from changing her nature thrice each year: spring, summer, and winter. She is also called "blue-

---

23.   The Egyptian name for the Nile was *Hep* or *Hapi*, probably a predynastic word for "river." Dynastic era texts state that Nunu, the primeval water of the abyss, was the "Father of the Gods."

eyed," not, as some of the Greeks have held, because she has blue eyes — for this is simpleminded — but from the sky's bluish cast.[24]

And they say these above-mentioned five gods do visit all the inhabited world, revealing themselves to men in the form of sacred animals, sometimes adopting even the appearance of men or divers other beings; nor is this merely fabulous, but entirely possible, if in truth these gods are the source of all life. Thus the poet, visiting Egypt and hearing such reports from the priests, somewhere in his works writes of them as true:

> And gods in alien forms from foreign shores
> The cities haunt in several shapes
> To see alike the perfidy, and righteousness, of man.
>
> [*Odyssey* 17.485-7]

This, then, is what the Egyptians say about the heavenly and eternal gods.

13   But they say other gods, having once been mortal, were born on earth and attained immortality through wisdom and benevolence to all mankind; and some of them had been kings of Egypt. Translated, some of their names are identical to those of the celestial gods; but some have names of their own, for example Helios, Kronos, Rhea, and Zeus (the one called Ammon by some), and also Hera, Hephaestos, Hestia, and finally Hermes.

Now Helios, with the same name as the sun, was the first of these to reign in Egypt, although some of the priests claim Hephaestos ruled before him, having been the discoverer of fire and having earned the sovereignty through this service to mankind.[25]   For when, one winter,

---

24.   Homer usually used the epithet "glaucopis" in reference to Athena. The word can also mean gleaming-eyed or grey-eyed (the word glaucoma derives from the same root). Diodorus' explanation of Tritogeneia is farfetched. The more usual derivation is from either lake Tritonis in Libya or the river Triton in Boeotia, alternative sites claimed as her place of birth.

25.   The oldest Egyptian accounts support Diodorus' contention that a god identified with the sun was the first ruler of Egypt. This deity, also usually seen as the creator, was Re', variously called Re'-Harakhty or Re'-Atum. As sun god, he was naturally identified with the Greek god Helios. Manetho, an Egyptian priest who lived about two centuries before Diodorus, wrote a history of Egypt widely known in antiquity, but surviving now only in fragments; he records

Hephaestos came upon a mountain tree struck by lightning with the surrounding forest ablaze, he enjoyed the warmth immensely; and, throwing on wood to sustain the expiring flame, he invited other men to the enjoyment of this find.[26]   Next ruled Kronos; and, having married his sister Rhea he begat, according to some mythographers, Osiris and Isis, but according to most of them Zeus and Hera who, through their virtue, came to rule the entire universe.   And of them five gods were born, one on each of the five days intercalated by the Egyptians.   Their names were Osiris and Isis, Typhon, Apollo, and Aphrodite.   Translated, Osiris is Dionysus, and Isis corresponds most closely with Demeter. Osiris married Isis and, having succeeded to the kingdom, accomplished many things of benefit to humanity.[27]

Hephaestos (Ptah in the Egyptian pantheon) as the first king in the reign of the gods, and his son Helios (Re') as the second. It may be that Manetho's lost *Aegyptiaca* was Diodorus' source for his statement that "some of the priests claim Hephaestos ruled before [Helios]...." Eusebius (*Praepar. Evang.* III.2) implies that most of Diodorus I.11-13 is a summary of Manetho, "who writes on this subject at great length."

26.   This does not reflect the traditional Greek tale of Prometheus and his gift of fire, nor does it seem to be an authentic Egyptian belief. Except for naming Hephaestos as the specific agent of discovery, this story closely parallels the naturalistic rationalization for the advent of fire as told by Vitruvius (*De Architectura* II.1): "The men of old were born like wild beasts, in woods, caves, and groves, and lived on savage fare. As time went on, the thickly crowded trees in a certain place, tossed by storms and winds, and rubbing their branches against one another, caught fire, and so the inhabitants of the place . . . drew near; and observing that they were very comfortable standing before the warm fire, they put on logs and, while thus keeping it alive, brought up other people to it, showing them by signs how much comfort they got from it." Vitruvius attributes the development of language and culture to the gatherings of men around their new-found campfires.

27.   For the Egyptian calendar, see chapter 50 and note 102, below. In one of several versions, the five gods born on the extra-monthly days of the solar year were Osiris on the first day, Seth (Greek: Typhon) on the second, Harmachis on the third, Isis on the fourth, and Nephthys on the fifth. Here Diodorus equates Apollo with Harmachis, which is unusual, and Aphrodite with Nephthys, although the goddess Hathor was the more commonly accepted Egyptian counterpart of Aphrodite. The Pyramid Texts substitute Haroeris for Harmachis and give a different order of birth on these five epagomenal days. Other identifications, highly tentative, are: Kronos and Rhea = Shu and Tefenet; Zeus and Hera = Geb and Nut. (However, Zeus was more usually equated with Ammon.)

14   For instance, he was the first to dissuade the human race from cannibalism: for after Isis had discovered the value of the wheat and barley which happened to be growing among the other grasses about the country, unappreciated by man, and Osiris had perfected their cultivation, all men were content to change their fare, both because of their delight in the quality of the new foods, and because it seemed wise to abstain from mutual savagery.   And as proof of the discovery of these food grains, the Egyptians point out the age-old custom they still observe: for even yet, at harvest time, the first-mown ears having been offered in sacrifice, the people gather around the sheaf to smite themselves and invoke Isis.   They do this to render praise to the goddess for her gifts, in the season appropriate to their first discovery.   Besides this, in some cities during the festivals of Isis, stalks of wheat and barley are borne in procession among the other cult objects in memory of these ingenious discoveries of the goddess in days of old.[28] Moreover, they tell how Isis established laws which encourage men to deal justly with each other and to refrain from unlawful violence and outrage through fear of punishment; for which reason the earliest Greeks called Demeter "Law-giver" [Thesmophorus], since she gave men the first laws.

15   Osiris, they report, founded in the Thebaid (the one in Egypt) a city with a hundred gates, which his contemporaries named after his mother, but which later generations call Diospolis [City of Zeus] and some call Thebes.   But the founding of this city is the occasion of a dispute, not only among historians, but even among the Egyptian priests themselves.   For many of them record that Thebes was established, not by Osiris, but many years later by another king about whom we will write in turn at the proper time.[29]   Osiris also dedicated to his parents,

---

28.   The cult of Isis spread to many parts of the Roman empire in the early years of our era.   In Book II of *The Golden Ass*, Lucius Apuleius recounts a procession at Cenchris in honor of Isis, and he enumerates many of the cult objects borne by the participants, such as a lamp, an altar, a golden palm tree, and a wine cup.   No ears of wheat are mentioned, but only a winnowing fan.   But this procession marked the festival of the opening of the sailing season, not the harvest festival described by Diodorus.

29.   See chapter 45, below, where Busiris is credited with founding Thebes. Diospolis is Greek, for "city of Zeus."   In the Egyptian language the city was called *níwt 'Imn*, or *níwt nt 'Imn* (*Waset* for short), meaning city of Ammon. Since the Greeks usually equated Zeus with Ammon, Diospolis is a literal Greek

Zeus and Hera, a temple remarkable both in size and richness, as well as two golden sanctuaries of Zeus, the larger for the heavenly god, the smaller for their father the king, whom some call Ammon. He also erected golden chapels to the other gods mentioned above, ordained rites for each of them, and appointed officiating priests. Osiris and Isis also honored those who discovered any of the arts or perfected any useful skills; thus, mines of copper and gold having been discovered in the Thebaid, men forged implements with which, hunting down the wild beasts and cultivating the soil, they vied in their efforts to tame the land. They also fashioned statues of the gods and resplendent golden sanctuaries.

Osiris was also a proponent of agriculture. A son of Zeus, he was raised at Nysa, in Arabia Felix not far from Egypt; in fact, the name Dionysus, which he bears among the Greeks, derives from both his father and the locale.[30]   Our poet, in his hymns, alludes to Nysa's proximity to Egypt when he says:

> There is a certain Nysa, wooded mount most high,
> In Phoenicê afar, near Egypt's watery stream.
>
> [*Homeric Hymns* 1.8-9]

It was near Nysa, they say, that he discovered the grape vine, and, having gone on to deduce the method of processing its fruit, he became the first to taste of wine; then he taught the rest of mankind to plant the vine, and the use, storage, and preservation of wine.

Above all others, Osiris esteemed Hermes, who was endowed with a superior natural faculty for inventing things of service to the human race.

---

rendition of the Egyptian name. The city of Nō, referred to in the Bible, is none other than *níwt*, or "the City" as the Egyptians familiarly called it. Where the name Thebes came from is more of a mystery. One theory holds it to be an Hellenic mispronunciation of the *Tápé* of the ancient Egyptian tongue, pronounced *Thaba* in the Memphis dialect, and which is said to mean "head," in the sense of head or chief city. This explanation, like all the others, is mere speculation, with no conclusive evidence behind it. See Chapter 45, note 94, below.

30.   This etymology is strained: from Dio- (a form of Zeus) and -nysus (Nysa). There is no agreement in scholarly circles on the correct etymology, just as there was no consensus among the ancients about where Nysa was located. Some said Arabia, others Libya, still others India or Scythia. But it was commonly agreed that Nysa, wherever it might be, was the birthplace of Dionysus.

16   For this god was the first to bring language to perfection; he named many nameless things, invented the alphabet, and ordained ceremonies governing divine worship and sacrifices to the gods. He was the first to perceive order in the stars and to discern the nature and harmony of musical sounds. He also was the first to establish a school of wrestling and to cultivate the graceful movement and proper development of the body. He invented the lyre, with three strings of sinew to represent the seasons of the year; that is, he prescribed three basic tones, treble, bass, and middle: treble evocative of summer, bass of winter, and the middle tone of spring. And he taught the Greeks eloquence [*hermeneia*], which is why he is called Hermes. In short, they hold him to have been the sacred scribe to whom Osiris confided all things, and on whose counsel he especially relied. And incidentally, it was he who discovered the olive, not Athena as the Greeks pretend.[31]

17   They go on to relate that Osiris, who was disposed to benevolence and anxious for renown, assembled a mighty host, intending to visit all the inhabited world and teach the race of men to plant the vine and sow crops of wheat and barley. For he reckoned that having once freed men of their brutishness and convinced them to adopt instead a civilized way of life, he would win eternal glory through the amplitude of these services. And this indeed came to pass. For not only the people of that age who received these gifts, but all those born afterwards who have enjoyed the benefit of these newfound foods, have honored as most glorious gods those who made them available.

Then, they continue, having ordered the affairs of Egypt and committed the government of the whole country to Isis his wife, Osiris set Hermes at her side as adviser, who was distinguished by his wisdom above his other friends. As general over all his dominions he left his kinsman Heracles, noted for his courage and strength of body; he appointed Busiris governor of the districts lying toward Phoenicia and the coastal areas and set Antaeus over those parts bordering Ethiopia and

---

31.   The Greeks usually identified Hermes with the Egyptian deity Thoth, based largely on the similarity of attributes. Both were gods of writing, of wisdom, and of language. Only Hermes, however, was associated with music and wrestling, which were accomplishments of far greater importance in the Greek world than in Egypt (see chapter 81). In chapter 96 Diodorus mentions the aspect of Hermes as conductor of souls to the underworld, a function which in Egyptian mythology was usually attributed to the jackal-headed Anubis.

Libya. He himself with his forces set out from Egypt for the campaign, taking with him his brother whom the Greeks call Apollo.

They say Apollo was the discoverer of laurel, with which all men crown this god in particular. But the discovery of ivy they ascribe to Osiris, and they consecrate it to him even as the Greeks do to Dionysus. Ivy, they continue, is known as the "plant of Osiris" in the language of the Egyptians;[32] they prefer it to the vine for offerings, since it stays green all the time while the other sheds its leaves. Indeed, the ancients did the same with other evergreen plants, devoting the myrtle to Aphrodite, the laurel to Apollo, and the olive to Athena.

18   But to resume: they recount that two sons of Osiris, Anubis and Macedon, both of excellent courage, took the field with him. Both sported singular battle cloaks made from animals like unto themselves in bold impetuosity: for Anubis wore about himself a dog's skin, and Macedon the foreparts of a wolf, for which reason these animals were revered by the Egyptians.[33]   Osiris also brought Pan on this expedition. Pan is honored extensively in Egypt, where the inhabitants not only have erected statues of him in every temple, but also have named a city after him in the Thebaid, called *Chemmo* by the natives but translated as City of Pan.[34]   With Osiris also went men of experience in agriculture: Maron in viniculture and Triptolemus in sowing grain and in every phase of the harvest. When everything was ready Osiris, vowing to the gods never to cut his hair until his return to Egypt, began his march through Ethiopia; this vow gave rise to the custom concerning the hair which prevailed until recent times among the Egyptians, that those traveling abroad would let their hair grow until their return home.

---

32.   Ivy does not seem to have been introduced to Egypt until Ptolemaic times.

33.   Diodorus later, in his general treatment of animal worship, gives several theories to explain the phenomenon in general (chapters 21, and 83-90), and particular reasons for the veneration of dogs and wolves (chapters 87 and 88), all of which differ from the rationale cited here.

34.   The Greeks commonly drew a correspondence between Pan and the Egyptian god Min, both of whom were ithyphallic deities. Chemmo or Chemmis, also called Panopolis by the Greeks, was the capital of the ninth Upper Egyptian nome, about a hundred miles downstream from the Thebaid proper. The name derived from the ancient Egyptian Khent-min. Today the site is known as Akhmim.

They relate that, while Osiris was in Ethiopia, the race of the Satyrs was presented to him. These folk, they claim, have hair upon their loins. Now Osiris was jovial and fond of music and dance; in fact, he was always attended by a company of musicians, including nine young maidens who could sing and who were skilled as well in the other arts. The Greeks call them Muses and say their leader was Apollo, who for this reason has been styled "Musegetes." So the Satyrs, with their inborn propensity for dance and song and every sport and frolic, were invited along on the campaign. For Osiris was not warlike; he employed neither battles nor skirmishes, since all nations accepted him as a god because of his beneficence. In Ethiopia he taught the people husbandry and, having founded illustrious cities there, he left behind him agents to govern and to collect the tribute.[35]

19 While the expedition was busy with these affairs, it seems the Nile, at its customary period of high water at the heliacal rising of the star Sirius,[36] burst its banks and submerged a large part of Egypt, particularly engulfing the districts governed by Prometheus. Nearly everything in the province was destroyed, at which Prometheus was so distraught that he gladly would have died. The river was indeed likened to an eagle [Aëtus] from the speed and violence with which its current swept along; but Heracles, never daunted and athirst for manly fame, promptly dammed the breach and turned the river back again into its proper channel. Hence certain Greek poets have spun the incident into the myth that Heracles slew the eagle feeding on the liver of Prometheus.[37]

---

35.   Maron, the Muses, and the Satyrs are Hellenic additions to the authentic Osiris myths of Egypt, borrowed from the story of Dionysus. See note 19, above.

36.   The heliacal rising of a star is its first appearance after a period of invisibility due to conjunction with the sun, that is, the first morning on which it becomes visible on the horizon just before sunrise. The peak of the Nile's annual inundation is in September.

37.   This is a good example of Diodorus' penchant for explaining myths by reference to real (or at least plausible) events. However, there is no evidence that the river Nile was ever called Aëtus, and in most other Greek versions of the myth it is Apollo who slays the eagle feeding on the Promethean liver, or Heracles who frees Prometheus by pleading with Zeus, at whose command he suffered (his crime was to give fire to men in violation of Zeus' wish). Arrian, however, agrees with Diodorus that Heracles slew the eagle (*Anabasis Alexandri*, V.3).

In the earliest days the river had the name Oceanê, which in Greek is Oceanus; next, they say, because of the occurrence of this flood it was called Aëtus or Eagle; later it was renamed Egyptus after one of the kings of the country, which the poet confirms, saying:

In River Egyptus I anchored by round-hulled ships.
[*Odyssey* 14.258]

(For the place called Thonis, where the river empties into the sea, was in olden times the trading port of Egypt.) Finally, the river received the name it now bears from Nileus, a former king.[38]

Now when Osiris arrived at the borders of Ethiopia, he separated the river from the land on either side by means of levees, so that at high water the countryside is not swamped and ruined; instead, the water is let in gently, no more than is necessary, through built-in floodgates.

Next Osiris took his course through Arabia, along the Red Sea as far as India and the extremity of the inhabited world.[39]   He also founded many cities in India, among which he named one Nysa, wishing to leave there a memorial of that city near Egypt in which he was raised. He also planted ivy at the Indian Nysa, and in this spot alone of all the parts of India and surrounding regions is ivy to be found.[40]   And he

38.   For the Egyptian name of the Nile, see note 23, above. The earliest use of the term Nilos, whose etymology is obscure, is in Hesiod (*Theog.* 338). For King Nileus, see chapter 63. The reference to Thonis, and its bearing on the discussion of the river's name, is puzzling. Thonis was the warden of the Canopic mouth of the Nile in the legend of Helen's visit to Egypt (see Herodotus II.113-116), not to be confused with Thon, whose wife Polydamna gave Helen the nepenthic drug (see chapter 97, below).

39.   The Red, or Erythraean, Sea was a name applied by the Greeks to the entire Indian Ocean and Persian Gulf, as well as to the modern Red Sea.

40.   J. B. Bury, in his *History of Greece*, suggests that the Indian Nysa was at the modern Nangenhar, in the Kabul valley near Jelalabad. In the *Anabasis Alexandri* V.2.5, Arrian places Nysa between the rivers Cophen and Indus. The head man of the town is said to have told Alexander: "Dionysus named this city Nysa and this land Nisaea in memory of his nurse, who bore that name; . . . If you wish for proof that Dionysus was our founder, here it is: this is the only place in India where ivy grows . . . ." Upon this Arrian comments "there is none in India elsewhere, not even in districts where the vine grows." Theophrastus (*H.P.* VI.3.7) doubted the discovery of ivy in India, while Cleitarchos (*Schol. Ap. Rhod.* II.904) said it was a plant "like ivy." Curtius, in his *Historiae*

likewise left in that country many other indications of his presence, by which the latter-day Indians were persuaded to claim the god and assert that he was born in India.

20   Osiris also busied himself with hunting elephants, and he left stelae everywhere commemorating his campaign. He traversed as well the other countries of Asia and crossed over into Europe at the Hellespont. In Thrace he slew Lycurgos, a barbarian king who opposed his plans.[41] He left there the now aged Maron, whom he commissioned to care for the plants introduced to this country, and made him the eponymous founder of a city which he called Maroneia. And he left his son Macedon behind as king of Macedonia, which was named after him, while to Triptolemus he entrusted the tillage of Attica.[42]

In conclusion, then, Osiris ranged over the entire inhabited world and enriched human society with the gift of our most widely cultivated foods. But if any country was unsuitable for vine growing, there he introduced the beverage made from barley, scarcely inferior to wine in fragrance and potency.[43]   When he returned to Egypt, he brought back most lavish presents from every country; and through the magnitude of his services he won, by universal consent, immortality and honor equal to that of the heavenly gods. Afterwards, when he had passed unto the gods from among men, he received sacrifices and other marks of the greatest respect from Isis and Hermes, who also established sacred rites and many mysteries to enhance the influence of the god Osiris.

21   Now although the priests privily transmitted from of old the circumstances surrounding the death of Osiris, eventually the secret was disclosed by some of them to the public. It is related thus: that Osiris,

---

Alexandri Magni Macedonis 8.10.7-18, would seem to place Nysa at an earlier point in Alexander's march, in the modern territories of Bajaur or Swat.

41.   The Lycurgos legend, of course, is from the Dionysus tradition, and it is attributed to Osiris because of the Hellenic identification of the two deities. In other variants of the same theme, Lycurgos is blinded or driven mad for his ill-timed opposition to the god's progress.

42.   The Ptolemies claimed descent from Dionysus (= Osiris), so the fable of Osiris' son Macedon as the eponymous founder of the Macedonian monarchy was perhaps a piece of propaganda, picked up and repeated by Diodorus, designed to legitimize Ptolemaic rule in Egypt.

43.   Egyptian beer, called zythos later in chapter 34.

while lawfully ruling Egypt, was assassinated by Typhon, his iniquitous and profane brother. Typhon dismembered the body of the murdered victim into six and twenty parts and gave a piece to each of his accomplices in the attack, wishing all to share in the defilement, and expecting by this device to acquire loyal confederates and guardians of his reign. But Isis, the sister and wife of Osiris, with the aid of her son Horus, avenged the homicide and, killing Typhon and his abettors, became queen of Egypt.

The battle occurred near the village now called Antaeus, which is situated, they say, beside the river on the Arabian side, and which is named after the Antaeus who was chastened by Heracles in the time of Osiris. After the battle, Isis recovered all the parts of her husband's body except the genitals. Wishing his place of burial to remain a mystery, yet to be venerated by all the people of Egypt, she accomplished her aim in the following manner. Around each of the parts, or so they relate, she formed, out of spices and beeswax, identical images of a man comparable in size to Osiris. She then summoned the priests, one group at a time, and made each party swear never to divulge the secret about to be entrusted to it. Then she told each group confidentially that to them alone was being committed for burial the body of Osiris. Reminding them of his good works, she entreated them to bury his corpse in their own locality, and to worship him henceforward as a god; she also asked them to consecrate at their choice one of their local species of animal, to honor it while alive as formerly they honored Osiris, and to deem it worthy of similar ceremonies at its death. And wishing also to bind the priests with self-interest to observe the stipulated veneration, Isis assigned a third of the land to them for the maintenance of the gods and for divine services. Thus the priests, it is said, recollecting the benefactions of Osiris, and anxious to gratify their supplicant, but motivated as well by their own cupidity, performed all that Isis suggested. And until this very day all the local priesthoods, thinking Osiris lies buried among them, continue their homage to the surrogate animals; and when one of them dies, they renew in its obsequies their mourning for Osiris.[44] In addition, the sacred bulls

---

44.   This is another of Diodorus' several contradictory explanations of Egyptian animal worship. For the others, see chapters 18 and 83-90. The dismemberment of Osiris was a relatively late addition to the Osirian tales, first mentioned in texts of the XVIIIth Dynasty (1550-1307 B.C.), but well established by the time Diodorus wrote. Diodorus mentions twenty-five rediscovered parts (not counting the genital organ) which were distributed for burial throughout

known as Apis and Mnevis were consecrated to Osiris, and their worship as gods was publicly proclaimed throughout all Egypt; for the bullock was of greater service than any other animal to the discoverers of the blessings of grain, such as in planting the seed and in other agricultural assistance of benefit to everyone.

22 After the death of Osiris, they say, Isis swore to accept thereafter the love of no other man, and she continued for the rest of her life to reign in perfect justice and to excel all monarchs in kindness to her subjects. Like Osiris, Isis attained immortality after her death and was entombed at Memphis, where her sepulcher is shown to this day in the temple precincts of Hephaestos. However, some claim the remains of these gods lie not in Memphis, but at the frontier between Egypt and Ethiopia, on an island in the Nile near the city of Philae; from which circumstance the island is named "the Holy Field." As evidence for this assertion they point out the tomb prepared for Osiris, universally venerated by all the priests of Egypt; to this day it remains on the island surrounded by three hundred and sixty libation bowls. Designated priests fill these bowls with milk every day and sing a dirge invoking the names of the gods. For this reason the island is forbidden to all passersby, except priests. Indeed, all the inhabitants of the Thebaid, the most ancient part of Egypt, deem it the most fearsome oath if anyone swears "by Osiris who lieth at Philae."[45]

Thus is it told how the honors of burial were paid to the rediscovered remnants of Osiris' body, except, they say, the lost genital organ;

Egypt. The original count was only fourteen pieces, but as the popularity of the Osiris cult increased, the number of parts multiplied until there were said to be forty-two, one for each Egyptian nome (see note 108, below).

45. Although Philae was considered sacred from the earliest historical period, its association with Isis and Osiris is of relatively late times, and its fame in Diodorus' day resulted from its beautiful temple complex begun by Nectanebo I (380-362 B.C.) and greatly enhanced by the Ptolemies. Once established, the cult of Isis persisted until finally suppressed by the Emperor Justinian in the middle of the sixth century A.D. The Egyptian etymology of Philae was "island of the time of Re'," but in hieroglyphics it is *Philak* or "boundary"; for its location, at the first cataract, was usually considered the frontier of Egypt proper (see plate 1). Actually, the tomb of Osiris was reputedly on the neighboring island of Senmut, now called Biga. Well attested sources support Diodorus both as to the inviolability of the island and the daily milk offerings. There were 365 bowls (not 360), one for each day of the year, for Osiris was the Year-god whose temples characteristically had 365 lamps, 365 trees, etc.

Typhon had flung this into the Nile, since none of his accomplices would have it. But to Isis, it was not less deserving of divine respect than his other members. So, setting up images of it in the temples, she taught how it should be worshipped; and in the ceremonies and sacrifices pertaining to the god Osiris she gave it the highest honors and obtained for it the greatest veneration. Therefore the Greeks, who learned from Egypt the custom of celebrating the "orgia" and the Dionysiac revels, in the mysteries, rites, and sacrifices of that god also give honor to this particular organ, which they call "phallus."

23   They record that ten thousand years elapsed from the time of Isis and Osiris until the reign of Alexander, who founded the city in Egypt named after himself; and some write that it was just short of twenty-three thousand years. But, they say, those who claim that Osiris was born of Semelê and Zeus in Thebes of Boeotia are just telling stories. This tale was started by Orpheus, who was a friend of the Cadmeans and honored by them; and having gone into Egypt, partaken of the rites of initiation, and adopted the Dionysiac mysteries, he pretended, to gratify the Cadmeans, that the god was born in Boeotia. The masses readily accepted the rites and mysteries, partly out of ignorance and partly because they wished the god to be considered Greek. Now the following is the occasion seized upon by Orpheus to relocate the birthplace of this god, and his worship, to Boeotia.

Cadmus was from Egyptian Thebes. Among other children he begat Semelê. It happened that this girl was seduced by someone, became pregnant, and after seven months gave birth to a child who was, in appearance, exactly as the Egyptians hold Osiris to have been. Now, it is unusual for a premature child of this sort to survive, either because it does not accord with nature, or because the gods will it not. So Cadmus, noting well this phenomenon, and having an oracle's command to respect the customs of his ancestors, swaddled the infant in gold and made the appropriate sacrifices to him, as if an incarnation of Osiris had occurred among men. He attributed the paternity to Zeus, thereby exalting the pretended Osiris as well as diverting reproach from his ravished daughter. And thus the story was spread abroad among the Greeks that Semelê, daughter of Cadmus, gave birth to Osiris by Zeus.

In later times Orpheus, enjoying great fame among the Greeks for singing, initiatory rites, and theology, was entertained as a guest by the descendants of Cadmus and was highly esteemed at Thebes. Being familiar with the theological tenets of the Egyptians, he transposed the nativity of the ancient Osiris to a later era and, to repay the Cadmeans, established new mystic rites in which he taught the initiates that Dionysus was born of Semelê and Zeus. As mentioned above, the people adopted these mysteries, partly through the deception practiced on their ignorance, partly through the trustworthiness of Orpheus and his reputation in these matters, but mostly because they gladly acquiesced in the recognition of this god as a Greek deity. Thereafter, the poets and mythographers seized on the story of this divine descent, the theaters were filled with it, and to succeeding generations it became a firm and unshakable article of belief.[46]

The Egyptians usually complain that the Greeks steal credit for all the most famous gods and heroes of Egypt, and even for their colonies.

24   For example Heracles, who courageously roamed much of the inhabited earth and erected his pillar in Libya, was of Egyptian birth; and the Egyptians take their evidence in support of this assertion from the Greeks themselves. For, although everyone agrees that Heracles fought alongside the Olympian gods in the war against the giants, the Egyptians point out that in no way is it conceivable for the earth to have harbored giants in the age at which the Greeks say Heracles was alive, a generation before the Trojan War; but it was rather, they argue, nearer the first origin of mankind: for from that time the Egyptians reckon more than ten thousand years, but from the Trojan War less than twelve hundred. And likewise both the club and the lion's skin cloak are more consistent with a primitive Heracles, since in those times, before the invention of arms, men defended themselves against enemies with wooden clubs and used wild animals' hides for defensive armor. Now this ancient Heracles they declare to have been the son of Zeus (though

---

46.   This is a good example of Diodorus attempting to rationalize a myth. He does not give the usual story either of Cadmus or Semelê. In his version, the origin of which is unknown, Cadmus is from Egyptian Thebes, and the pretended incarnation of Osiris occurred there before Cadmus emigrated to Greece and founded Boeotian Thebes. Later, Orpheus cleverly substituted Dionysus for Osiris and Boeotian for Egyptian Thebes. In the standard version of the myth, Cadmus was from Phoenicia (although his father came from Egypt). His daughter Semelê was wooed by Zeus in mortal disguise. Jealous Hera persuaded Semelê to demand a glimpse of Zeus in his true form, which he granted, and the girl was consumed in thunder and lightning. But Hermes rescued her unborn child, who grew up to be Dionysus. There were other traditions of the birth and parentage of Dionysus, so contradictory that Diodorus assumes there were three different personages of that name (Book III, chapter 74). In Book IV, chapter 4, he gives yet a fourth version. Cicero, in *The Nature of the Gods* III.23, counts five.

his mother, they say, is unknown). But the son born of Alcmenê over
ten thousand years later, called Alcaeus at birth, later took the new name
Heracles, not because he achieved fame [kleos] through Hera, as Matris
claims, but because in emulating the same course of life as the Heracles
of old, he fell heir to his name as well as his reputation.[47]

Indeed, their story agrees with the legend handed down among the
Greeks from remote antiquity, that Heracles rid the earth of wild beasts;
for this feat can hardly be attributed to one living near the time of the
Trojan War, when most parts of the known world had been reclaimed by
cities, tilled fields, and the multitudes inhabiting the land everywhere.
This taming of the earth accords better with the Heracles living in
earlier times, when men were as yet oppressed by many ferocious
predators — a situation especially true in Egypt, where to this day the
land upriver is a desert overrun with savage beasts. For it is not
unreasonable that Heracles, having provided for this, his fatherland, and
having cleared the countryside of wild animals, should have gained
honor equal to that of the gods. The priests claim that Perseus likewise
was born in Egypt; and that the Greeks also transplant the birth of Isis
to Argos, in their myth recounting the metamorphosis of Io to the shape
of a heifer.[48]

25   In general, there is considerable disagreement concerning these
gods. For the same goddess that some call Isis others will call Demeter,
others Thesmophorus, others Selenê, others Hera, and yet others all these

---

47.   Diodorus was not alone in distinguishing between an ancient and an
"historical" Heracles. In Book III, chapter 74 he also alludes to a third Heracles
in between these two. Diodorus gives a much fuller treatment of the Heracles
legends in Book IV, chapter 9ff where, incidentally, he accepts the fake
etymology of the name that he has here rejected! Indeed, since Heracles achieved
fame by his own efforts despite the active hostility of Hera, the idea that his
name reflects Hera's patronage is patently ridiculous; and Diodorus, in alternately
dismissing and then adopting the hypothesis, demonstrates an uncritical acceptance
of whatever source he was consulting at any given time — the fault for which he
is most often criticized as an historian. The Greeks sometimes identified the
Egyptian god Herishef (or Harsaphes), sometimes the god Shu, with the "ancient"
Heracles. The "historical" Heracles was first named Alcaeus (or Alcides) after his
grandfather.

48.   For Perseus, see Appendix 1, Proper Names. Io, one of Zeus' lovers, was
changed into a bird by a jealous Hera. Zeus changed her into a cow until her
pregnancy neared its end. The connection with Isis was partly because both were
moon goddesses, partly because the cow was sacred to Isis (see chapter 11).

names. As for Osiris, some call him Serapis, some Dionysus, some Pluto, some Ammon, and others Zeus; many have held Pan to be the same god, while some say Serapis is the god called Pluto by the Greeks.[49]
The Egyptians credit Isis both with the discovery of many therapeutic drugs and with having skill in understanding the art of healing. Thus, having become immortal, her greatest delight is to bestow cures on mankind, and to give remedies during sleep to those who have implored her aid, openly displaying to men who seek her assistance her beneficence as well as her very apparition. And in proof of these miracles, they claim to adduce not myths, as do the Greeks, but palpable evidence: for nearly all the world bears witness to them, and renders praise to Isis because of her manifestations through healing. For hovering near the sick while they slumber, she grants them succor in their afflictions, and those who have submitted to her are miraculously made well. She even saves many of those for whom, from the stubbornness of their maladies, the doctors have despaired; and many, entirely deprived of sight or some other bodily function, are restored to their former healthy condition when they have recourse to this goddess. Isis also discovered the elixir of immortality, and when her son Horus fell victim to the plots of the Titans and was found dead beneath the waves, she not only raised him from the dead and restored his soul, but also gave him eternal life. But Horus, it seems, was the last of the gods to rule Egypt after the departure of his father Osiris from among men. They say Horus, in the Greek tongue, is Apollo, who was taught both

---

49.   The cults of Isis and, to a lesser extent, Osiris spread throughout the Mediterranean lands during Hellenistic times and continued to grow in influence under the Roman empire. The former geographical barriers began to fall, and the collision of cultures led to a blurring of distinctions among local gods. In *The Golden Ass* of Apuleius (XI.2), Isis appears in a dream to the hapless quadruped and introduces herself in these terms: "I am she that is the natural mother of all things, mistress and governess of all the elements, the initial progeny of worlds, chief of the powers divine, queen of heaven, the principal of the gods celestial, the light of the goddesses. At my will the planets of the air, the wholesome winds of the seas and the silences of hell are disposed. My name, my divinity, is adored throughout the world, in divers manners, in variable customs and in many names, for the Phrygians call me the mother of the gods; the Athenians, Minerva; the Cyprians, Venus; the Candians, Diana; the Sicilians, Proserpina; the Eleusians, Ceres; some Juno, others Bellona, others Hecate; and principally the Ethiopians who dwell in the Orient, and the Egyptians . . . do call me Queen Isis." (Wm. Addlington translation). For Serapis, see Appendix I, Proper Names.

medicine and divination by his mother Isis, and who showers benefits on the race of men through his oracles and his cures.[50]

26   The Egyptian priests, computing the time elapsed from the reign of Helios until Alexander crossed into Asia, say it is about twenty-three thousand years. Their myths have it also that the most ancient gods each ruled more than twelve hundred years, and those of later times not less than three hundred apiece. But since this length of years strains credibility, some people try to explain that in olden days, when the course of the sun was not yet understood, it is obvious that the "year" was marked by the orbit of the moon. Therefore, it was not impossible for some individuals to have lived twelve hundred "years" which were only thirty days long; and in fact even now, when a year is twelve months, not a few survive over a hundred years. They also offer the same explanation for those who seem to have ruled three hundred years: for in those days the "year" consisted of four months, corresponding to the seasons of the calendar, namely spring, summer, and winter; from which fact, even among some of the Greeks, the years are called seasons [horoi], and yearly annals are called horographs.[51]

The Egyptian myths also say that in the time of Isis there were beings of enormous size whom the Greeks call giants, but who called themselves . . .;[52] their colossal forms are depicted upon the temple

---

50.   In chapter 13, Diodorus said Apollo was brother to Isis, but it was more normal for the Greeks to equate him with Horus, her son. Indeed the Greek deity came to be called Horapollo in some cases.

51.   This unusual explanation of the one-month and four-month years is unsupported by solid evidence, but it is mentioned by several ancient authors besides Diodorus. Manetho seems to be the earliest extant writer to give this account (e.g., fragments 1 and 2, Loeb edition). Plutarch, in *Numa*, repeats it briefly, and various authors allude to it, including Pliny and Augustine. Censorinus in *De Die Natale* XIX, published c. 238 A.D., gives a slightly different version: "Thus, it is reported that in Egypt, in the most ancient time, the year was composed of two months, then King Isone made it four months . . . . The same thing in Achaia; the Arcadians commenced by having years of three months . . . . On the other hand, the people of Caria and of Acarnania had years of six months . . . ." These types of mini-years in the Greek world are well attested. Censorinus also explains that the terms *horoi* and *horograph* were based on the name of Horus, whom some credit with the institution of the trimensual year. Horus was also said to have first divided the day into *hours*, which still reflect his name.

52.   A proper noun seems to be missing from the manuscripts.

walls being defeated by the adherents of Osiris. Some say the giants were born of the earth when the origin of life, rising up from the soil, was still recent. But others insist that the fable of their huge bodies arose because they excelled in strength of body and accomplished many feats. Yet nearly everyone agrees that when they started a war against the gods Zeus and Osiris they were exterminated one and all.[53]

27   They say the Egyptians, in defiance of the usual custom among men, made it legal to marry their own sisters, because of the success Isis had in this regard. For having married her brother Osiris and vowed, upon his death, never to accept the love of any other man, she not only avenged her husband's murder but continued to rule most lawfully, and on the whole she was the source of great and numerous blessings for all mankind. Now for these reasons it became the rule that the queen enjoys greater authority and honor than does the king; while among the common people the wife is likewise master of the husband, since in the marriage contract the man promises to obey his wife in all things.[54]

And they say Isis was entombed at Memphis, where her sepulcher is shown to this day in the temple precincts of Hephaestos. But some claim the remains of these gods lie at the frontier of Egypt and Ethiopia, on an island in the Nile near Philae; from which circumstance the island is named "the Holy Field." As evidence for this assertion, they point out the tomb prepared for Osiris, universally venerated by all the priests of Egypt, which remains on the island to this day surrounded, they say, by three hundred and sixty libation bowls. Designated priests fill these bowls with milk every day and sing a dirge invoking the names of the gods. For this reason the island is forbidden to all, except priests. Indeed, all the inhabitants of the Thebaid, the most ancient part of Egypt, deem it the most fearsome oath if anyone should swear "by Osiris who lieth at Philae."[55]

---

53.   In Greek myth, the giants were earthborn creatures who attacked Olympus in revenge for Zeus' confinement of their kinfolk, the Titans, in Tartarus. Heracles aided the gods in defeating the giants.

54.   Consanguinous marriage was practiced in Egypt to a limited extent, but Diodorus is mistaken in his assertion that women were more exalted than men.

55.   This paragraph, found with variations in only some of the manuscripts, is almost a verbatim repetition from chapter 22. In the next paragraph, Diodorus cites an inscription at Nysa attributed to Isis. Two Greek inscriptions remarkably similar to this in wording have been discovered on the islands of Ios and Andros.

Of course, I am not ignorant of the opinion of some historians that the graves of these gods are really in Nysa of Arabia (after which place, by the way, Dionysus is called "Nysaeus"). There is even, in Nysa, a stele for each of the two deities, inscribed with the sacred writing. Thus upon the stele of Isis it is engraven:

> Isis am I, queen of all the land, the one taught by Hermes; no one can abrogate the laws that I have made. I am the eldest daughter of Kronos the youngest god; I am wife and sister to Osiris the king; I am she who first discovered grain for the race of men; I am the mother of King Horus; I am the star rising in the constellation of the dog; I raised the city of Bubastis. Farewell, 0 Egypt who nurtured me; farewell!

On the column of Osiris the following is said to be written:

> My father is Kronos, youngest of all the gods, and I am the king, Osiris, the one who campaigned in every country, even to the deserts of India and the regions lying as far to the north as the springs of the river Ister, and back again through other lands unto Ocean itself. I am the eldest son of Kronos, sprung from a fair and noble line, an offspring born akin to Day. And there is not a place in the populous world I have not visited, sharing with all men the things which I discovered.

They say that only this much of the writing on the columns is legible and that the rest, the larger part, has been effaced by time. Be that as it may, most writers disagree over the burial place of the two gods. This is because the real facts in the case were handed down in secret tradition by the Egyptian priests, who cared neither to share the truth with the populace, nor to incur the retribution threatened for any who should reveal the mysteries of these gods to the vulgar.

28   Now the Egyptians go on to relate that after this period a large number of colonies were sent forth from their land into all the civilized world. Belus, for example, acknowledged son of Poseidon and Libya, led colonists into Babylon; there, having settled on the banks of the Euphrates River, he appointed priests who were exempt from taxes and free of all civic obligations, just like those of Egypt. The Babylonians call them Chaldeans, and they make observations of the stars, imitating in this the practice of the priests and philosophers, not to mention the astrologers, among the Egyptians.[56] In like manner, they continue, those who set out with Danaus colonized Argos, which is nearly the oldest city in Greece;[57] and likewise the nation of the Colchians on the Pontus, and that of the Jews lying between Syria and Arabia, were also settled by certain expatriates from Egypt. This explains the traditional circumcision of male children practiced among these races, an age-old custom imported from Egypt.[58] Even the Athenians, they claim, were colonists from Saïs in Egypt, and they endeavor to show proof of this connection: for alone of all the Greeks the Athenians call their city "Astu," adopting this name from the city of Astu in Egypt.[59] What is more, their commonwealth was divided originally into three parts and had the same organization and class structure as that found in Egypt. Foremost was the class of nobles, called "eupatridae;" those who, like the priests in Egypt, devoted the most time to their education and who were judged worthy of the highest honors. The second order was that of the landowners, or "geomoroi," who were obliged to possess a suit of armor and to fight for the state, exactly like the caste (called husbandmen) which furnishes the soldiery of Egypt. Finally was reckoned the class of "demiurgoi," or artisans, who followed the vulgar trades and performed the most basic social functions, doing the same work as the corresponding class among the Egyptians.

They also say a number of the Athenian rulers were from Egypt. For example Petes, the sire of that Menestheus who served in the war

---

56.   In Greek myth, Belus was a king of Chemmis in the Thebaid. His wife was the daughter of Nilus, and his twin sons were Egyptus and Danaus. The Greeks connected him with the Mesopotamian deity title *Ba'al* (the *Bel* of the Bible). Babylon was not an Egyptian colony, and Chaldean astronomy and astrology owe little, if anything, to Egyptian influence. See note 157, below.

57.   The traditional date of the arrival of Danaus was 1511-1509 B.C. Archaeological evidence from the Argolid does show Egyptian cultural influence at about this period. Danaus became king of Argos and by the time of Homer the term *Danaoi* had come to refer to all the Greeks.

58.   Circumcision as an hygenic measure and as a condition for entry into some priesthoods was certainly practiced in Egypt, but written references to the practice are sparse. See also note 109, below.

59.   The Egyptian colonization of Athens is imaginary, and Diodorus rejects the claim in chapter 29, below. The Athenians did call their city "Astu," as did the Alexandrians in Egypt, but the Greeks of Alexandria probably borrowed the term from Athens.

against Troy, was without doubt an Egyptian, but afterwards he obtained
Athenian citizenship and the monarchy as well. . . . [There is a lacuna
at this point. What follows must apply to Cecrops, whose lower body
was that of a serpent.] He is represented as being of a double form; yet
the Athenians, with all their subtlety, are not able to explain the cause
of this dual nature; though it is obvious to all that since he had two
citizenships, Greek and barbarian, he was customarily held to be of a
twofold nature, part man and part beast.

29   And in just the same way, they add, the Egyptian-born
Erechtheus was also made king of the Athenians, for which they offer
specific evidence such as this: that when the well-known droughts of
wide extent oppressed nearly all the known world — except Egypt, due
to the peculiar nature of that land — and ruin ensued both for crops and
for many of the people, Erechtheus, through his kinship in Egypt,
brought a great quantity of food from there to Athens. In return for this
boon, the Athenians appointed their benefactor king. Then he, once
having acquired the sovereignty, established at Eleusis the religious rites
and mysteries of Demeter, importing the relevant customs from Egypt.
Now tradition also preserves a legend that a manifestation of Demeter
occurred in Attica during this time of drought; for since this was the
period when the cereal grains bearing her name were supplied to the
Athenians, it seemed as if Demeter had repeated her original discovery
and bestowal of grain. The Athenians themselves corroborate that this
advent of Demeter with her gift of grain took place among them at the
time when Erechtheus was on the throne and the crops had been
destroyed by drought; that, in addition, it was this occasion when the
religious rites and mysteries of the goddess were introduced at Eleusis;[60]
and that the ceremonies of the Athenians, both in style and antiquity, are

---

60.   Diodorus is almost the only writer to give this Egyptian version of the
Erechtheus story, or to credit him with the introduction of the mysteries of
Demeter at Eleusis. There is no archaeological evidence of Egyptian influence at
Eleusis, which was the chief center of the worship of Demeter and Persephone.
The famous mysteries celebrated in honor of these goddesses were the most
sacred in Greece until the town was destroyed by Alaric the Visigoth in A.D. 396.
The commonest version of the legend is that Erechtheus forcibly incorporated
Eleusis into the Athenian state, but Eleusis was allowed to maintain control over
the celebration of the mysteries until about the fifth century B.C. The reign of
Erechtheus is given as the late fifteenth century, and the advent of Demeter and
her gift of grain a generation earlier. Erechtheus was the grandfather of Petes and
great-grandfather of Menestheus.

the same as those of Egypt: for the Athenian Eumolpidae were derived from the priests of Egypt, and their Ceryces or Heralds from the pastophoroi.[61] Besides, of all the Greeks, only the Athenians swear by Isis; and in their manner and character they are quite like the Egyptians. And because of the fame of Athens, the Egyptians utter many other arguments such as these to prove that the city is their colony. But this is more vainglory than truth, at least in my opinion.

In general, the Egyptians assert that their ancestors, because of the large surplus population and the ascendancy of their kings over other lands, sent numerous colonies to many parts of the known world. But since no one produces any clear proof of this, and no competent historian endorses it, we have judged their stories not worth recording.

But to preserve due proportion, let what we have said about the gods of Egypt suffice. We shall now attempt a brief description of everything pertaining to the country of Egypt, the Nile, and anything else worth hearing about.

30 Now Egypt, in general, extends mainly toward the south, and it seems far to surpass in natural strength and scenic beauty the places bordering on the kingdom. On the west it is protected by the desert and the beast-infested wilderness of Libya, so vast in extent, whose aridity and total lack of food make a passage not only difficult but extremely dangerous. And the southern parts are defended by the cataracts of the Nile and the mountains surrounding them. Indeed, beyond the land of the Trogodytes and the highest uplands of Ethiopia, for almost five thousand and five hundred stades, it is not easy to sail via the river nor to travel overland, unless one has the wherewithal of a king or an absolutely enormous fortune.

Now of the parts lying to the east, some are protected by the river while others are surrounded by deserts and the marshy plains called Barathra. For there is a lake called Serbonis between Coele-Syria and Egypt, of extremely narrow breadth but wondrous deep, and in length stretching almost two hundred stades; and to those who approach it unwarily it offers unexpected dangers. Since the lake is narrow like a

---

61. The Eumolpidae (descendants of Eumolpos, last king of Eleusis) and Ceryces were two noble families, originally of Eleusis, whose sacerdotal offices were hereditary. The pastophoroi were Egyptian priests who bore small shrines of the gods in processions. The line of the Ceryces (or Kerukes) apparently had died out by the fourth century B.C. and was replaced by the Lukomidae of Phyle.

ribbon and surrounded on every side with vast dunes, a great quantity of sand is hurled onto it whenever a steady southwest wind is blowing. This sand, spread over the surface, hides the water, and obscures the boundaries between lake and land, making them indistinguishable. For this reason, many people unfamiliar with the peculiarity of this place — even whole armies — have strayed from the established road and have been swallowed up. For the sand of this abyss, when trodden underfoot, gives way but gradually; and it deceives those venturing upon it as if by malevolent cunning until, when they realize the truth of what is about to happen and seek to save themselves, there is no longer escape or deliverance. After being sucked down into the water they are able neither to swim, since the silt hampers bodily movement, nor to climb out, having nothing firm for a foothold. The sand and water are intermixed, and the nature of each is altered, with the result that the place is impassable either afoot or afloat; wherefore those who enter it are carried away to the depths without a handhold to save themselves, the sand within the rim slipping and caving in with them. For these reasons the flats just described have earned a name in keeping with their singular nature, and are called Barathra, or Perdition.[62]

31   Having discussed the features of the three regions defending Egypt by land, we will proceed to what is said about its remaining frontier. The entire fourth side is protected by the Egyptian Sea, and it is washed by a stretch of water almost without harbors. The coast extends a very great distance, and landing in the country is a problem; for except Pharos, not a safe haven is to be found between Paraetonium in Libya and Iopê in Coele-Syria, a coasting voyage of nearly five thousand stades. Besides this, a sandbar stretches along practically the whole coast of Egypt, imperceivable to anyone without experience of sailing in those waters. Therefore, those who imagine they have survived the dangers of the sea and in blissful ignorance head toward the shore, suddenly run their vessels aground and suffer unexpected shipwreck. And many, unable to see the land from afar because the country lies so low, are wrecked without warning, some in marshy fens and swampy places, others in desert regions.

---

62.   The word comes from a root meaning "to devour." The Barathra was on the main military road between Egypt and Palestine. At Athens, condemned criminals were thrown into a rocky cleft known as Barathron, or the Pit.

Egypt, then, is protected by nature on all sides in the ways just described; it is oblong in shape, with a seaboard of two thousand stades, and it extends nearly six thousand stades into the interior. In times gone by its vast population greatly exceeded that of any known place in the inhabited world, and even in our own day it seems inferior to no other. In olden times it had more than eighteen thousand considerable towns and cities, as can be seen recorded in the sacred archives, and in the era of Ptolemy son of Lagus there were enumerated over thirty thousand, most of which have remained until our own times. They say the total population of old was about seven million, and even today it is no less than this.[63] Wherefore, say historians, through this abundance of labor the ancient kings of Egypt raised massive and wondrous works and left for posterity imperishable memorials of their own glory. We will, however, relate the facts about these monuments a little later, in their turn; for now we are concerned with the nature of the river and the unique features of the country.

32   The Nile flows from south to north. It has secret sources in spots unknown: they lie in the deserts of farthest Ethiopia, where the country is inaccessible because of the intolerable heat. It is the greatest of all rivers and passes through a wide extent of land, and it makes great windings, bending at one time to Arabia and the east, at another turning toward Libya and the west. Inclusive of these meanders, it traverses approximately twelve thousand stades in all from the mountains of Ethiopia to its mouth at the sea. In the lower reaches of the river its volume of flow grows ever less as the water is diverted to the lands on either side. Of the two branches which thus split off, the one flowing into Libya is swallowed up in sands of unbelievable depth, while the one coursing in the opposite direction through Arabia empties into vast swamps and marshy lakes of enormous size, around which many races dwell. The Nile enters Egypt ten stades or less in width and flows not in a straight line, but making detours of all kinds; for at one time it turns sharply to the east, at another to the west, and sometimes it even takes a backward course to the south. For hills skirt each bank of the

---

63.   Herodotus II.177 says there were twenty thousand inhabited cities in the time of Amasis, 570-526 B.C.   In the first century A.D. Josephus (*Jewish War* II.385) estimated a population of over 7,500,000, closely agreeing with Diodorus a century earlier. Diodorus must be counting even small hamlets as "cities," for the average population based on his figures is a scant 233 inhabitants per location.

river, extending along much of the land on either side, and cleft with deep ravines and narrow defiles. Dashing against these hills, the river abruptly rushes back through the flat lands once more until, having retreated a considerable distance to the south, it is restored again to its natural course.[64]

And such is its preeminence in all respects, that this river alone of all the rest pursues its way without turbulence or agitation, except at what are called the cataracts. One such place is about ten stades in length, and hemmed into a narrow gorge by overhanging banks; it is rugged throughout and full of ravines, and besides this it is crowded with massive and closely packed rocks sticking up like peaks. As the water violently breaks against these boulders, it is often spun around by these obstacles into a reverse plunge, creating incredible whirlpools. The surge of water fills the entire middle of the chasm with spray, to the great astonishment of anyone coming near. And indeed, the descent of the river is so rapid and violent that it seems as fast as an arrow in flight. When the Nile is in flood and the boulders submerged, and the whole length of rapids is covered by the fullness of the river, boats sometimes sail downstream through the cataracts in the face of contrary winds;[65] but none are ever able to sail upstream, since the force of the river frustrates all human endeavor. There are many cataracts like this one, but the greatest is that at the border between Egypt and Ethiopia.[66]

33   The river also contains many islands, and amongst others in Ethiopia is one of good size called Meroë, in which there is a famous city of the same name which was founded by Cambyses and named

---

64.   Diodorus exaggerates the Nile's width, but his estimate of its length from the mountains of Ethiopia to the sea is far too short; and, not knowing the source of the Nile, he could not have known that its full length is over 4,100 miles. His description of the streams diverted to Libya and Arabia (i.e., at the Delta) reflects the ancient convention that the Nile was the dividing line between them. Diodorus is correct that the Nile occasionally makes detours to east and west of its generally northward course, and in some instances actually flows in a southerly direction.

65.   This seems to mean that the wind was used as a sort of brake. See plates 1 and 4 for scenes of the "closely packed rocks sticking up like peaks" at the first cataract, near Philae.

66.   Ethiopia was the term describing the lands south (upriver) of Egypt, and the dividing line was usually considered the first cataract near Philae. See note 45, above.

after Meroë, his mother.[67] They say this island is shaped like an oblong shield and is the largest by far of all the islands in these parts, for they claim it is three thousand stades long and a thousand broad.[68] It has many cities, of which the most illustrious is Meroë. Hills composed of an infinite quantity of sand flank the entire shore of the island facing Libya, but jagged rocks line the side across from Arabia. There are mines of gold, silver, iron, and copper in this island and, in addition to these, it has great store of ebony[69] and valuable gemstones of all descriptions. In truth, this river boasts more islands than those who hear of it can well believe. For aside from the water-girt regions of the place called the Delta, there are more than seven hundred other islands, some of which are irrigated by the Ethiopians and planted with millet, while others are overrun with serpents and dog-faced apes and are thus unapproachable by men.

Now in Egypt the Nile branches into many channels to create an area called, by reason of its shape, the Delta [Δ]. The two outermost channels demarcate the sides of this Delta, while the sea, which receives the outlets of the river, constitutes the base. The Nile discharges into the sea by seven mouths, of which the first and farthest toward the east is called the Pelusiac, second the Tanitic, then the Mendesian, the Phatnitic, the Sebennytic, and then the Bolbitine and finally the Canopic, which some call the Heracleotic mouth.[70] (There are also other, artificial, outlets which are not worth writing about.) At each mouth a walled city has been built, divided in two by the river, and provided on each side of the outlet with gates and watch towers at well-placed intervals. There is a man-made canal from the Pelusiac mouth to the Gulf of Arabia and the Erythraean Sea. Necho, the son of Psammetichos, initiated the construction of this canal. After him, Darius

---

67.   This explanation of the name is incorrect. Cambyses never reached Meroë. It seems *Meroë* had some general meaning, perhaps "city." The city of Meroë is about 600 miles south of Thebes near modern Kabushiya, Sudan. In Diodorus' day, it was the capital of the powerful Meroïtic kingdom.

68.   The territory of Meroë lies between the Nile and Atbara rivers and is not a true island in any sense. The shape and dimensions given by Diodorus are roughly correct.

69.   Our word ebony comes directly from the Egyptian *hbny*.

70.   Ancient writers agreed that the Nile had seven mouths, but their names varied. The Tanitic mouth was sometimes called the Saïtic or Cataptystic, and the Phatnitic was sometimes known as the Bucolic.

the Persian advanced the work for a while but finally left it incomplete, for he learned from certain people that to dig through the isthmus would cause Egypt to be flooded; for they pointed out that the Erythraean Sea is higher than the land in Egypt. But Ptolemy the Second later finished the work and installed an ingenious lock at the most appropriate spot. This he opened whenever he wished to sail through and quickly closed it again after it had successfully served his purpose. And the rivulet flowing through this canal is called the Ptolemy, after he who created it, and it has at its mouth a city named Arsinoë.[71]

34   So the Delta, then, is very much like Sicily in shape, seven hundred and fifty stades on each side, while the base, which is washed by the sea, has a length of thirteen hundred stades.[72]   This island is intersected by numerous man-made irrigation ditches and comprises the most fertile land in Egypt. As an alluvial soil under irrigation, it yields crops of every description; for each year the inundation of the river regularly deposits a fresh layer of silt, and men easily irrigate the entire

---

71.   The Nile-Red Sea canal really existed, and Diodorus' account of it is accurate in the main. It originally may have been a natural feature, and may have been improved as a canal as early as the XIIth Dynasty, 1991-1783 B.C. Strabo, indeed, credits Sesostris with the earliest work on it. Most sources, however, agree with Diodorus that Necho II, 610-595 B.C. began it, yet left it incomplete when an oracle warned him that it would only benefit the barbarians. Apparently the oracle was right. Darius the Persian, 521-486 B.C., completed the canal primarily from military motives, and it was in active operation in Herodotus' day, c. 484-430 B.C. Commemorative stelae of Darius have been found along the canal route, one of which reads: "Says Darius the King: I am a Persian . . . . From Persia I seized Egypt. I gave command to dig this canal from the river named Nile, that flows through Egypt, to the sea which extends from Persia. After this canal was dug even as I had ordered, ships went from Egypt through this canal to Persia, as was my desire." The canal apparently silted up frequently, and was restored by Ptolemy II Philadelphus, Trajan and Hadrian, and Amr ibn el-'Asi the Moslem conqueror. According to Strabo, its chief use was military, not commercial. The route was east from Bubastis through Wadi Tumilat to Ismailia, then south along the Bitter Lakes to the Gulf of Suez. It was 100-200 feet wide, and 16-17 feet deep.

72.   These dimensions are fairly accurate. The seaboard seems to have diminished since chapter 31, where Diodorus incorrectly says it is 2000 stades.

region by means of a certain machine which Archimedes of Syracuse invented, and which from its shape is named the snail shell [cochlea].[73]

Because the Nile has a sluggish current and also carries down silt of all kinds in great amounts, and since moreover it forms flood-pools in the low ground, fertile marshlands abound. Edible roots of many a flavor grow about these bogs, as well as fruits and leafy vegetables of peculiar varieties, which contribute greatly to self-sufficiency among the poor and feeble of the populace. For not only do these plants supply a variety of plentiful and convenient comestibles for all who have a need, but they furnish materials as well for many of the other necessities of life. Here the lotus grows in profusion, from which the Egyptians prepare a bread well suited for satisfying the physical needs of the body; and the "ciborium," also found here in great abundance, yields the so-called Egyptian bean. There are also many kinds of fruit trees, of which the one called the "persea" bears a fruit of surpassing sweetness; this tree was imported from Ethiopia by the Persians at the time when Cambyses conquered those regions. There are mulberry trees too, of which some bear the black mulberry proper, while some yield a fruit resembling the fig which, since it is produced almost year-round, helps the poor with an unfailing source of food to be had in times of scarcity. The fruit called the blackberry is gathered at the seasonal retreat of the river, and for its delectable sweetness it is consumed as a dessert. The Egyptians also prepare a drink from barley, calling it "zythos," which is little inferior to wine in fragrance. And they use a liquid pressed from a certain plant named "kiki" for burning in their lamps, pouring it in rather than olive oil. Many other plants which are able to furnish some of man's basic necessities also grow widely in Egypt, but it would be tedious to write of every one.[74]

---

73. This refers to Archimedes' screw, a spirally broad-threaded tubular core encased snugly in a cylinder. It was used to raise water by utilizing the efficiencies of continuous circular motion. Vitruvius, *De Architectura* X.6 gives exact directions for constructing such a device. See plate 2.

74. Of the plants described in this paragraph, the lotus or water lily (*Nymphaea lotus*) was a staple of the Egyptian diet. The seeds and roots were made into loaves; the tubers are almost solid starch and can also be boiled or roasted. For the Egyptian bean, see chapter 10, note 13, above. Both of these plants are more fully described in Herodotus II.92 and in Theophrastus, *History of Plants* IV.8.7-11. Zythos is, of course, beer. Kiki is the castor plant, and the illuminant is castor oil, used throughout Egyptian history. Persea is an unidentified tree important in Egyptian myth and art. It is strange that Diodorus

35   Now the Nile is home to many wild animals unique in their form, but two are especially remarkable: the crocodile and the beast known as the "horse." Of these animals, the crocodile grows to the greatest size from the tiniest beginning; for although it lays eggs like those of a goose in size, yet after birth its hatchlings grow to almost sixteen cubits in length. It is as long-lived as man; and it has no tongue. Its body is marvelously protected by nature, for the skin is completely covered with scales and is extremely tough. It is well-provided with teeth in either jaw, having two tusks that greatly exceed the others in size; and it devours not only men, but any other land animals which venture near the river. The bites it inflicts are large and grievous, and it rends terribly with its claws; and the wounds it leaves in the flesh are extremely difficult to heal. Long ago, the Egyptians hunted these monsters using hooks baited with the meat of swine; but later they came to catch them, like certain fish, with stout nets, or else with iron spears, striking them repeatedly to the head from light skiffs. The vast number of crocodiles, both in the river and in the marshes lying nearby, is beyond all reckoning, since they are prolific breeders; also, they are rarely destroyed by man: for most of the natives are accustomed to worship the crocodile as a god, while strangers find no profit whatsoever in hunting it, since its flesh is inedible.[75] But nature has provided nonetheless an effective safeguard, lest the increase of this multitude should overrun mankind. For the animal called the ichneumon, about the same size as a small dog, goes about breaking open the crocodile's eggs (which the creature lays on the riverbanks) and, most astonishingly, it neither eats them nor derives any advantage therefrom, but only fulfills a sort of instinctive and preordained duty by doing this service for the human race.[76]

---

fails to mention papyrus, which besides its use as food (see chapter 80) had many other uses, most notably for making paper, and figured prominently in Egyptian decorative arts (see plate 3).

75.   The crocodile formerly was found throughout Egypt, but its range has now retreated far to the south. Crocodiles were not worshipped everywhere in Egypt, as Diodorus implies, but only in some localities, and they were despised and hunted, even eaten, in others, such as Apollinopolis (Plutarch, *On Isis and Osiris*, 50). They were also hunted for sport. For crocodile worship, see chapters 84 and 89, below, and note 178. See also plate 4.

76.   The ichneumon is a mongoose. See chapter 87 for a more detailed account, and also plate 5.

Now the animal called the "horse" is no less than five cubits in height. It is a quadruped, of cloven hoof like a cow, and has tusks larger than those of a wild boar, three on each side of its mouth; its ears, tail, and sound are somewhat like those of a horse, and the whole trunk of its body is not unlike an elephant's, with the toughest hide of nearly any animal. As it is a creature of both land and river, it spends the day in the water sporting in the deep pools, while at night it browses the grain and hay of the countryside so voraciously that, if it were prolific and produced offspring every year, it would completely destroy the tillage of Egypt. But even this beast is killed by hunting parties, who attack it with iron lances. For wherever it surfaces, their boats converge upon it, and surrounding it, they wound it all over with their barbed, chisel-like weapons of iron; then, tying the end of a rope to one of these embedded harpoons, they let the beast go until it drops from loss of blood. Yet for all this, its flesh is tough and hard to digest, and none of its innards are edible, neither the viscera nor the intestines.[77]

36 Besides these two animals just described, the Nile is home to many species of scaly fish in unbelievable numbers, providing the natives with all the freshly caught fish they can eat and yielding an inexhaustible supply for salting as well. And in truth, the Nile surpasses all other rivers of the known world in its usefulness to man. For, beginning to rise at the summer solstice, it swells until the autumnal equinox; and, bringing fresh silt all the while, it overflows alike the fallow lands, the croplands, and the orchards, for as long as the farmers of each place may wish. As the water flows gently along, they impound it easily with little earthen dams, and let it out again just as simply by breaking these dikes whenever the time seems right. And on the whole, it renders such ease to the work and such convenience to men, that most of the farmers, standing in the parts of the fields that are drying out, simply scatter the seed, let in their flocks to trample it down, and return

---

77. The "horse" is the hippopotamus, or "horse of the river." It is no longer found in Egypt proper. It does not have cloven hooves, and its tail resembles a pig's more than a horse's. The method of hunting hippos with barbed harpoons is described very accurately. (See plate 5a.)

four or five months later for the harvest.[78]   Others, superficially applying
a lightweight plough to the surface of the damp fields, gather in heaps
of produce with practically no toil or expense.   For although farming in
other nations generally is carried on with considerable labor and
expenditure, yet among the Egyptians alone is the harvest brought in
with minimal cost and drudgery.   Likewise the vineyards, which are
flooded along with everything else, yield an abundance of wine to the
inhabitants.   And those who, after the deluge, leave their fields
unplanted as a grazing land for flocks, are blessed with sheep which,
thanks to the luxuriance of the pasturage, bear young twice each year
and twice are shorn.

Now the phenomenon of the Nile's annual rising seems miraculous
enough to those who have witnessed it, but it is quite unbelievable to
those who have it only by hearsay.   For although all other rivers subside
about the time of the summer solstice and dwindle continually for the
remainder of the summer, the Nile alone begins to increase at this very
time and rises so much as the days go by that finally it covers nearly all
of Egypt.[79]   Likewise, when it has exhausted its momentum, it falls a
little each day for the same length of time until it has returned to its
former level.   Since the land is flat, while the cities, villages, and even
farmsteads are raised up on artificial mounds, Egypt during floodtime
begins to look like the Cyclades Islands.   Most of the feral beasts that
live on land are trapped by the rising river and drowned, although some
save themselves by escaping to higher ground; but while the inundation
persists, the cattle are maintained in the villages and farmhouses, eating
fodder prepared for them in advance.   For the duration of the flood, all
the people are freed of their labors and turn to relaxation, feasting
continually and indulging without restraint in everything pertaining to
pleasure.   But since a nagging anxiety remains about the height of the
river, the kings have installed at Memphis the niloscope, by means of

---

78.   Diodorus and other ancient authors undoubtedly exaggerate the ease of
farming in Egypt, but the use of cattle, sheep, and even swine to trample in the
seed is mentioned by many authors and depicted in a number of Egyptian reliefs
and paintings.   See plate 6.

79.   When Diodorus claims that the Nile behaves oppositely to "all other
rivers," he reflects the conventional meteorological knowledge of most
Mediterranean lands, that is, rainy winters with swollen streams, versus arid
summers with dry riverbeds.   The enigmas of the Nile were two: its unknown
source, and its mysterious reversal of normal riverine behavior by rising in
summer (without rain or tributaries) and subsiding in winter.

which responsible officials precisely gauge the rate of increase; and they dispatch bulletins to inform the cities of how many cubits or fingers the river has risen, and on what day it begins to fall. In this way the entire populace is relieved of its uncertainty once it has learned that the river has ceased to swell and started to diminish; and straightaway everyone knows the size of the coming harvest, since the Egyptians have kept accurate records of this phenomenon from time immemorial.[80]

37   There is great perplexity concerning the flooding of the river, and many philosophers and historians have attempted to explain its cause. We will summarize the question here, that we may neither make the digression tiresome, nor yet leave unmentioned a topic of such general interest. Actually, however, some writers simply have not bothered to say anything at all about the overflow of the Nile, nor about its sources, its egress to the sea, or the other points in which this, the greatest river in the inhabited world, differs from other rivers (although these same authors can wax prolix at times about an ordinary rain-swollen torrent). Others, while undertaking to treat of these mysteries, are quite wide of the truth. As for Hellanicus and Cadmus, and even Hecataeus, and all such as these, being thoroughly old-fashioned, they tend toward mythological answers. Herodotus also, as full of curiosity as anyone ever was, tried to elucidate what is known of these subjects, but is found to have followed discredited conjectures; while Xenophon and Thucydides, who are lauded for the accuracy of their researches, totally neglected the vicinity of Egypt in their writing. Even Ephorus and Theopompus, who worried more about these subjects than anyone else, were the farthest of all from attaining the true facts. All these writers have failed, not through carelessness, but because of the peculiar nature of the country. For from remote antiquity down to the time of

---

80.   Rainless Egypt was almost totally dependent on one source of water, the Nile; and a life-or-death anxiety about its annual inundation is understandable. In *Natural History* V.10, Pliny explains that "the country has reason to make careful note of either extreme [in river height]. When the water rises to only 12 cubits they experience the horrors of famine; when it attains to 13, hunger still results; a rise of 14 cubits produces gladness; a rise of 15 sets all anxieties at rest, while an increase of 16 meets with unbounded transports of joy . . . ." The nilometer, which Diodorus incorrectly calls the niloscope, was simply a well on the river bank calibrated with lines indicative of water height. There were nilometers at Elephantine, Philae, Edfu, Esna, and Fustat as well as at Memphis, where the mean normal rise was fourteen cubits according to Plutarch (*On Isis and Osiris* 43). See plate 7.

Ptolemy who was called Philadelphus, not only had no Greeks penetrated into Ethiopia, but none had ascended even so far as the borders of Egypt, so inhospitable and altogether hazardous was everything about these places; but the above-mentioned monarch, with a Greek army, was the first who marched into Ethiopia, from which time the facts about that country have been more accurately known.[81]

Such, then, are the reasons for the ignorance of the earlier historians about these matters. And even down to the time of writing this present history, no one has claimed actually to have seen the sources of the Nile or the spot from which the river starts its course, nor published a report derived from anyone proven to have seen these places. So the matter boils down to guesswork and plausible conjecture. For instance, the priests of Egypt say the Nile originates in the world-encircling ocean; but they are dealing in riddles, merely explaining one puzzle with another and offering to prove it with a proposition which itself sorely lacks proof. Those of the Trogodytes called the Bolgii, on the other hand, who migrated northward out of these regions to escape the withering heat, report certain facts concerning those places, from which one might infer that the Nile stream owes its existence to the confluence of many springs in one spot; and that for this reason it is the most life-sustaining of all known rivers. But those who dwell near the island of Meroë, whom one might be most likely to trust (since they live nearest the places in question and are the least inclined to sophistical speculations of plausibility) possess so little definite information on these matters that they have even named the river "Astapus;" which translated into Greek means "water from darkness"! These folk, then, have given the Nile a name consonant with their lack of knowledge about these places and in keeping with their own ignorance; but to us the most truthful explanation seems to be the one most free of fabrication.

Of course, I am not unaware that Herodotus, distinguishing between the Libya to the east of the river and that to the west, attributes to those Libyans known as Nasamonians an accurate knowledge of its course: he claims the Nile has its origin in a certain lake and flows forth through the untold vastness of the land of Ethiopia. Yet surely, without proof

---

81.   Ptolemy II Philadelphus, 285-246 B.C., sent an expedition beyond the old frontier at the first cataract early in his reign; but Diodorus is wrong in asserting that no Greek had ever before ascended as far as the border. Herodotus was there, and describes his visit (II.29-32); Greek forces were stationed there under Alexander and Ptolemy I; and Greek mercenaries had accompanied Psammetichos II on a campaign to Napata in 591 B.C., leaving graffiti along their route.

one should heed neither what Libyans say (even if, indeed, they have
spoken the truth), nor what Herodotus reports about their stories.[82]

38   Having now written of the sources of the Nile and of its course,
we will next attempt to explain the causes of its flooding. Thales, who
is called one of the seven sages, says that the etesian wind, blowing
against the outlets of the river, impedes the progress of the stream to the
sea and thus causes it to back up and overflow Egypt, which is low-
lying and flat.[83]   But, convincing as this reasoning appears, its error is
easily proven. For if this were the true explanation, all rivers having
their mouths exposed to the etesian winds would experience a similar
increase: and since this happens nowhere in the known world, one must
seek elsewhere for the real cause of the Nile's swelling. Anaxagoras the
natural philosopher proclaims that melting snow in Ethiopia is the reason
for the increase. Euripides, his disciple, agrees with this; or at least he
says

> He left behind Nile's fair cascade,
> The fairest far of all the earth,
> Whose stream pours forth from Negro land:
> The land of Ethiopia,
> Whence waters flow from melting snow
> [And wander far through plains below].
>
> [Frag. 228, Nauck.]

---

82.   Diodorus misquotes Herodotus II.32-34, who does not mention a lake as
the source of the Nile. In fact, he asserts truthfully that the source was
unknown. He claims that five adventurous Nasamonians (Libyans of the regions
near the Syrtis) traveled south, then west, on a journey of exploration "for many
days over a wide extent of sand." Captured by short black men while gathering
fruit in a wooded plain, they were conducted across extensive marshes to a town.
"A great river flowed by the town from west to east, and containing crocodiles."
Only the Niger river fits this description. But Herodotus, on the analogy of the
Danube, assumed that the Nile must also flow from west to east, dividing Libya
(= Africa) the way the Danube divides Europe. Then, because of the crocodiles,
which in Greek experience of that day existed only in the Nile, he assumed that
this river must be the upper Nile, a misconception that persisted for over two
thousand years. Ibn Batuta in A.D. 1352 sailed on the Niger and reported that it
extended to Egypt and became the Nile. See plate 8.

83.   Etesian (or "annual," from *etos* or "year" in Greek) in this context must
mean the northwest winds which blow in summer from the Mediterranean; but the
term did not refer to any precise set of winds.

But it happens that this explanation, like the last one, admits of an obvious refutation, as it is manifestly impossible for snow to fall in Ethiopia because of the burning heat. For generally in these regions there is neither ice nor cold, nor so much as the hint of winter, especially at the season of the Nile's increase. But even should one concede that immense fields of snow exist in the territory beyond Ethiopia, the fallacy of this assertion can be proven nonetheless: for it is well known that every river formed from melting snow exhales cool breezes and thickens the air; but around the Nile, unique among rivers, no cloud masses arise, no cool breezes occur, and the air does not grow thick.

Now Herodotus claims [at II.24-25] the Nile's normal height is that which it attains at its fullness, but that in winter the sun, passing directly over Libya, draws much of the moisture to itself out of the Nile, thereby causing the river to become unnaturally lower during this season. Then when summer is at hand the sun, retreating in its course to the north, evaporates and lowers the rivers in Greece and in other countries similarly situated. Consequently, he says, the behavior of the Nile is a mystery no longer, since it does not increase in the summer at all, but merely diminishes during the winter for the reason just mentioned. Now one must admit even this conjecture to be acceptable if, just as the sun draws moisture to itself from the Nile during the winter months, it would also take up some of the water from the other rivers in Libya and reduce their flow. But since this phenomenon is not observed anywhere in Libya, the writer is plainly caught in an improvisation. And as for the rivers in Greece, surely they are swollen in winter by the ample rains, not by the sun withdrawing to a greater distance!

39   Democritos of Abdera says that it is not the southern climes that are covered with snow, as claimed by Euripides and Anaxagoras, but those of the north; and this is plain to all. The great accumulation of snow in the northern zone remains frozen during winter, but as summer's warmth unlocks the grip of ice, a great melting takes place; and this causes the formation of many dense clouds in the upper elevations as thick vapors ascend into the atmosphere. These clouds are driven before the etesian winds until they run up against the highest mountains in the known world, which, he says, are in Ethiopia. Then disintegrating upon impact with these towering peaks, they beget immense downpours which swell the river to a prodigious extent at the season of the etesian winds. Yet this theory too is easily refuted, by accurately observing the timing of the Nile's inundation. For it begins to rise at the summer solstice, when the etesian winds are not yet blowing, and ceases after the autumn equinox, long after the said winds have stopped. Since, therefore, the certainty of fact outweighs the plausibility of speculation, we must not believe what Democritos says, though we may acknowledge his fertile imagination.[84]   Besides, need I point out that the etesian winds are seen to blow as often from the west as from the north?   For not only the Borean and Aparctian winds, but the Argestean winds as well, which blow from the summer sunset, have a right to be called etesian.[85]   Also, as it happens, the statement that the world's highest mountains are in Ethiopia is not only unprovable, but lacks the credence yielded by direct observation.

Finally, Ephorus propounds a most novel hypothesis and tries to back it with convincing arguments, but in no way does he hit upon the truth. For, says he, since all the land in Egypt is alluvial and porous with a nature like pumice stone, it is riddled with an extensive and unbroken network of fissures by which it absorbs a prodigious quantity of water; it holds this fast within itself during the winter season, but in summer releases it like perspiration from every pore; and in this way the river is filled up.   But this writer, it seems to me, not only has never seen the true nature of the different places in Egypt, but has not even accurately learned the facts about this country from those who know.   For to begin with, if the Nile derived its increase from within Egypt itself, it would not flood in its upper reaches, where it flows through lands both rocky and impervious; yet in fact, flowing more than six thousand stades through Ethiopia, it attains its full height before reaching Egypt. Furthermore, if the Nile's waters were lower lying than the vacuities in the alluvial soil, it follows that these cavities would be exposed on the surface and unable to retain so great a quantity of water.   But on the other hand, if the river occupied a higher level than the fissures, the water would not be able to flow up from the hollows to the higher plane.

---

84.   Heavy rains in central Africa from April to September are, of course, the cause of the Nile's inundation in Egypt from June to November.   The time lag is due to the enormous length of the river's course.   Diodorus rightly rejects the role of the etesian winds in this cycle, but not the rain itself.   See his discussion of the hypothesis of Agatharchides, chapter 41.

85.   The Borean and Aparctian were northerly winds; the Argestean was a northwesterly.

But, in any case, can one believe it possible for exudations from cracks in the ground to make so great an increase in the river that nearly all of Egypt is submerged thereby? And indeed I make no comment on the false assertion that the soil is alluvial and that the water is stored in its crannies, since the refutation of these things is self-evident. For in Asia the river Meander has deposited great expanses of alluvial soil, yet in its case not one of the phenomenon connected with the overflow of the Nile is to be observed. Likewise, both the river called the Acheloüs in Acarnania, and the Cephisus which flows into Boeotia from Phocis, have each built up a lot of alluvial land, and both clearly prove the mistake of this writer. But of course one should never expect accuracy from Ephorus, seeing that he values truth so lightly in so many ways.

40   Now, certain philosophers of Memphis have tried to offer an explanation for the rising of the Nile, which is not so much convincing as it is merely impossible of disproof, but to which many have subscribed. For dividing the earth into three zones, they claim that one includes the world we know, a second is opposite to ours in its seasons, and between them lies a third which is uninhabitable because of the awful heat. If, they continue, the Nile were to rise in wintertime, we could be certain that it receives its influx from within our zone, owing to the especially copious rainfall we experience in that season. But on the contrary, since it rises in the summer, it is probable that winter storms are then raging in the regions lying opposite to our own, and that the excess water from those places is being carried to our part of the earth. And naturally, no traveler is able to reach the sources of the Nile, since from this antipodean zone the river flows through the uninhabitable one. They also avow that the fine purity of the Nile's water bears further witness to their theory: for in flowing through the torrid zone it is tempered, and because of this it is the freshest of all rivers, inasmuch as fire and heat by their nature always purify water.

But this argument has an easy and obvious rebuttal, since it seems totally impossible for a river to flow up out of the world opposite to our own, especially if one holds the earth to be a sphere.[86]   And indeed, although men's sophistry would thus brazenly contradict observational

---

86.   Diodorus, like all men of his day, had no concept of gravity. Without such a frame of reference, it is excusable for Diodorus, who was no scientist, to confuse his own northern side of the globe with "up." Yet this ignorant error is amazingly prevalent even today.

evidence, at least the nature of the facts will in no way support them. For by offering an assertion impossible to refute, and by placing an uninhabitable land between the other two zones, they expect by this dodge to avoid close scrutiny of their ideas. However, it is incumbent on those arguing strongly for any point of view either to offer factual proof themselves, or to cite generally accepted evidence at the outset. For why is the Nile the only river flowing up from that hemisphere to our own? It is probable that other rivers exist there, just as among us. And their reason for the purity of the water is absolutely absurd! For were the river to become sweet by being tempered in the heat, it would not teem with life nor support so many species of fish and game, for water changed by the action of the fiery element is most hostile to the generation of animal life. And since, therefore, the real nature of the Nile is contrary to this supposed tempering, we may conclude that the causes they advance for the increase of the river are untrue as well.

41   Next, Oenopides of Chios doth contend that the waters in the earth are cold in summer but, on the contrary, warm in winter. This fact becomes quite clear at deep wells: for their waters are the least cold in the middle of winter, whereas the coolest water is drawn from them on the hottest days. Therefore it is logical that the Nile is low in winter and reduced in volume, since the heat in the earth evaporates the greatest part of its own water, and because there are no rains in Egypt. But in summer, when this vaporization is no longer occurring in the bowels of the earth, the river channel is filled up naturally without hindrance. But again, to this explanation one may object that many of the rivers in Libya, whose mouths have the same orientation and whose courses are substantially similar, do not experience a rise analogous to that of the Nile; indeed, on the contrary, by swelling in the winter and abating during the summer they attest the falsehood of one who is trying to obscure the truth with clever arguments.

But it is Agatharchides of Cnidos who has come closest to the truth. For he says there are incessant rainstorms in the mountains of Ethiopia from the summer solstice until the autumnal equinox. Thus it is reasonable that in winter the Nile is low, since it gets its water only from its sources, while in summer it increases by the runoff from these storms. And since no one until now has been able to explain the origin of the flood waters, he contends that it is not fair to scoff at his own theory; for nature presents many such contrary phenomena for which men find it difficult to discover the precise causes.[87]   He points out that occurrences in certain parts of Asia lend support to his own statements; for instance, near the confines of Scythia, in the vicinity of Mount Caucasus, every year after winter has already passed, violent snow storms blow continuously for many a day; and in districts lying in the north of India hailstones of unbelievable size and number crash down at certain seasons; while near the river Hydaspes unceasing rainstorms occur, beginning in summer; and the same thing happens for days at a time in Ethiopia, for this recurrent climatic condition always raises storms in adjacent regions.   It is therefore nothing marvelous if in Ethiopia, which lies above Egypt, incessant rainstorms descending on the mountains in summer fill up the river, especially as the plain fact itself is so testified by the barbarians dwelling in these places.   But although the phenomena just mentioned are opposite in nature to those existing among us, they should not for this reason be disbelieved; for with us the south wind is indeed stormy, but in Ethiopia it is fair; while the north winds, boisterous in Europe, are weak and languid in that country.

So concerning the flooding of the Nile, although we could well have answered all these theories in more detail, we will rest content with what we have said, that we may not deviate from the brevity we promised at the start.   And since we have divided this book into two parts because of its great length, we shall for the sake of due proportion conclude the first volume of our chronicle, and in the second we shall relate what comes next in the history of Egypt, starting with an account of those who were kings of Egypt, and the earliest manner of life among the Egyptians.

---

87.   See note 84 to chapter 39, above.   Agatharchides' hypothesis was essentially correct, but he too ignored the length of time it takes for the Nile to rise in Egypt following the rains three thousand miles upstream.   The rains begin in April, but flooding does not reach Egypt until June.   Agatharchides considered this theory a "contrary phenomenon" which his Greek readers, conditioned to consider dry summers and wet winters as normal, would scarcely believe.   See note 79 to Chapter 36, above.

Part Two

42   The first book of Diodorus having been divided into two volumes because of its great size, the first contained the introduction to the whole work, and those things the Egyptians have to say about the origin of the world and the first foundation of the universe, and about those gods who founded cities in Egypt named after themselves; also what they say about the first genesis of mankind and his earliest manner of life; about the worship of the gods and the building of their temples; and about the topography of the land in Egypt, the wonders related of the river Nile, and the causes of its flooding, with the theories of the historians and philosophers concerning it as well as a refutation of each writer.[88]

In this book we shall relate in detail the subjects next in order to what we have said before. We begin with those who were the first kings of Egypt. We shall expound the achievements of each in turn up to king Amasis, after, however, we have first given in summary fashion an account of the most primitive mode of existence among the Egyptians.

43   They say that in primeval times the meadows supplied the earliest foods to the Egyptians, who ate of the stalks and roots growing in the marshlands. They tried the taste of every plant, but first and foremost in their diet was the one called Agrostis,[89] both because of its superior sweetness and because it afforded adequate nutrition in itself for the human body; and indeed men saw for themselves that the cattle preferred it and rapidly waxed fat upon it. And therefore until this very

---

88.   This paragraph seems to be the addition of an editor.

89.   This could be dog's-tooth grass, *Cynodon dactylon,* mentioned in Theophrastus *History of Plants,* I.6.7, I.6.10, and IV.10.6.

55

day, whenever men approach the gods, they call to mind the usefulness of this plant, holding it in their hands as they offer their prayers; for they believe that man is a creature of the swamp and marsh, judging from both his smooth skin and his physical qualities, and moreover because he requires moist food rather than dry.

Later on, they say, the Egyptians subsisted by eating fish, of which the river supplied a great store, especially when it was low and drying up after the annual flood. And some in like manner also ate the flesh of cattle, making clothes from the skins of those they ate. They also built homes for themselves out of reeds. Vestiges of this way of life still remain among the herdsmen in Egypt, all of whom, they say, have no other habitations than those they make of reeds, and with these they see fit to be content.

After living in this fashion for a considerable length of time, men progressed at last to the use of cultivated foods, including the bread made from the lotus. Some attribute the discovery of these foods to Isis, others to a certain king of olden time named Menas.[90] Now, the priests tell in their myths that Hermes was the father of learning and the arts, but that the kings discovered the things necessary to life; wherefore, kingship in antiquity was not bequeathed to the progeny of those who ruled, but to those who conferred on the populace the greatest or most numerous benefits, either because the people would thus inspire their kings with concern for the common good, or else because they were really so instructed by their sacred books.

44   Now some of them relate the fable that the first rulers in Egypt, for nearly eighteen thousand years, were gods and heroes, and that the last of the gods to hold sway was Horus, son of Isis; but they say the country has been ruled by mortals now for close to five thousand years, down to the One Hundred and Eightieth Olympiad, at the time of my visit to Egypt in the reign of Ptolemy surnamed "The New Dionysus."[91] Native kings held the throne for the greater part of this period, and

---

90.   For lotus bread, see chapter 34 and note 74, above. Menas (or Menes, Menis, Menon, Meinios, Minaios, Min, etc. in other classical authors) was said to be the first mortal king of Egypt, after the reigns of the gods and heroes (see chapter 45, below). Modern Egyptologists identify him with either Na'rmer, one of the last predynastic kings, or 'Aha of the Ist Dynasty. See plates 9a and 9b.

91.   The 180th Olympiad was 60/59 to 57/56 B.C. Ptolemy XII Auletes (or Neos Dionysus) reigned for most of the period 80-51 B.C.

Ethiopians, Persians, and Macedonians for a small part: to be exact, four Ethiopians ruled a bit less than thirty-six years, not all at once but with an interval.   The Persians ruled for a hundred and thirty-five years after Cambyses the king had subdued the nation by force of arms; this includes the rebellion staged by the Egyptians when they could no longer endure the harshness of the Persians' yoke nor brook their impiety toward the native gods.   Last of all have the Macedonians and their descendants reigned for two hundred and seventy-six years.   In all the remaining periods, natives of the country ruled continuously, four hundred and seventy being men and five women.[92]   The priests have a record concerning every one of them in their sacred books, which have been handed down without interruption to each succeeding generation. These records tell the stature and temperament of each king and the achievements of each in his own day.   But it would be wearisome and unnecessary for us to write the deeds of every one in succession, since the majority of their acts offer no instruction.   Therefore we shall only undertake to explain briefly the most critical facts of historical significance.

45   They say, then, that Menas was the first to rule Egypt after the gods, and that he taught the people to worship the gods and offer them sacrifices.   But he also taught them to provide themselves with tables and couches and to make use of sumptuous bed furnishings; in short, he introduced them to luxury and a lavish style of life.   They say, however, that many generations later, when Tnephachthos (father of Bocchoris the Wise) was king and had marched into Arabia, where provisions failed him in the rough and desolate terrain, he was forced by necessity to sup

---

92.   Diodorus is correct in saying that four "Ethiopian," i.e. Nubian, kings ruled Egypt, in that the last four kings of the Nubian XXVth Dynasty controlled all or most of the country.   Two earlier Nubian kings, Kashta and Piye or Pi'ankhi, held only partial or imperfect sway.   The duration of the later XXVth Dynasty was fifty-five years, c. 712-657 B.C.; the "interval" in their rule must be the two years 671-669 when Esarhaddon the Assyrian temporarily drove the Nubian king Taharqa out of the country.   The Persians ruled from 525-404 B.C., or 121 years, being ejected by Amyrtaios, sole king in the native XXVIIIth Dynasty.   The Persians briefly regained control in 343 B.C., but lost it to Alexander in 332.   The 276 years of Macedonian rule mentioned by Diodorus proves that he wrote this passage in 56 or 55 B.C. (see note 6, above).   Diodorus greatly overestimates the number of native Egyptian kings, and does not seem to know of foreign rulers such as the Hyksos kings of the XVth Dynasty.   But he is correct in the number of native queens.

one day at the extremely poor abode of some ordinary common citizens. But he enjoyed himself immensely, and he thereupon denounced luxury and called down a curse on Menas, the king who had set the first example of extravagance. And so much to heart did he take this change in meat, drink and sleep, that he had the curse inscribed in sacred letters on the temple of Zeus at Thebes, which undoubtedly seems to be the reason that the fame and glory of Menas did not persist into future ages.[93]

It is said that fifty-two descendants of this last-mentioned king [Menas] ruled one after another for more than a thousand and forty years in all, during which time nothing worth writing occurred.

Next, Busiris became king and eight of his descendants in turn. They say that the last of this line, who had the same name as the first, founded the great city which the Egyptians named after Zeus, but which the Greeks call Thebes.[94] He made it a hundred and forty stades in circumference and embellished it wondrously with huge buildings, splendid temples, and other ornaments; he likewise built houses for the private citizens, some of four stories, some of five; and generally speaking, he made this city more opulent than the others in Egypt or anywhere else. Its fame spread abroad to every corner of the world

---

93.   Bocchoris, c. 717-712 B.C., was an historical king of the XXIVth Dynasty, mentioned also in chapters 65, 79, and 94 below. Tnephachthos is probably his predecessor and father Tefnakhte, c. 724-717 B.C.

94.   Thebes existed as a provincial town, capital of the 4th Upper Egyptian nome, under the Old Kingdom, c. 2575-2134 B.C., but remains of this period are scarce. It rose to prominence during the XIth Dynasty, c. 2134-1991 B.C., and reached its peak in the XVIIIth Dynasty, c. 1550-1307 B.C., when it became the capital of Egypt. The temples, tombs, and other archaeological monuments of the Theban area are among the most extensive and astounding in the world. That Busiris was the founder of Thebes is a myth. In fact, the ancient traditions about Busiris are so contradictory (and so lacking in support from Egyptian sources) that it is no surprise that Diodorus, who was not the most critical of historians, is utterly confused on the subject. In chapter 17, he mentions a Busiris who governed part of Egypt in the absence of Osiris. Here, he notes two later kings of that name, one a descendant of the other and founder of Thebes (also in chapter 15). But in chapter 88, he denies there was a king Busiris at all, and explains the name to mean Tomb of Osiris. Both in chapter 88 and earlier in chapter 67 he denies the standard Greek legend of Busiris, the ruler who killed all foreigners setting foot in Egypt, but he gives contradictory reasons for the story; and later in Book IV he accepts the legend without comment. In chapter 85 he gives another etymology, this one ridiculous, for the name itself.

because of its unrivaled wealth and power, and they point out that even
the poet takes note of it in the passage where he says

> Not even Thebes, of Egypt far,
> Where great domestic riches are;
> Whose hundred gates, swung full ajar,
> Send forth each one in time of war
> Two hundred men with horse and car.

[*Illiad*, 9.381-384]

Some deny the city had a hundred gates but say that it possessed many
grand temple porticoes, from which it got the name "the Hundred-gated,"
exactly as if it had numerous gates.[95]   But twenty thousand chariots did
in fact go forth from it to the wars; for there were a hundred remount
stations along the side of the river opposite Libya, stretching from
Memphis all the way to Thebes, and each one accommodated up to two
hundred horses. The foundations of these facilities are still pointed out
today.

46   We have heard that not this king alone, but also many others
who ruled later, made liberal contributions to the enhancement of this
city. For no other city under the sun has been adorned to this extent
with so many and such splendid decorations of silver, gold, and ivory;
with such a number of colossal portrait statues, and, in addition to all
this, with obelisks hewn from single blocks of stone. Four temples were
raised there, the oldest of which is noteworthy both in size and grace;
for it is thirteen stades in circuit and forty-five cubits high, with
courtyard walls twenty-four feet thick.[96]   This scale of magnificence was

---

95.   A play on words. The Greek term for temple porticoes, "propylaea," is
similar to its epithet for many-gated, "polypylaea."   The monumental pylon
entrances to the numerous temples at Thebes (see plate 12) give some plausibility
to this etymology of the epithet "Hundred-gated."

96.   Thebes proper is on the east bank of the Nile. There were more than
four temples in the city, but perhaps Diodorus refers only to the four largest: that
of Ammon or Min at Luxor; and at Karnak, the temple precincts of Montu, Mut,
and Ammon. (See plate 11.) To judge by the dimensions, this last must be the
one described by Diodorus as the "oldest," for none of the others approach it in
size. If anything, Diodorus underestimates its magnitude. The brick enclosure
wall, which must have been impressively intact in his day, is over 8,000 feet in
circumference (slightly exceeding 13 stades of 606.7 feet). The temple itself is

60 Diodorus Siculus

matched by its style of decoration, which was astounding for its expense and outstanding in point of craftsmanship. But while the structures themselves have survived until our era, the silver, gold, and ivory, and a king's ransom in precious stones, were carried off by the Persians at the time when Cambyses burned the temples of Egypt. They say it was at this period that the Persians, having stolen away this wealth to Asia and kidnapped artisans by force out of Egypt, built for themselves the celebrated palaces in Persepolis, Susa, and Media. But of so vast an extent, they boast, was the wealth of Egypt in those days, that the amount salvaged here and there from the burnt ruins of the pillage was found to total more than three hundred talents in gold and not less than two thousand three hundred in silver!

They assert that in that city the tombs of the ancient kings were so wonderful that they left nothing to be surpassed by those of later birth who aspired to the like. Now the priests claim to find records of forty-seven royal tombs, but they say that by the reign of Ptolemy son of Lagus only seventeen remained; and many of these were in ruins at the time of our visit to those parts in the One Hundred and Eightieth Olympiad.[97] And it is not only the priests of Egypt quoting from their archives who corroborate what we have said, but also many of the Greeks who traveled to Thebes in the days of Ptolemy son of Lagus and who wrote books on Egyptian history: Hecataeus is one of these.

47   Now Hecataeus tells us that ten stades from the oldest tombs (in which, according to tradition, the concubines of Zeus lie buried) there stands a monument to the king named Osymandias.[98]   And at its

---

1,220 feet long and 370 feet wide at its widest point. The west pylon is 142.5 feet high, double the 45 cubits given by Diodorus. The oldest part of the complex still standing dates to Tuthmosis I, c. 1500 B.C., but evidence of buildings from the reign of Senwosret I have been found in the enclosure, c. 1950 B.C. (See plates 10a and 10b.)

97.   There are over sixty king's tombs known in the vicinity of Thebes, mostly in the famous Valley of the Kings in the western desert. This barren valley was the site of King Tut'ankhamun's tomb. (In the same general area are a number of queen's tombs, and hundreds of non-royal burials.)   But Diodorus probably refers not to the actual burial sites themselves, which are mostly remote, secluded, and hidden below ground, but the many mortuary temples lining the foothills at the edge of the irrigated plain. (See plate 11.)

98.   The name Osymandias occurs nowhere else in ancient literature. The temple described in the next several chapters is almost certainly the well-known

entrance is a pylon of variegated stone, two plethra in length and forty-five cubits tall; within this gate is a square peristyle court of stone, each side being of four plethra; and instead of pillars, it is supported by monolithic statues sixteen cubits high of figures executed in the ancient manner. The entire ceiling is made from one slab of stone almost two fathoms in width decorated with stars on a dark blue background. Next beyond this peristyle is another entranceway and a pylon resembling the first in all else, but more profusely wrought with every kind of carving. Beside the entrance are three portrait statues, each carved out of a single block of black stone from Syene. Of these, one seated figure is the largest statue in Egypt, the foot of which measures more than seven cubits. The other two, standing near its knees to the right and left, are inferior in size to this one and represent his daughter and mother. But this work of art deserves praise not only for its size, but also for its admirable workmanship and for the excellent quality of the stone, since despite such great bulk, neither crack nor flaw can be seen therein. And this has been written upon it:

> I am Osymandias, King of kings. Should any man seek to know how great I am and where I lie, let him surpass one of my works.

There is another statue also of his mother alone, a monolith of twenty cubits; on its head it has three diadems, which symbolize that she was the daughter, the wife, and mother of a king.[99]

"Ramesseum," the mortuary temple of Ramesses II, c. 1290-1224 B.C. If the concubines' tombs are conjectured to be those in the Valley of the Queens a little over a mile away, this fits the ten stades of Diodorus almost perfectly. See plate 11. "Osymandias" may be a corruption of Userma'atre' or Usimare, part of the praenomen (royal name) of Ramesses II.

99. As he himself says, Diodorus is merely paraphrasing a description of this temple complex given by Hecataeus of Abdera (in his *Aigyptiaka*, now lost, written two centuries earlier). Diodorus himself apparently never saw the temple. If it is indeed the Ramesseum (see note 98, above), his account is accurate in general, but not in every detail. For instance, the first pylon is of sandstone, not "variegated" stone such as marble or porphyry. The dimensions given for this pylon are roughly accurate, but those of the first peristyle court are exaggerated, and the portrait columns are not monoliths. The astronomical ceiling is misplaced; it may have covered what Diodorus calls, probably erroneously, the "library" (chapter 49, below). The well-preserved astronomical/astrological ceiling in this second hypostyle hall is not monolithic. The colossal black stone portrait

Beyond this pylon is another peristyle even more remarkable than the first. Within it are reliefs of all kinds to illustrate the war that Osymandias waged against the Bactrians, who had rebelled, and against whom he took the field with four hundred thousand infantry and twenty thousand cavalry. The whole army was divided into four parts, all of which were commanded by sons of the king.

48   On the first wall the king is depicted besieging a fortified city encircled by a river. With the aid of a lion, he bears the brunt of the fight against the enemy, and the ferocious animal spreads terror with his assault. Concerning this scene, some commentators say that there really was a pet lion raised by the king to share the dangers of battle with him and break the ranks of the enemy by its onslaught; but other historians claim that the king, though extremely brave, basely desired to extol himself by representing the spirit of his own disposition in the image of a lion. On the second wall the carvings show captives being led away by the king. These prisoners have neither genitals nor hands, which seems to imply that they were devoid of manly courage and had no skill in the terrible art of war. The third wall has carvings of all descriptions and magnificent paintings which show the king sacrificing oxen and leading a triumph after the war.[100]   In the center of the peristyle, an open-air altar has been built of the most beautiful stone, excellent in workmanship and remarkable in size. At the final wall of the peristyle are two monolithic seated statues of seven and twenty cubits in height; nearby, three doorways have been built leading from the peristyle into a

---

statue, though now toppled and badly mutilated, still exists (although its three smaller companions are gone) and still excites amazement, being over 57 feet in height. No trace remains of the inscription; nineteen centuries later these lines preserved by Diodorus inspired Shelley's celebrated poem, *Ozymandias.* See plates 12-15.

100. The battle reliefs in the Ramesseum depict the siege of Kadesh (or Qadesh), a town on the upper Orontes river in Syria, where Ramesses II won a minor engagement against the Hittites early in his reign, c. 1288 B.C. The vanity of Ramesses, or perhaps his need for favorable propaganda, magnified the encounter into a great victory, and he carved the details not only on the pylon walls of the Ramesseum, but also in temples at Karnak, Luxor, Abu Simbel, Abydos, and Derr. See plates 16a and 16b. Two official reports and one poem survive which describe this fight, making it the earliest battle in history whose details are known. Diodorus' description of these reliefs, and of the others in the temple, are fairly reliable.

hypostyle hall made in the form of an Odeum, or music hall, each side of which is two plethra in length. This hall contains many wooden statues depicting men engaged in legal disputes, their gaze directed toward those who decide the cases; and the judges themselves have been carved upon one of the walls, to the number of thirty, but without any hands. The chief judge is in their midst with his eyes shut. Round his neck hangs the icon of Truth, and many books lie scattered about him. These images convey symbolically that judges ought to accept no bribes, and that the chief judge ought to see nothing but the truth.

49   Next to the hypostyle hall stretches a gallery crowded with all manner of rooms, in which are depicted many kinds of food most pleasant to the taste. Here one finds reliefs decorated with bright colors, in which the king presents the god with the gold and silver he was wont to receive annually from all the mines of Egypt; and also, inscribed below, is the stupendous amount of this tribute, which, reckoned up in terms of silver, is thirty-two million minas. The next building is the sacred library, upon which are inscribed the words "Balm of the Soul;" adjoining this are statues of all the gods of Egypt, and likewise of the king bringing presents which are appropriate to each one, as if demonstrating both to Osiris and to the lesser divinities that he has fulfilled a life of piety and justice toward men and gods. Separated from the library by a party wall is a well-built dining room with capacity for twenty couches, which contains statues of Zeus and Hera as well as the king, and in which it seems that the body of the king lies interred.[101]   Surrounding this, many chambers have been constructed which show admirable paintings of all the animals held sacred in Egypt. There is an ascent through these apartments to the roof of the tomb, mounting which one formerly reached a golden cornice running round the entire monument, three hundred and sixty-five cubits long and a cubit thick. On this were engraved, one for each cubit, the days of the year, beside each of which were noted both the risings and settings of the stars as they naturally occur, as well as the seasonal changes that these portend according to the Egyptian astrologers. They say, however,

---

101. Much of the hypostyle hall still stands (see plate 17). The three entrances from the second peristyle court are identifiable, as are the two colossi of the latter, but no trace of an altar remains. The gallery, "library," and dining hall all seem to be part of the House of Life, a feature of many Egyptian temples. However, the king was not buried anywhere in the temple complex.

64   Diodorus Siculus

that this encircling border was carried away by Cambyses and his Persians at the time they conquered Egypt.

Such then is the description they give of the funerary temple of Osymandias the king, which seems to exceed all others not only in the vast scale of its expense, but also in the genius of its builders.

50   The Thebans assert that they themselves are of all men the most ancient, and that they were the first to discover philosophy as well as scientific astrology, since their country facilitates a very clear observation of the risings and settings of the stars. Their ordering of months and years is also peculiar to them, for they do not count off the days according to the moon, but rather by the sun, fixing the month at thirty days; and they intercalate five days and a quarter in every twelvemonth, in this way bringing the yearly cycle up to full measure. But they neither make use of intercalated months, nor do they subtract days, as do most of the Greeks.[102]   Also, they seem to have studied with care the eclipses of the sun and moon and make predictions concerning them, infallibly foretelling every particular.

Now the eighth descendant of King Osymandias, who was called Uchoreus after his father, founded Memphis, the most illustrious city in Egypt. For he sought out the most fitting site in all the land, the place where the Nile divides into many branches to create the Delta (so called by reason of its shape); wherefore it came to pass that the city, opportunely situated, as it were, at the gateway to Egypt, was master of

---

102. The Egyptians had an ancient lunar calendar, of 354 days, for religious purposes. But possibly as early as July 19, 4241 B.C. (no later than 2781 B.C.) the Egyptians adopted a civil calendar of 365 days, composed of twelve conventional months of thirty days, plus five epagomenal days at yearend (not five and a quarter, as Diodorus says). With no leap year or other adjustment to compensate for the one quarter day shortfall, the civil year gradually crept out of synchronization with the seasons, coming back to its starting point once in approximately 1459 natural (or 1461 civil) years. Hence to keep the agricultural season from utter confusion, a "Sothic" year was also used, which always began at the heliacal rising of the star Sopdet (Greek Sothis = Sirius, the "dog star") which is July 19 in our calendar (see note 36, above). The civil year theoretically started on the same day, but of course an actual correspondence only occurred once every 1460 Sothic (or 1461 civil) years. Ptolemy III tried to legislate adoption of the more accurate 365-1/4 day civil year in 238 B.C., but failed. Julius Caesar adopted from the Egyptians the idea of a conventional month in his reform of the Roman calendar, and the 365-1/4 day year was finally imposed on Egypt by the Romans in 30 or 26 B.C.

the commerce passing upstream to the country above. And indeed he gave the city a circuit of a hundred and fifty stades, and he rendered it exceedingly secure and of marvelous convenience in the following way: since the Nile flowed near the city and used to flood it during the period of high water, he threw up before the south side an earthen rampart of massive dimensions to serve as both a barrier against the inundation of the river and a citadel against enemies from the land. On the other sides he dug a lake great and deep, which, absorbing the force of the river and covering all the space round the town (except where he had built the mound), afforded unparalleled protection. And so perfectly did the founder of this city discern the advantage of the spot, that nearly all the succeeding kings, forsaking Thebes, established their courts and palaces in Memphis.[103] Wherefore from this time onward the fortunes of Thebes began to sink; but those of Memphis increased until the time of Alexander the king; for Alexander established the city named for himself by the sea, and all the kings of Egypt after him contributed liberally to its ascendancy. Some adorned it with sumptuous palaces, others with dockyards and harbors, and others with yet additional impressive ornaments and buildings, in such manner that most people count it the first or second city in the inhabited world. But we will write the story of this city in its turn at the appropriate time.[104]

51 After building the mound and the moat, the founder of Memphis erected a palace which, while not inferior to those in other lands, yet was not equal to the lordliness and love of beauty of former kings. For the Egyptians regard the time spent in this life as completely worthless; but to be remembered for virtue after one's demise they hold to be of the highest value. Indeed, they refer to the houses of the living as "inns," since we dwell in them but a short time, while the tombs of the

---

103. Diodorus, like many classical writers, erroneously ascribes greater antiquity to Thebes than to Memphis, whereas in reality Memphis dates from the Ist Dynasty, c. 2920-2770 B.C., much earlier than Thebes (see note 94, above). After Theban political ascendancy faded with the XVIIIth Dynasty, Memphis again became the capital under Tut'ankhamun, c. 1330 B.C. Memphis had long been the chief city of Egypt, and served as the capital for much of the millenium preceding the advent of the Macedonians. Most ancient authors ascribed the foundation of Memphis to Menas, not Uchoreus (see note 90, above). There is today no trace of either the dike or the lake described by Diodorus.

104. Diodorus reserves his description of Alexandria until Book XVII, not Book 1.

dead they call "everlasting homes," since in Hades we remain for an endless span. For this reason they trouble themselves little about the furnishings of their houses, but betray an excess of ostentation concerning their places of burial.

Some say that the above-mentioned town was named after the daughter of the king who founded it. Mythologically, they tell that the river Nile, in the form of a bull, made love to her, and that as a result she gave birth to Egyptus, whom the natives admired for his virtue and from whom the land as a whole took its name. For having ascended the throne, he proved a benevolent and righteous lord, generally superior in every way; and therefore, since in the eyes of every man he was deemed worthy of great praise for his goodness, he obtained the honor just mentioned.

Moeris succeeded to the sovereignty twelve generations after Egyptus. In Memphis he built the north propylaea, which far surpasses the others in splendor. Upriver from the city, at a distance of ten schoinoi, he excavated a lake which is admirable for its usefulness and unbelievable in the scale of the labor involved. For they say its circumference measures three thousand and three hundred stades and its depth, in most places, fifty fathoms. And who indeed, contemplating the immensity of this endeavor, can help but wonder (and with good reason) how many myriads of men and how many years were required to finish the work? For one cannot praise highly enough the general utility of this lake, the advantages it yields to all the inhabitants of Egypt, and what is more, the genius of the king.

52   For since the extent of the Nile's inundations used to be ungovernable, while the land derived its fertility from just the proper amount of flooding, the king dug this lake as a reservoir for excess water, that through ill-timed flooding a surfeit of moisture might not turn the country to bog and swamp; also that, through a failure of the river to rise to its proper height, the fruits of the earth might not perish for want of dampness. He built a canal from the river to the lake, eighty stades in length and three plethra broad; and sometimes letting the river through this cut into the lake, and at other times diverting it, he provided the right amount of irrigation for the farmers, opening the floodgate and closing it up again ingeniously but at great expense. For if anyone wished to open or close the aforesaid mechanism, the cost was no less than fifty talents.

The reservoir has continued to be of use to the Egyptians until our own times. It takes its name from he who made it, being called the lake of Moeris to this day. Now the king, when he excavated this lake, left in the middle an island on which he erected a tomb, and two pyramids a stade in height, one for himself and the other for his wife; atop of these he placed stone statues seated on thrones. By these works he fancied that he could leave behind himself an everlasting memorial to his virtue. And he granted the revenue derived from the fish in the lake to his wife, for her perfumes and other cosmetics. The catch yields a talent of silver each day; for they say there are twenty-two varieties of fish in the lake, and that the number caught is so great that those engaged in salting the fish, though very numerous, have difficulty keeping up with the task.

This, then, is what the Egyptians have to say about the history of Moeris.[105]

53   They relate that seven generations later Sesoösis became king and accomplished deeds greater and more famous than those of his predecessors.[106]   But since not only the Greek writers differ among

---

105. Lake Moeris, described in chapters 51 and 52, is the Greek rendition of *Mer-Wer*, or the "Great Lake," in Egyptian. Shrunken to a fifth of its former size by thousands of years of land reclamation, its modern name is Birket Qarun. It is located west of the Nile twenty-five miles southwest of Memphis, in the Faiyum depression (Faiyum = Peiom or "lake" in Coptic). See plate 18. The credulous belief of ancient authors that the lake was man-made is sheer fantasy. Engineering work to regulate the flow of Nile waters into the lake via the Hawara Channel was apparently initiated by Amenemhet III of the XIIth Dynasty, c. 1844-1797 B.C., whose praenomen Nema're' could easily have been confused with the name of the lake. A pyramid of Amenemhet III stands on the eastern bank of the Hawara Channel, whose length matches Diodorus' description of the "canal." At Byahmu, in what formerly must have been the middle of the lake, are the remains of two colossi of Amenemhet III, estimated to have been sixty feet in height. These structures and the mortuary temple (the Labyrinth? see notes 119 and 132, below) near the pyramid may be the source of Diodorus' description of the monuments erected by Moeris.

106. The great legendary king whom Diodorus calls Sesoösis is usually called Sesostris by other ancient writers. Manetho says Sesostris was the third king of the XIIth Dynasty; if taken literally, this would be Amenemhet II, whose reign (1929-1892 B.C.) was unremarkable. Many classical authors, impressed by the ubiquitous and boastful military reliefs and self-adulating monuments of Ramesses II (c. 1290-1224 B.C.) obviously identified that king with Sesostris. Modern scholars lean toward the view that the legend of world-conquering Sesostris was a much exaggerated reminiscence of the Nubian and Palestinian campaigns of Senwosret I (1971-1926 B.C.) and Senwosret III (1878 -c. 1841 B.C.) of the XIIth

themselves concerning this king, but even the priests of the Egyptians disagree with the poets who sing his praises, we shall attempt to recount only the most probable facts about him, and those most strongly corroborated by evidence still existing in the country. Now when Sesoösis was born, his father did something princely and of befitting greatness; for he gathered together out of the whole land of Egypt all the boys who were born on the same day, and appointing governors and teachers for them, ordered identical education and training for them all, on the assumption that those who have grown up together most intimately and who share the same familiarity will make the best friends and the noblest comrades in arms for the wars. And though he lavishly supplied their every need, yet he subjected the youths to a discipline of unremitting bodily training and fatigues. For example, none of them was allowed to eat a meal until he had first run a hundred and eighty stades. And therefore, when they reached manhood they were all like athletes, strong of body, fit for command, and indomitable in spirit because of their training in the noblest pursuits of life.

Accordingly, Sesoösis was first dispatched by his father to Arabia, with an army, and was accompanied by those who had been raised with him. He was hardened by the hunting of wild beasts, and he overcame drought and failure of provisions to subdue the entire nation of the Arabians, which had never been conquered ere this time. Next he was sent against the western regions and, though very young in age, he reduced the greatest part of Libya to subjection. When his father died, he succeeded to the monarchy; and, emboldened by his earlier achievements, he elevated his thoughts to the conquest of the world. Some relate that he was encouraged to seek the sovereignty of all the earth by his own daughter Athyrtis, who, some say, excelling more than others in wisdom, convinced her father that the campaign would be quite easy. Others assert that she was skilled in the art of divination and that,

---

Dynasty, the first serious extensions of Egypt's power and influence beyond its traditional boundaries. Some Egyptologists continue to use the name Sesostris rather than Senwosret in transliterating the names of these kings. See plate 19.

through sacrifices, dreaming in the temples,[107] and the portents in the heavens, she could foresee the events that were destined to happen. Some have also recorded that, at the birth of Sesoösis, his father fancied that Hephaestos addressed him in his sleep, announcing that the son who had been born would conquer all the inhabited world; this, then, was the reason that the father collected together those of the same age as his son and afforded them a noble upbringing, preparing in advance for an assault on the entire world. And Sesoösis himself, having grown to manhood, and trusting in the prediction of the god, was led to prosecute the above-mentioned campaign.

54   And with a view to this attempt he first of all made sure of the loyalty of all the inhabitants of Egypt toward himself: for he thought it imperative, if he were to accomplish his intended purpose, that those joining in the expedition should be willing to die for their commanders, and that those at home in their native places should attempt no revolution. He therefore lavished kindness on everyone by all possible means, winning some with gifts of money, others with gifts of land, still others by release from punishment; and he endeared himself to all by fair words and the natural mildness of his temperament. For he acquitted without punishment all those who were accused of treason, and he discharged the debts of any who were imprisoned for want of money, of whom the gaols were full.

He divided the whole country into six and thirty districts, which the Egyptians call nomes, and he appointed a nomarch over each to superintend the royal revenues and manage all the public affairs of each locality.[108] He next selected the most able-bodied men of each nome to

---

107. "Dreaming in the temples" refers to the practice of incubation, which entailed sleeping in the temple of a god in hopes of receiving a prophetic dream or vision. There was also therapeutic incubation, wherein the subject hoped to be healed by the temple deity; the cures attributed to Isis in chapter 25, above, are of this nature. Temple incubation seems to have existed in Egypt as early as 1450 B.C., but it became more popular under Greek influence.

108. Nomes were the administrative subdivisions of Egypt. Although varying in number, name, capital, and extent, by Diodorus' day the arrangement of forty-two nomes had become traditional (not thirty-six as Diodorus relates). There were twenty in Lower Egypt, from Memphis to the sea, and twenty-two in Upper Egypt. The latter had become fixed by the Vth Dynasty, and extended as far south as Elephantine. Neither the Faiyum (see note 105, above) nor the oases were included in the scheme. It is not known which king established the nomes,

form an army suitable to the greatness of his enterprise, enrolling six hundred thousand infantry, twenty-four thousand cavalry, and twenty-seven thousand war chariots. He entrusted command over the various units of soldiery to the companions of his youth, who by now were tried in battle, who from childhood had cultivated heroic virtue, and who felt a brotherly love toward both the king and one another. There were more than a thousand and seven hundred of these companions. They say that he granted them the most fertile estates in all the land so that, having a sufficient income and lacking naught, they could devote themselves to the practice of war.

55   Making ready the army, he marched first against the Ethiopians dwelling to the south, overcame them in battle, and forced them to pay tribute of ebony, gold, and elephants' tusks. He then launched a fleet of four hundred ships in the Erythraean Sea, being the first of his nation to build warships. He not only conquered the islands in those waters, but subjugated the coasts of the mainland as far as India; but he himself with the army made the journey by land and conquered all of Asia. He invaded not only the territory later won by Alexander of Macedon, but also some nations to whose lands Alexander never came. Indeed, he crossed the Ganges River and overran all of India as far as the ocean, and he conquered the Scythian tribes all the way to the river Tanaïs, which divides Europe from Asia. It was at this point, they claim, that certain of the Egyptians were left behind near the Maeotic lake and became the race of the Colchians. The proof of their Egyptian descent is that their males are circumcised, as are those in Egypt; for these colonists retained that custom, just as did the Jews.[109]

---

but the kiosk of Senwosret I at Karnak records the extent of the Upper Egyptian nomes, which could account for Diodorus' opinion that they were instituted by Sesoösis (see note 106, above). The nomes probably developed from predynastic petty kingdoms. In dynastic times, the independence of the nomarchs waxed and waned in inverse proportion to the power of the royal authority, but the semiautonomous status which the nomarchs sometimes exercised was submerged forever by the coming of the Macedonians.

109. The river Tanaïs is the Don; the Maeotic lake is the Sea of Azov. Colchis, the land of the Colchians, was near the Caucasus range at the eastern extremity of the Black Sea. Since the conquests of Sesoösis in this area are imaginary, the Colchians obviously were not descendants of his soldiers. But abundant evidence in classical authors suggests that they were strikingly different from neighboring peoples. Herodotus, Pindar, and the Scholiast to Apollonius of

In similar fashion Sesoösis subdued all the rest of Asia and most of the Cyclades islands. But crossing over into Europe and passing all the way through Thrace, he was in danger of losing his army from lack of food and from the hazardous terrain of those places. He therefore made Thrace the limit of his campaign. In many parts of the lands he had conquered he set up stelae with inscriptions in the so-called sacred characters of the Egyptians, to this effect: "Sesoösis, King of kings and Lord of lords, overwhelmed this country by the might of his arms." The stelae he thus erected among warlike nations bore the likeness of a man's genitals, while those of a woman were featured among peoples base and cowardly; for he thought that the quality of each nation's spirit would be quite evident to posterity by means of these appropriate organs. In some places he also set up stone statues of himself with bow and javelin. These statues were four cubits and four palms in height, his own true stature.

Having thus finished the campaign in nine years and dealt equitably with all he subdued, he ordered every nation, according to its wealth, to bring annual tribute to Egypt. And having amassed a multitude of war prisoners and other booty without measure, he returned to the land of his birth with greater deeds to his credit than anyone else before him. He adorned all the temples of Egypt with remarkable offerings and spoils of war, and any of his soldiers who had acted bravely he honored with gifts according to their deserts. And in general, as a result of this campaign, not only did the army through its conserted valor return triumphantly loaded with wealth, but it also transpired that all Egypt was filled with riches of every kind.

56 Sesoösis then relieved his people from the burdens of war and allowed his brave soldier-companions to rest and enjoy the fruits of victory. But he himself, athirst for glory, and wishing to be remembered for all time, built many great works that were wonderful for their design and their rich embellishment. He thus attained undying fame for himself

---

Rhodes all say that the Colchians were dark- or black-skinned, and Hippocrates reports their "yellowish color, as though they suffered from jaundice." Herodotus also claims that the Colchians had "woolly hair" as did the Egyptians, but like Diodorus he relies mainly on the fact of circumcision to connect the two peoples, and the Jews as well (see note 58, above). Circumcision is not sufficient evidence of any cultural or ethnic connection; but strangely enough, some proof exists for a small negroid community near Sukhumi in the Gruzinskaya S.S.R., perhaps the relict of an earlier aboriginal population.

and left the Egyptians with ease and security for all time. Attending first to the gods, he constructed in every city of Egypt a temple for the divinity most revered by the local inhabitants. However, he subjected none of the Egyptians to servile toil, but built every temple with the labor of war prisoners, wherefore he inscribed on every structure that none of the natives had worked upon it.

A story is told that the captives brought from Babylonia, unable to endure the hardship of their servitude, revolted against the king. They seized a stronghold for themselves beside the river, and, maintaining war against the Egyptians, plundered the land thereabouts. But eventually they were granted immunity and settled in that place, which they named Babylon after their fatherland. They say likewise that the Egyptian Troy, which even yet exists beside the Nile, was named under similar circumstances; for Menelaus, sailing home from Ilium with many prisoners of war, is said to have landed in Egypt, where the Trojans rose against him. Seizing some territory for themselves, they waged war until such time as assurances of safety were granted them; then they founded this city, which they gave the same name as their fatherland. I am not unaware that Ctesias of Cnidos gives a different account of the cities just mentioned, saying they were established by some who came to Egypt with Semiramis and who named them after their own homelands. It is not easy to disentangle with certainty the truth of these matters; but the points of dispute among historians must be deemed worthy of record, so that the judgment of what is valid may be left to the readers.[110]

---

110. For Menelaus, Ctesias of Cnidos, and Semiramis, see Appendix I, Proper Names. The stories Diodorus gives to explain the names of Egyptian Troy and Babylon are fictitious; the places themselves are not. Strabo (*Geog.* XVII.1.34) mentions the Trojan tale and locates Egyptian Troy at a village not far from the great pyramid complex at Giza; it may be the modern Tura. The site of Babylon is certain. It is at el-Fustat, or, Old Cairo, whose Egyptian name P(er)-Ḥapu-l'ōn sounded like "Babylon" to the Greeks. It was a fortress, not a town. Diodorus is the earliest writer to mention it, and Strabo (*Geog.* XVII.1.30) gives a similar account of its origin. Josephus (*Ant. Jud.* II.15) thinks it was first built by the Persians under Cambyses, c. 525 B.C. Eutychius, Patriarch of Alexandria under Justinian, credits it to Artaxerxes III Ochus, who conquered Egypt in 343 B.C. But John of Nikiou assigns its foundation to Nebuchadnezzar II of Babylon (the original) who attacked Egypt in 601 B.C. Whatever the truth of its origin, a famous Roman fort was built on its ruins by Trajan and survived until the nineteenth century fairly intact, despite the bloody siege under the Moslem conquerors, 640-641 A.D. Its few remaining towers have been incorporated in Cairo's Coptic Museum. Even after the Arab foundation of Cairo, European

57 But to continue: Sesoösis raised many great mounds of earth, and onto these he relocated all the cities that were not elevated by nature on rising ground, so that both people and animals would have a safe place of refuge when the river was in flood. He also built many canals out from the river, all through the land from Memphis to the sea, in order to hasten and facilitate the gathering in of the produce of the countryside, and so that there might be ease of communication among the people and among all localities, as well as ready availability of all commodities for man's enjoyment. But even more importantly, he thus rendered the land difficult to invade and secured it against the attacks of enemies. Before this time, nearly all the best portion of Egypt offered easy riding for cavalry and was passable by chariots. But from this day forward it became quite intraversable, thanks to the numerous canals branching out from the river.[111] In addition, to foil incursions from Syria and Arabia, Sesoösis built a wall along the eastern border of Egypt, extending through fifteen hundred stades of desert from Pelusium to Heliopolis.[112] He also constructed for himself a ship of cedar wood two hundred and eighty cubits long, the exterior surface of which was covered with gold and the interior with silver.[113] He dedicated this to the god most adored at Thebes, along with two obelisks of hard stone one hundred and twenty cubits in height, upon which he recorded the vastness of his empire, the magnitude of his revenues, and the number of nations he had conquered. He also consecrated, in the temple of

writers of the Middle Ages almost invariably referred to that city by its earlier name of Babylon. See plate 20.

111. The primary purpose of the canals was for regulating irrigation, not for communication, transport, or defense. The canal system was the work of many continuous generations, not of a single king such as Sesoösis. As for horses and chariots, they were not introduced into Egypt until the Hyksos period, c. 1600 B.C. (Camels, incidentally, were first brought in by the Persians over a thousand years later.)

112. There is no archaeological evidence of such a defensive wall, but in the Story of Sinuhe, known from demotic papyri of c. 715 B.C. though undoubtedly reflecting earlier traditions, there is mention of the "Wall of the Prince," ascribed to Amenemhet I, 1991-1962 B.C.

113. Ceremonial barks were common features of the temples of various gods, including that of Ammon at Thebes. Several examples remain to this day, as well as numerous representations. The largest known is less than half the rather incredible length given by Diodorus.

Hephaestos at Memphis, monolithic statues thirty cubits high of himself and his wife, and another twenty cubits high of his sons, the occasion of which was as follows: when Sesoösis had returned to Egypt after his great campaign and was staying at Pelusium with his wife and sons, his brother contrived a plot against them, even while serving as their host. For after strong drink had put them to sleep, he set fire to a pile of dry reeds which had been prepared in advance and had been strewn about their pavilion after nightfall. Now when the fire suddenly blazed up, the king's attendants were clumsy in coming to the rescue because they were drunk; but Sesoösis, lifting up his hands in supplication and begging the gods to save his wife and children, dashed out through the flames. For this unexpected escape he repaid the other gods with votive offerings, as earlier described; but he honored Hephaestos especially, since through him deliverance had come.[114]

58   Of the many grandiose things ascribed to Sesoösis, it seems that the most lordly was his treatment of the other kings whenever he chanced to go abroad. For both the kings of the subject nations who still ruled the kingdoms they had surrendered, as well as those others who had received the greatest princedoms from Sesoösis, all brought gifts to Egypt at prescribed intervals. The king would welcome them with special courtesy and do them honor in every way, except that when he wished to visit a temple or city, he would loose the horses from his chariot and yoke in their place the kings and other grandees in teams of four. By this he thought to show the world that, having subjected the mightiest kings and those most famous for valor, he had no competitor in the rivalry for greatness. And it does appear that this monarch outstripped all previous kings in his military exploits, in the number and size of his oblations, and in the works he constructed in Egypt. After a reign of thirty-three years he took his own life because his eyes had failed him. He was much praised for this action, not only by the priests, but also by the rest of the Egyptians, who were of opinion that

114. In other words, the monolithic statues of himself and family mentioned above were erected in the temple of Hephaestos at Memphis as a thank offering to that god. Just outside the south enclosure gate of the gigantic temple of Ptah (whom the classical authors identified with Hephaestos), at Memphis, archaeologists have discovered a colossus of Ramesses II a little short of the thirty cubits mentioned by Diodorus as the height of the statue of Sesoösis. Herodotus II.110 gives the same dimensions, and says the image stood in front of the temple. See plate 21.

the termination of his life was accomplished in harmony with the lofty spirit of his other achievements.

So well established and persistent was the fame of this king that many generations later, when Egypt came under the sway of the Persians, and Darius the father of Xerxes had determined to set up his own statue at Memphis in place of that of Sesoösis, the high priest, in a speech delivered at the ecclesiastical assembly, denounced the plan on the grounds that Darius had not as yet surpassed the achievements of Sesoösis. Now the king not only took no umbrage at this, but on the contrary, pleased with such frankness, said that he would strive to be inferior to Sesoösis in nothing, if only he lived as long; and he charged them but to compare their achievements at equivalent ages, for this was the fairest way to measure worth.[115]

We will now rest content with what has been said about Sesoösis.

59   His son, however, who inherited his father's kingdom and adopted his name, accomplished no feat of arms or anything else worth mentioning, although a peculiar occurrence did once befall him. For it seems he lost his sight, either through inheritance of his father's infirmity or, as certain legends relate, through his impiety toward the river, into whose onrushing current he once hurled a spear because he was jostled in a storm. In any event, because of this affliction he was forced to seek relief from the mercy of the gods, and long he sought to appease them with offerings and sacrifices aplenty, though all to no avail. But in the tenth year an oracle advised him both to adore the god of Heliopolis, and to wash his face in the urine of any wife who had never known a man outside of wedlock. Many a wife he put to the test, starting with his own; but he found none of them chaste except a certain gardener's spouse, whom he married as soon as he regained his sight. But the rest he burned alive in a certain village which the Egyptians, because of this incident, call the "Holy Ground." He rendered gratitude for this favor to the god of Heliopolis, and in accordance with the oracle's command he dedicated to him two monolithic obelisks eight cubits wide and a hundred tall.[116]

---

115. Herodotus II.110 tells a similar story and identifies the statue in question as that mentioned above in chapter 57 (see also note 114).

116. This wry folk tale is no more than a snide lampoon on the virtue of women (although urine sometimes was considered a cure for poor eyesight in Egypt, and even in Rome). Herodotus II.111 relates the same fable, giving the

60   After this king, many of his successors on the throne attained nothing at all worth writing about. But many generations later Amasis became king, and he ruled the people with a rod of iron; for he punished many people unjustly, deprived many others of their property, and bore himself arrogantly in every way, with contempt for all. Now up to a point the suffering populace endured their lot with patience, since they were unable to defend themselves against his superior strength. But their hatred found an opportunity at last. When Actisanes, the king of Ethiopia, marched against Amasis, most of the people rose in revolt; wherefore, since Amasis was easily defeated, Egypt passed under the sway of the Ethiopians. But Actisanes bore success as a man should and treated the vanquished with moderation.[117]

He contrived a unique solution to the problem of bandits, neither putting to death those condemned for brigandage nor yet letting them go completely unpunished. For he brought together from throughout the land all who were accused of this crime; then, having made the most impartial investigation of them, he assembled all of those found guilty, cut off their noses, and settled them as colonists in the farthest reaches of the desert, where he founded a city named Rhinocolura ["Clipped-nose"] from the plight of its inhabitants. Situated at the border of Egypt and Syria and lying close beside the coast, this colony is bereft of nearly everything requisite to human life. Salt flats surround it, while inside the walls the scanty water of the wells is brackish and very bitter to the taste. He settled them in this country so that, should they persevere in their original mode of life, they could neither harm the innocent nor, being unknown, escape detection in their dealings with others. But notwithstanding their exile in a wasted land devoid of nearly every useful resource, they devised a way of life well attuned to the scarcity around them, because nature perforce constrained them to enlist all means available against their poverty. For they cut reeds in the neighboring countryside, and split them to fabricate long nets; and setting these along the shore for many stades, they lay in wait for the vast droves of quail which were driven in from the open sea. By

---

son of Sesostris the name Pheron, probably a corruption of the term Pharaoh. Two obelisks sixty-six feet high (forty-four cubits) made of red granite from Syene stood at Heliopolis until about A.D. 1160. Only one remains in place. They are attributed to Senwosret I, 1971-1926 B.C. See plate 22.

117. Neither Amasis (not to be confused with the much later authentic Amasis; see chapter 68, below) nor Actisanes are historical figures.

trapping these birds, they could collect a quantity sufficiently large for their subsistence.[118]

61 After King Actisanes died, the Egyptians regained the sovereignty for themselves and chose as king their countryman Mendes, whom some call Marrus. This king performed no martial deeds whatever, but he did build himself a place of burial known as the Labyrinth, a work remarkable not so much for its size as for its unrivaled cleverness of construction: for it is hard for anyone venturing inside to find his way out again, unless he has obtained a guide of fully proven experience. And some say also that Daedalos, who during a visit to Egypt had marveled at the ingenuity of the building, made for King Minos of Crete a labyrinth similar to the one in Egypt, and in which, say the myths, lived the so-called Minotaur. But the one in Crete has wholly disappeared, either because one of the rulers demolished it or because time has destroyed the work; while the one in Egypt has been preserved in its entirety down until our lifetime.[119]

---

118. Rhinocolura, or Rhinocorura as it is more often called, is the modern el-Arish, situated near the sea about seventy miles east of Pelusium at the "Brook of Egypt," the *wadi* which marked the frontier between Egypt and Palestine. Rhinocolura is sometimes mentioned by ancient writers as belonging to one country, sometimes to the other. But it was originally an Egyptian penal colony, as Diodorus states. Strabo repeats the story of its origin, as does Seneca, who ascribes it to a Persian king. The netting of migrating quails was common both in Egypt and Sinai; the exhausted birds to this day alight for rest after crossing the sea, just as they did in ancient times: "And there went forth a wind from the Lord, and brought quails from the sea, and let them fall by the camp" (*Num.* 11.31). The netting of quail at el-Arish goes on to this day.

119. Diodorus gives several conflicting versions of the Labyrinth's origin and purpose, of which this is the first. See chapters 66, 89, and 97, and notes 132 and 179, below. From these later chapters and from other classical accounts (Herodotus II.147-148; Manetho II; Strabo XVII.1.37; Pliny *Nat. Hist.* XXXVI.84ff; and Pomponius Mela I.56) we know that the building called the Labyrinth was near the Hawara channel, which regulates the flow of Nile water into the Faiyum (Lake Moeris, see note 105, above). The archaeological debris of an enormous edifice 800 x 1000 feet in extent was found there, but not before most of the ruins had been hauled away for constructing a railway grade. Almost all that remains is a vast field of limestone chips. The exact function of the building is uncertain. Early authorities called it variously a central administrative complex, or a joint temple for the local animal cults, but current opinion declares it was a mortuary temple of Amenemhet III, c. 1844-1797 B.C., agreeing with Manetho's attribution of the structure.

62   After the death of King Mendes, anarchy prevailed for five generations. Then a certain man of ignoble birth was chosen king, whom the Egyptians call Cetes, but who, among the Greeks, is thought to be the Proteus who lived at the time of the Trojan War. Tradition holds that Cetes knew the secrets of the winds and also knew how to change his shape, sometimes into the form of an animal, sometimes into a tree, or fire, or any other thing; and it happens that the priests tell things about him which corroborate these stories. For they say the king acquired this kind of knowledge by his constant practise of consorting with astrologers. But among the Greeks the myth about his change of shapes derives from a custom prevalent with the kings: for it was the wont of Egypt's lords to wear about their brows the likeness of a lion's, bull's, or serpent's head as emblems of their sovereignty; and they sometimes wore on their heads the image of a tree or fire, and sometimes a considerable amount of sweet smelling incense; and by these means they enhanced their comeliness while simultaneously reducing the populace to awe and a kind of religious dread.[120]

Now after the demise of Proteus, his son Remphis inherited the kingship, who never ceased to heap up wealth from every source, and to worry about his revenues his whole life long; and from mean paltriness and a miserly disposition he spent nothing either on the worship of the gods or the welfare of his people. Being a good steward, therefore, rather than a true king, he left behind him, not a reputation for virtue, but a pile of treasure greater than any of his predecessors on the throne; for as tradition has it, he amassed approximately four hundred thousand talents of silver and gold.

63   After this king's death, there succeeded to the throne seven generations of thoroughly idle rulers who were devoted to every kind of relaxation and luxury; wherefore the sacred writings preserve no record of any costly works made by them, nor so much as a single act worthy of historical note, except for those of a certain Nileus, from whom the river came to be called the Nile, whereas before it had been named

---

120. Cetes cannot be definitely connected with any actual Egyptian ruler. The Homeric Proteus was a prophetic sea god living off the coast of Pharos in Egypt, who could assume any shape to deceive would-be questioners and avoid the necessity of prophesying. Diodorus makes a connection between this mythical deity and the equally fabulous King Proteus of Egypt, who figures in the weird story of the phantom Helen who went to Troy while the real Helen remained anonymous and chaste in Egypt.

Egyptus. For because this king excavated a large number of conveniently situated canals and enthusiastically undertook many projects to enhance the usefulness of the Nile, he became the source of this name for the river.

The eighth king after Remphis was Chemmis of Memphis. He ruled fifty years and built the largest of the three pyramids which are accounted among the seven most famous works of the world.[121] These pyramids are located a hundred and twenty stades from Memphis and forty-five from the Nile on the Libyan side. All who behold them are struck with a kind of wondrous awe at the size of the structures and the skill of their workmanship. The largest of them is square in its groundplan; each of its sides has a base length of seven plethra, and its height is more than six plethra; but it slopes gradually from the base to the apex, until at the top each side is but six cubits long.[122] It is built entirely of a hard stone which is difficult to work but lasts forever; for although they say no less than a thousand years have since elapsed until our lifetime (or, as some writers have it, more than three thousand and four hundred years), yet the stonework has lasted until now in its original condition, and the entire structure is preserved undecayed. And 'tis said the stone was transported a great distance from Arabia,[123] and that the edifices were raised by means of earthen ramps, since machines

---

121. Diodorus, probably following Herodotus II.124-125, badly mistakes the age of the pyramids at Giza and confuses the real chronology of Egypt. He has just been discussing kings of the XIIth Dynasty (1991-1783 B.C.) and later; now he brings in the IVth Dynasty pyramid builders, c. 2575-2465 B.C. Next, in chapter 65 below, he skips back to the XXIVth and XXVth dynasties, c. 724-664 B.C. Manetho, writing later than Herodotus, gives the correct chronological placement to the IVth Dynasty, but Diodorus unfortunately follows Herodotus.

122. Diodorus gives reasonably accurate dimensions for the Great Pyramid, but either he greatly overestimates the height, or he refers to the diagonal rather than the vertical dimension. The former possibility is not only likely, but understandable, for the pyramid presents to the untrained eye an optical illusion of being almost as lofty as it is broad. The true dimensions (minus the now missing facing stones) are approximately 755 feet at the base and 482 feet in height.

123. Most of the materials for the pyramids at Giza are locally quarried limestone, but the facing is of higher quality limestone from Tura, about seven miles upriver on the "Arabian" side; to Diodorus, this was considered part of Arabia. Almost the entire facing has been stripped off since the Middle Ages for buildings in Cairo and vicinity, and the top six courses and the capstone are missing; aside from these losses, the stonework today is almost as "undecayed" as it was when Diodorus wrote two thousand years ago. See plate 23.

for lifting had not yet been invented in those days; and most surprising it is, that although such large structures were raised in an area surrounded by sand, no trace remains of either ramps or the dressing of the stones, so that it seems not the result of the patient labor of men, but rather as if the whole complex were set down entire upon the surrounding sand by some god. Now some Egyptians try to make a marvel of these things, alleging that the ramps were made of salt and natron and that, when the river was turned against them, it melted them clean away and obliterated their every trace without the use of human labor. But in very truth, it most certainly was not done in this way! Rather, the same multitude of workmen who raised the mounds returned the entire mass again to its original place; for they say that three hundred and sixty thousand men were constantly employed in the prosecution of the work, yet the entire edifice was hardly finished at the end of twenty years.[124]

64 When Chemmis died, his brother Cephren succeeded to the throne and ruled for fifty-six years; however, some claim it was not his brother, but his son named Chabryes who received the crown. Yet everyone agrees that the next king, imitating the policy of the previous ruler, built the second pyramid; this equals the first in skill of execution but falls quite short of it in size, since each side of the base is but a stade in length.[125] Now, upon the greater of the pyramids is an inscription recording the large sums expended on it: for instance, the writing reveals that over sixteen hundred talents were spent just on vegetables and radishes for the workmen. The smaller pyramid has no inscription, but an ascent has been cut into one of the sides. But it came to pass that neither of the two kings was buried in the pyramid

---

124. The building method used to construct the pyramids is still a subject of dispute among scholars. The only proven technique (based on remains at a pyramid near el-Lisht) was mud-brick ramps; but how these were placed; whether the stones were moved by rollers or sledges (wheels and pulleys were unknown), by men or animals; and whether they were lifted by rockers, counterweight cranes, or wedges, are questions unlikely to be resolved. Whatever the details, the labor involved was stupendous. The Great Pyramid alone weighs over six million tons; it is comprised of 2,250,000 stone blocks; and it would have required twenty-three years to complete, even if the stones were laid at the incredible rate of three hundred per day!

125. A stade was about six plethra, one short of the seven which Diodorus says was the base length of the first pyramid. See note 122 above.

which he had built as a tomb for himself. For the people, after the onerous labor of construction, and because of many cruel and violent outrages on the part of these kings, became exasperated with the authors of their misery and threatened to rend their bodies in pieces and cast them forth with violence from their tombs. Therefore each king, on his deathbed, commanded his kinfolk to bury his body secretly in an unmarked grave.[126]

After these two, Mycerinos became king; some call him Mencherinos, and he was the son of the king who built the first pyramid. He attempted to build a third one, but he died before the work was brought to completion. He laid out the base with sides that were three plethra in length and constructed the first fifteen courses of the walls out of a black stone resembling the Theban; but he finished the rest of the pyramid with stone like that of the others. But although this pyramid is inferior in size to the two just described, it greatly exceeds them in architectural mastery and in the costliness of the stone.[127] Upon its northern face an inscription records that Mycerinos was the builder. They say this king, deploring the cruelty of his predecessors, aspired to a life free from blame and dedicated to the good of his people. He constantly performed many acts which won for him the good will of the multitude; and among other things, he spent great sums of money especially in the administration of justice, bestowing gifts on those worthy men who appeared to depart the courts of law without obtaining justice.

There are also three other pyramids of one plethra per side, and these works on the whole resemble the others except in size; for they explain that the above-mentioned three kings built them for their wives.[128]

There is no doubt that these structures greatly exceed all others in Egypt, not only in size and splendor, but also in the craftsmanship of

---

126. There is no proof that the kings were not buried in their pyramids.

127. Diodorus is very accurate in describing the third pyramid. Mycerinos intended to face the entire structure with red granite, but work apparently stopped abruptly, presumably because of the king's death. Only the lower sixteen courses (not fifteen) were faced with granite, and even some of these blocks were left undressed, while the remaining courses were finished in limestone by his son. This pyramid is about 365 1/2 feet in base, 218 feet in height.

128. There are three smaller queens' pyramids beside the Great Pyramid, and three beside that of Mycerinos. A small pyramid also sits next to the middle pyramid.

the builders. Indeed, it is said that one ought to admire the architects of these works more than the potentates who paid for them: for the former brought their plans to completion through their own genius and thirst for fame, whereas the latter relied on inherited wealth and the oppression of others.

But there is lack of unanimity concerning these pyramids, both among the natives of the place and among historians. Some say the above-mentioned kings erected them. But some say it was certain others: for example, some claim that Armaeus made the largest one, Amosis the second, and Inaros the third; and some people assert that this last is the burial place of Rhodopis the courtesan, of whom they relate that certain of the nomarchs, who were her lovers, built the structure in common out of affection for her.[129]

65   Now after the kings enumerated above, the sovereignty passed to Bocchoris, who was thoroughly undistinguished in body but who far surpassed his royal predecessors in wisdom. Afterwards, many years later, Sabaco ruled Egypt; he was of the Ethiopian race, but he greatly surpassed all earlier kings in goodness and piety.[130]   Proof of his kindliness, for example, may be found in his abolition of the supreme penalty of law, by which I mean the deprivation of life; for instead of death, he used to sentence the condemned, in chains, to perform public

---

129. Armaeus (or Harmais) was a king assigned by Manetho to the XVIIIth Dynasty, and was said to be the same as Danaus (see chapter 28 and note 57, above). Amosis was the first king of the same dynasty, according to some versions of Manetho ('Ahmose, c. 1550-1525 B.C.). Inaros was a son of Psammetichos III who gained Athenian support for an unsuccessful revolt against Persian rule in the Fifth Century B.C. The actual builders of the pyramids at Giza were not these three, but the kings of the IVth Dynasty. Khufu or Cheops, c. 2551-2528 B.C., whom Diodorus calls Chemmis, built the Great Pyramid; his son (?) Cephren or Kephren, c. 2520-2494 B.C., built the second, and the variant name Chabryes of Diodorus is probably an attempt to translate his Egyptian name Khafre'; Menkaure' or Mycerinos, c. 2490-2472 B.C., built the third pyramid. The Rhodopis story is ridiculous, as Herodotus II.134-135 recognizes, although Rhodopis was a real and famous courtesan of the Greek town of Naucratis, active c. 600 B.C.

130. Bocchoris of Saïs, c. 717-712 B.C., was killed in battle when the "Ethiopian" (actually Nubian) king Shabaka (Sabaco) extended the rule of the XXVth Dynasty over all Egypt. Shabaka ruled until about 698 B.C. To get to this point in his narrative, Diodorus unwittingly skips over about a thousand years of Egyptian history. For more on Bocchoris, see chapters 79 and 94, below.

duties for the cities; and by means of them he built extensive levees and many convenient canals. His motive was to mitigate the rigor of punishment for those under sentence, while providing substantial benefits to the towns in place of useless penalties.

Again, his extreme piety may be inferred from the vision he saw in a dream and his subsequent renunciation of the sovereignty. For he imagined that the god of Thebes announced to him while he slept that he would not be able to rule Egypt happily or long unless he should hack in two every priest and then pass with his court through the midst of them. Now when this apparition had come repeatedly, he sent for the priests from all sides and said to them that by remaining in the country he was offending the god; for were it not so, these visions would not be sent to him in his sleep. Therefore he wished to depart free of sin and surrender his life to the dictates of fate, rather than to vex the god, or to rule in Egypt after staining his own life by impious homicide. So at length he restored the kingdom to the native inhabitants and returned to Ethiopia.[131]

66   Anarchy then prevailed in Egypt for two years, and the people turned to fratricidal strife and murder. Finally the twelve most powerful leaders formed an oath-bound league. Meeting in council at Memphis, they wrote out covenants of mutual accord and good faith, then declared themselves kings. And after they had ruled for fifteen years in observance of their oaths and compacts, preserving unity with one another, they began to build for themselves a single tomb so that, as in life their mutual support brought equal honors to all, in death as well their bodies would lie together, and their monument built in common would enshrine the glory of those entombed therein. Being quite enthusiastic for this project, they exerted themselves mightily to

---

131. In this edifying (but untrue) fable Diodorus alludes to a bloody sacrificial rite widespread throughout the Old World in many eras. Passing between the severed halves of a sacrificial victim, human or animal, had deep ritual significance in various contexts and is mentioned in Livy, Quintus Curtius, the Bible, and Apollodorus among others. Seneca (*De Ira* III.16.4) refers to the Persian army marching out between the severed halves of a man's body (perceived by Herodotus VII.39-40 as a simple act of revenge) and contends that the purpose was to purify the army. Other motives for this grisly proceeding were to effect a cure, or to sanctify an oath. Similar ceremonies have been reported of the Israelites, the Macedonians, the Boeotians, the Persians, the Hittites, the Tartars, and some southern African tribes.

surpass in size the works of all who had gone before. So they chose a spot beside the inlet to Lake Moeris in Libya and built a sepulcher there of the most beautiful stone, making it square in shape with dimensions of one stade on each side. Its stone carvings and other artistic embellishments left nothing to be surpassed by future generations. For as one entered the enclosure wall there was a peristyle hall, with forty columns comprising each side, and with a recessed coffered ceiling made from one block of stone, and decorated with excellent paintings. This hall also contained ingeniously executed and very beautiful paintings as memorials of each king's home district, with its temples and sacrificial rites. And indeed it is said that the kings planned a tomb so large and costly that, had they not been deposed before completing their design, they would have left no room for anyone else to surpass them in the building of monuments.[132]

But when they had ruled Egypt for fifteen years, it came to pass that the sovereignty devolved on one of them alone, for the following reason. It seems that Psammetichos of Saïs, who was one of the twelve kings and who was lord of the regions beside the sea, used to supply goods to all the merchants, and especially to the Phoenicians and the Greeks. In this way he profitably disposed of the surplus of his own country in exchange for the products made by other nations, and he acquired not only great wealth, but the friendship of peoples and rulers abroad. Now because of this, they say, the other kings envied him and began a war against him. But instead of this tale, some early historians tell instead the legend of an oracular response the strongmen received, to this effect: that whichever of them should first pour libation from a

---

132. The structure described is none other than the Labyrinth, already attributed to Mendes in chapter 61, above (see note 119). Although Diodorus does not mention its name in this story of the twelve kings, Herodotus II.148 does; and Herodotus also gives a much fuller description of the edifice: "It has twelve courts, all of them roofed, with gates exactly opposite one another, six on the north side and six on the south, in continuous lines. A single wall surrounds the entire building. There are two different kinds of rooms throughout: half are above ground, half below, amounting to three thousand in all . . . . [The underground rooms] contained, as they said, the tombs of the kings who built the Labyrinth, and also those of the sacred crocodiles . . . . The upper chambers . . . excel all other human productions . . . . The roof was throughout of stone, like the walls; and the walls were carved all over with figures; every court was surrounded by a colonnade built of white stones, exquisitely fitted together." Strabo (XVII.1.37) confirms that the ceiling of each chamber was a single slab of stone.

bronze vessel to the god in Memphis, he should become master of all Egypt; so, although one of the priests brought twelve golden bowls out of the temple, Psammetichos doffed his bronze helmet and poured his own libation therefrom. Now the council of rulers mistrusted what he had done; but as they were unwilling to have him killed, they banished him and ordered him to live in the marshland along the sea.

Now, whether the rupture came about for this reason, or, as first explained, through envy of his good fortune, Psammetichos summoned mercenary troops from Caria and Ionia and won a battle near the city called Momemphis. Some of the kings ranged against him perished in the encounter, and the others were driven away to Libya, where they were no longer powerful enough to dispute the sovereignty with him.[133]

67 Psammetichos being now lord of the entire kingdom, he built for the god of Memphis the east propylon and also the enclosure of the sanctuary, which he supported upon colossi twelve cubits high instead of on columns. He distributed lavish gifts to the mercenaries besides their stipulated pay, gave them the so-called "Camps" as a place to live, and assigned them extensive lands a little way above the Pelusiac mouth of the Nile (although Amasis, who reigned many years later, removed them from that place and resettled them in Memphis).[134] And since Psammetichos had established his authority by means of the mercenaries, he afterwards entrusted the affairs of the empire especially unto them

---

133. The tale of Psammetichos and the twelve "kings" probably derives from Herodotus II.147-154. In very general outline, its basis in historical fact is as follows: Nubian rule was firmly established in all Egypt by Shabaka about 712 B.C., but local nomarchs in Lower Egypt retained considerable power, which grew even stronger after Assyrian attacks began in 674. Necho I, ruler of Saïs in the Delta, supported the Assyrians and assumed the title of king, but he died in the fighting about 664. His son Psamtik or Psammetichos helped oust the Nubians for good, then he systematically eliminated his rival nomarchs to reunite Egypt under Assyrian suzerainty by 656. By 653 he had capitalized on Assyrian preoccupation with a Babylonian revolt to make Egypt independent once more. He relied heavily on Greek and Ionian mercenaries and began to expand Egyptian military and political influence into the Levant.

134. This garrison town was Daphnae, the modern Tell Dafana and the Tahpanhes of Jeremiah the Prophet, who once lived there. It held a Greek garrison from about 664 B.C., and sometimes a Jewish one. Other major military "camps" were at Marea, on the western side of the Delta, and at Elephantine, the former held by native troops and the latter (at least in one period) by another Jewish contingent.

and continued to maintain large forces of foreign soldiers. In a campaign to Syria, however, he gave excessive honor to the mercenaries by placing them on the right wing in the line of battle, while he deployed the native troops less honorably by assigning them the left side of the phalanx.[135]   The Egyptians, more than two hundred thousand of them, were outraged by the insult and deserted; and proceeding toward Ethiopia, they chose to win a country of their own. At first the king sent some of the army commanders to make excuses for the slight. But since the soldiers paid no attention to them, he with his kinsmen followed along in boats. He implored them, as they marched up the Nile and were crossing the boundaries of Egypt, to change their purpose, reminding them of their homeland and temples, their wives and children. But clashing their pikes against their shields, they all cried out at one time, declaring that as long as they were masters of their weapons, they would easily find homelands; and lifting up their undergarments to display the generative parts of their bodies, they boasted that, having these organs, they would be in want of neither wives nor children. Thus they showed their proud determination and scorned the things of greatest value to other men. So, taking possession of the best part of Ethiopia, they divided a great stretch of land among themselves, and therein did dwell.[136]

Now Psammetichos was much aggrieved at this defection, but having settled the affairs of Egypt and put the revenues in order, he concluded alliances with the Athenians and some of the other Greeks. He was also wont to offer hospitality to foreigners who came to Egypt of their own accord; and, being especially fond of the Greeks, he gave his sons an Hellenic education. Indeed, he was the first king of Egypt to open the interior trade of the country to other nations, and he provided great personal security to visiting strangers. For earlier rulers had made Egypt inaccessible to foreign travelers, slaying some of the mariners who put

---

135. Traditional tactics of the phalanx called for the right wing to outflank and attack the enemy line; the best troops were usually posted there to drive the attack home, while the weaker left was supposed to engage and pin down the enemy's right, or at least not to give way before victory had been secured.

136. Herodotus II.30 gives a different version of the saga of the deserters from Psammetichos. Putting their number at 240,000, he records that their disaffection resulted from three years of unrelieved garrison duty at various frontier posts. He interprets their name, the Asmach, as meaning "those who stand on the left hand of the king," and places their country sixty days' journey south of Meroë, much further than either Pliny (seventeen days) or Strabo (fifteen days).

in there, and enslaving others. In fact, the impiety ascribed to Busiris became notorious among the Greeks based on the inhospitality of the natives; for although there was no truth to this tale, the excessive lawlessness of the Egyptians made a plausible myth of it.[137]

68   Four generations after Psammetichos, Apries held the throne for twenty-two years. This king waged war with strong forces by land and sea against Cyprus and against Phoenicia, where he seized Sidon by storm; whereupon the other Phoenician cities, stricken with panic, rallied to his side. He also defeated the Phoenicians and Cypriots in a great sea battle; and having collected a great mass of spoils, he returned to Egypt. After this he sent a mighty host of native Egyptians against Cyrenê and Barcê; but when the greater portion of it was destroyed, the survivors became alienated from the king and revolted. For they suspected him of plotting the annihilation of the army, that he might rule the rest of the Egyptians more securely. So the king sent to them a prominent man of Egypt named Amasis. But Amasis disregarded the royal orders to effect a reconciliation with the troops, and on the contrary, encouraging their disaffection, he joined them in rebellion and was chosen their king. When shortly thereafter all of the other natives also joined the insurrection, King Apries in consternation was forced to flee to the protection of his mercenaries, who numbered about thirty thousand. A battle ensued near the village of Marea, wherein the Egyptians were victorious. Apries was captured alive and hung up on a gibbet, where he died of strangulation.[138]

Amasis then ordered the affairs of the kingdom as seemed best to him. He ruled the Egyptians in conformance with the laws and was held in great esteem. He also subdued the city-states of Cyprus and beautified many of the temples with stately votive ornaments. After a

---

137. For Busiris, see note 94, above.

138. Diodorus gives a tolerably correct, although incomplete, sketch of the reign of Apries, 589-570 B.C. He is the Hophra of the Old Testament (Ha'i'bre' in Egyptian), upon whose ineffectual support Zedekiah and other local rulers relied in their disastrous revolts against Babylonian overlordship. Apries' victories in the Levant were ephemeral in result, and he was unsuccessful in opposing Babylonian interests in the area. Domestically, however, Apries was at first more fortunate, and Egypt prospered. But excessive reliance on mercenaries proved his downfall, much as Diodorus relates. The last several years of his life seem to have been spent in armed exile, contesting the popular usurpation of Amasis, and he seems to have died in 566 B.C., after two pitched battles.

reign of fifty-five years he died, about the time when Cambyses, king of the Persians, invaded Egypt, in the third year of the sixty-third Olympiad, in which Parmenides of Camarina won the stadion.[139]

69   We have now sufficiently discussed the affairs of the kings of Egypt, from the earliest times until the death of Amasis, and we shall write of the remainder at the proper times in our history. For now, however, we shall give a summary treatment of the customs of Egypt, both the strangest ones and those most liable to be of use to our readers. For many of the ancient customs that were current among the Egyptians were valued not only among the native inhabitants, but also were admired greatly by the Greeks. For this reason, Greeks of the highest repute for learning were eager to visit Egypt, that they might gain knowledge of its noteworthy laws and customs. For albeit the country of old was inhospitable to strangers for the reasons just mentioned, yet nonetheless in ancient times Orpheus and the poet Homer were anxious to voyage thither, as were many others as well in later days, including Pythagoras of Samos and even Solon the lawgiver. What is more, the Egyptians assert that both the invention of writing and the observation of the stars originated among them, besides the discovery of geometrical principles and most of the arts, and that they promulgated the best laws. And they say the surest proof of these claims is that most of the kings of Egypt for over four thousand and seven hundred years were natives, while the country was the most prosperous on the face of the earth. This fortunate condition could never have existed had not this people possessed the most excellent laws, and customs, and those institutions concerned with all branches of learning.

We shall omit from our history the stories invented by Herodotus and certain other writers on the affairs of Egypt, who deliberately prefer fables to facts, and who spin yarns merely for the purpose of amusement. We shall, however, set forth the things written by the priests of Egypt in their sacred records, which we have examined diligently and minutely.

---

139. Amasis reigned forty-four years, 570-526 B.C. He briefly ruled Cyprus between the waning of Babylonian power and the waxing of the Persian. It was also he who granted the Greeks the city of Naucratis, which soon became the commercial center of the whole area. (The stadion was the famous 202-yard foot race at the Olympic games.)

70   In the first place, then, their kings led lives unlike those of other monarchs who hold royal sway and govern all things according to their absolute will. Instead, in Egypt, everything was preordained for the kings by order of law, not only the affairs of public business but even their daily life and diet. For none of their servants were slaves either bought with money or bred in the home, but all were sons of the most eminent priests, at least twenty years of age and better educated than any of their countrymen; so that the king, his person entrusted to the best of men to attend him constantly day and night, might fall into no evil ways. For a ruler never makes much progress in vice if he has no one to humor his base desires.[140]

The hours both of day and night were governed by a schedule, according to which the king must perforce do what was ordained, and not what might seem best to himself. For example, after being awakened in the morning, he was first obliged to read the dispatches sent in from every quarter, so that, precisely apprised of all events throughout his realm, he might aptly perform his duties and tend to all affairs of the state. After this, he bathed. Then, clothing his body in magnificent robes with the regalia of his sovereignty, he made sacrifice to the gods.

When the victims had been brought to the altar, it was customary for the chief priest to stand beside the king, surrounded by the common people of Egypt, and to pray in a loud voice for the gods to bestow good health and every other blessing on a king who was just to his people. The priest was also required to proclaim the king's virtues one by one, saying that he was both reverent to the gods and most gentle toward men; that he was self-disciplined, just, and magnanimous, as well as truthful, generous with his wealth, and generally superior to all passions. He punished transgressors less than they deserved, and repaid his benefactors in measure greater than the services rendered. The high priest recited much else in a similar vein and finished by pronouncing a curse over things done amiss, absolving the king from blame and demanding that the evil and the punishment should fall upon his servants and on those who had led him astray. He uttered these prayers in part to encourage the king to fear the gods and to live a life pleasing

---

140. Royal slaves, who often reached positions of great power, were notorious for pandering to their masters' lusts. Diodorus contrasts the reputed moral safeguards in Egypt with the degeneracy more common in Eastern monarchies of Hellenistic times.

to them, and in part to accustom him to act properly, using not stern admonitions, but agreeable praise with special emphasis on his virtues.

After these preliminaries, when the king had inspected the entrails of the sacrificial calf and had obtained favorable omens, the sacred scribe would read to the multitude, from the holy books, certain worthwhile sayings and deeds of the most eminent men. Thus their sovereign lord, having turned over in his mind the noblest of precepts, might then apply himself to the management of each successive task that was ordained for him to do. For not only was there a properly appointed time for him to hold court or render justice, but even for taking a walk, bathing himself, sleeping with his wife, and in general for all the activities of his daily life. And it was customary for him to eat simple foods, only the flesh of calves and geese being served to him, and to drink only a prescribed measure of wine, which was not enough to occasion unseemly satiety or drunkenness. Taken all together, the admirable rules laid down for his diet were such as might seem to have been drawn up, not by a legislator, but by the ablest physicians, whose aim was the health of the body.[141]

71   Although strange it may seem that the king had not the full control of his daily life, far stranger was it indeed that he was not allowed to judge cases nor transact public business at his own discretion, nor to punish anyone in haughtiness or anger or for any other improper motive, but only as the established laws provided in each case. Yet the kings were not averse in any way to doing such things according to

---

141. Scholars differ concerning the accuracy of Diodorus' account of the ritual surrounding the daily life of Egyptian kings. Actual evidence is scant, but analogy with the circumstances in other theocratic monarchies of long duration make it not improbable that, at least in certain periods (not necessarily in late Ptolemaic times), the kings were required to live according to the strictest of religious, superstitious, and magical taboos. The concept is widespread both temporally and geographically. Prominent examples can be found in Chinese, Japanese, Aztec, and Inca history. (". . . the king is often thought to be . . . an incarnation of a deity, and consistently with this belief the course of nature is supposed to be more or less under his control [but] . . . partly independent of his will. His person is considered . . . the dynamical center of the universe . . . . He is the point of support on which hangs the balance of the world, and the slightest irregularity on his part may overthrow the delicate equipoise; . . . his whole life, down to its minutest details, must be so regulated that no act of his, voluntary or involuntary, may disarrange or upset the established order of nature." Sir James Frazer, *The Golden Bough*, chapter XVII.)

custom, nor did they take offense in their hearts. On the contrary, they believed themselves to live the happiest of lives: for they considered that other men, thoughtlessly indulging their natural passions, did many things that caused them harm or hazard, and that often a man, knowing that he was about to do wrong, yet overcome by love or hate or some other emotion, did sin nonetheless. But they themselves, striving after a way of life sanctioned by the wisest men, fell into the fewest ignorant errors.

Now the kings were so full of justice toward their subjects, that the love of the people for their rulers exceeded even the natural affection reserved for their own kinsmen, and the general populace as well as the confraternity of priests were as concerned for the welfare of the kings as for their own wives and children and the rest of their possessions. Therefore, indeed, during most of the times of the kings we know about, they maintained an orderly government and continued to be blessed with the happiest way of life so long as the above-mentioned system of laws was unchanged; in addition to which, they conquered the largest number of foreign nations, enjoyed the greatest wealth, adorned their lands with works and wonders unexcelled, and beautified their cities with sumptuous monuments of every kind.

72   Now a signal proof of the love the Egyptians bore their sovereigns is the grief they showed after a king had died: since when marks of affection are rendered unto one who can no longer be sensible of them, it is a sure warrant of their sincerity. For whenever a king took leave of life, all the people of Egypt without exception went into mourning, and for seventy-two days they closed the temples, stopped the sacrifices, and kept no feasts; men and women alike, rending their garments, casting dust on their heads, and girding their bodies round with linen bands below the breasts, went about twice each day in groups of two or three hundred, and droning a dirge in rhythmic chant they honored the dead with paeans of praise and recitations of his virtues. They ate no food of flesh or wheat and abstained from wine and all other luxuries. No one deemed it proper to indulge in baths, perfumes, or soft beds, nor even less had they the heart to partake of sexual pleasure; but each person, full of grief as if a dearly beloved child had died, passed these seventy-two days in lamentation (see plate 24). During this time they made elaborate preparations for the burial. On the final day, they laid the coffin containing the body before the mouth of the tomb and according to custom convened a court to inquire into the actions of the deceased during his life. Then, after permitting

accusations from anyone who wished to make them, the priests enumerated and praised everything the king had done well; upon hearing which, the common people, who had gathered in myriads for the funeral, applauded one and all if they knew that he had lived worthily; but on the contrary, if he had not, they raised an uproar. And many a king has been denied the customary public burial through the opposition of the throng. Wherefore it came about on this account that all successive occupants of the throne used to behave with integrity, not only for the reasons aforementioned, but also because they feared ill treatment of their bodies after death and an infamous reputation for all eternity.[142]

These, then, are the most significant customs concerning the ancient kings.

73   Egypt as a whole was subdivided into numerous districts, which are called nomes in the Greek language, and a nomarch was appointed over each one to have charge and care of all therein.[143]   All the lands are distributed into three allotments. The first share belongs to the order of priests,[144] who enjoy the highest respect among the native population because of their attendance on the gods and because these men, through their education, are of the highest intelligence.   From their landed revenues they pay for all the sacrifices throughout Egypt, provide for their servants, and supply their own wants; for the Egyptians believe it imperative never to interrupt the worship of the gods, but to continue it both by the same men and in essentially the same way forever.   Also, they believe that the priests, who intercede for the interests of all, should not be lacking in the necessities of life.   For some of them are generally with the king at all times, as associates discussing the weightiest matters,

---

142. The Egyptians believed that continued spiritual existence after death depended upon the preservation of the body; hence the elaborate precautions taken to protect the corpse, such as mummification and strongly constructed tombs with booby traps, false passages, and secret burial chambers.

143. See note 108, above, on the subject of nomes.

144. The Harris Papyrus gives some definite statistics from the reign of Ramesses III, c. 1194-1163 B.C.   Since an organized priestly class first came about during the New Kingdom, which began with the XVIIIth Dynasty, c. 1550 B.C., this developing caste had not yet attained the heights of power and influence it was later to possess.   But even in this early period, the temples owned about fifteen percent of the cultivable land, two percent of the population, 169 towns, and 500,000 head of cattle.

as advisers and teachers, or foretelling the future through astrology and entrail divination; they also read from the sacred books the incidents recorded therein which can be of help. Now unlike the custom of the Greeks, no one man or woman in Egypt succeeds to the priesthood, but many people devote themselves to the sacrifices and honors of the gods, and bequeath the same way of life to their descendants. Furthermore, the priesthood is free from all taxation and second only to the king in authority and public esteem.[145]

The second share of the lands belongs to the kings by inheritance. It furnishes their revenues, out of which they finance their wars, maintain their regal pomp, and reward with gifts, according to merit, those who have acted in any praiseworthy manner; and by means of the income derived from these lands they avoid drowning the common citizens with taxes.

The final portion of the lands is possessed by those called the warriors, who are subject to military service. The men who run this risk are thus, through their ownership of land, quite patriotic, and they willingly face the hazards of war. For it would be absurd to trust the defense of the realm to soldiers who own nothing worth fighting for in the country! But even more importantly, if the warrior caste be prosperous, it will beget many children and by this means build up a large population, so that the country may never stand in need of foreign mercenaries. Soldiers, like priests, inherit their calling from their forebears, and the bravery of their fathers inspires them with courage;

---

145. The standard Greek view of Egypt as a land dominated by priests was not true for early periods, but it was fairly accurate for the centuries just preceding Diodorus' visit. The hereditary nature of the priesthood developed gradually from New Kingdom times, c. 1550-1070 B.C. The resulting priestly class included all religious ranks, from the temple administrators down to the lowest lectors and scribes. The priests were primarily servants of the gods, not spiritual counsellors or shepherds of the people, and their chief sacerdotal function was to ensure the observance of every scintilla of religious ritual, taboo and tradition. They were also the intellectual and cultural leaders of society, tending always to a conservatism verging, in Diodorus' day, on antiquarianism. By his time, of course, their real political power was extinguished, but their social influence was still great.

and practicing the arts of war from very childhood, their skill and daring renders them invincible.[146]

74   Now there are three other classes of citizens, namely: farmers, herdsmen, and artisans. The farmers rent small plots of productive land from the king, the priests, and the warriors, and they spend all their lives tilling the ground. Since they grow up from childhood concerned only with agriculture, their expertise far exceeds that of farmers in other nations; for indeed they understand more perfectly than anyone else the nature of the soil, the channeling of waters, and the proper times for sowing, reaping, and other steps in harvesting the crops, having inherited some of their knowledge from the empirical observations of their ancestors, and having learned some from their own experience. The same can also be said about the herdsmen, who receive the care of the flocks from their forefathers as if by the law of inheritance, and who pass their entire lives in pastoral pursuits. Although they have learned many traditional things from their ancestors about the best way to raise and feed the herds, they also continually discover many new techniques by their own zeal in these pursuits. And it is most incredible how the keepers of poultry and geese, through their excessive application to these matters, raise a prodigious number of birds by their own artifice, and contrary to the natural way in which other men hatch these fowls. For they do not allow the hens to incubate the eggs, but, on the contrary, hatch them artificially with such cleverness and ingenuity that they are unsurpassed by nature's own endeavors.[147]

Yet again, we find that the Egyptians have been most diligent in cultivating the manual crafts and have mastered them to the highest state of perfection. For only in Egypt are the artisans all forbidden to belong to any occupation or class of citizens except those dictated by custom and handed down from their parents; and as a result, neither the malice of teachers, nor political turmoil, nor anything else interferes with their application to their trades. For in other lands we see the artisans distracted in mind about many things; and through covetous ambition

---

146. The invincibility of the Egyptian soldier class must be understood to be theoretical, at best. Egyptian warfare had been dominated by Greek mercenaries for centuries. Although the native military class still existed, its martial prowess was more despised than esteemed.

147. In *Historia Animalium* VI.2, Aristotle says that the eggs hatched after being buried in heaps of dung.

they will not confine themselves to their own proper business: for some try farming, others take up commerce, and yet others practice two or three trades at a time. And, in cities of a democratic temperament, huge crowds of people thronging to the assemblies make a mockery of government, though earning their stipends from their employers all the while.[148] But among the Egyptians, any artisan who works at more than one trade or meddles in the government incurs a severe punishment.

The foregoing, then, is the class structure possessed by the inhabitants of ancient Egypt, and their attachment, through their ancestors, to their own orders of society.[149]

75   The Egyptians took their legal proceedings very seriously, believing that decisions in court have a far-reaching influence, in two ways, on life in the community: for they saw clearly that the best safeguards against wrongdoing are the punishment of lawbreakers, on one hand, and on the other the relief of the victims. But they realized that civil life would be undone if transgressors should be able to overcome, through bribery or favoritism, their fear of condemnation; wherefore, by appointing the ablest men from the most prominent cities as judges over all the nation, they failed not to achieve their goal of impartiality. For they would select ten judges apiece from Heliopolis, Thebes, and Memphis, and this judicial council, it seems, was not a bit

---

148. This passage is a sarcastic gibe at the rambunctious populace of many Greek city-states, Athens in particular, who were addicted to neglecting business to attend popular assemblies and the law courts. This mania is devastatingly satirized in *The Wasps* of Aristophanes.

149. Diodorus lists priests, warriors, farmers, herdsmen, and artisans as the five social classes in Egypt. Herodotus II.164 enumerates seven: priests, warriors, cowherds, swineherds, tradesmen, interpreters, and boatmen. A thousand years earlier in the reign of Tuthmosis IV, c. 1401-1391 B.C., a census tabulated priests, warriors, royal serfs, and craftsmen or artisans. The once powerful class of landed nobles had dwindled into utter insignificance by Herodotus' day, as had the class of bureaucrats and officials which succeeded it. Like the priestly class, that of the warriors did not reach real importance until the New Kingdom, but by Diodorus' time its influence and power long had been eclipsed. Slaves constituted a large proportion of the population, but they were non-persons in the political sense and not even deserving of mention. Egyptian society was rigid in structure compared to the Hellenic norm, and social class and occupation tended to be hereditary in its later stages; but it was not as inflexibly stratified as Diodorus says. Throughout his account, Diodorus seems to be paraphrasing sources from earlier centuries, rather than indulging in independent contemporary observation.

inferior to the Athenian Areopagites or to the elders of the Lacedaemonians. Now whenever the thirty convened, they decided which of their number was most worthy; and he was elected chief justice, while his city would send another judge to fill up his place. The king provided each judge with a fixed allowance of supplies which was just enough for his maintenance, but he gave many times this amount to the chief justice. The chief justice wore around his neck, suspended from a golden chain, a little image made of precious stones which they called "Truth," and the pleas would not begin until the chief justice held up this icon of the Truth.

Now all their laws were written down in eight volumes, and after these were laid before the judges, it was the custom for the plaintiff to write down one by one the substance of his accusations, in what manner they came about, and the value of the injury or damages done to him; then the defendant, after receiving the instrument thus executed by the plaintiff, wrote in reply to each charge, either that he had not done what was alleged or that, if he had done it, it was not wrong; or that, if it was wrong, yet he deserved a reduced penalty. The law then required the accuser to write a rebuttal and the defendant again to offer counter arguments. After both parties had twice given their written arguments to the judges, the thirty were obligated then and there to share their opinions with one another; and finally the chief justice would place the small figure of Truth on one of the two briefs.

76   The Egyptians conduct all their court cases in this way, from a belief that all too frequently the eloquence of advocates would obscure the truth, and that indeed the wiles of orators, the witchery of declamation, or the tears of the accused would lead many men to disregard the rigor of the laws and the strictness of the truth; in fact, they observe that even those renowned for their probity can be swayed by the skill of pleaders, whether by their guile, their persuasiveness, or their appeals for compassion. But by requiring the litigants to write out their suits, the Egyptians knew that verdicts would be impartial and based solely on the unadorned facts. For this method ensures that the clever of tongue will gain no advantage over the slower, nor the experienced advocates over the inexperienced, nor the liars over the lovers of truth, nor the brash over the mild-mannered; but all will have their rights on an equal basis, since the law allows ample time for the opponents to examine each other's arguments and for the judges to consider the case from either side.[150]

77   But since we have broached the subject of their laws, we believe it not inconsistent with the scope of our researches to elaborate upon those statutes of the Egyptians which are of the greatest antiquity or have the strangest form, or which, by and large, are able to furnish instruction to those fond of reading. To begin with, they punished perjurers with death, because these miscreants commit two of the most serious breaches of the law, namely, impiety toward the gods, and violation of the most sacred trust among men. As another example, if anyone saw a man being murdered upon the highway in this country or suffering violence in any way and did not rescue him if at all possible, he was himself condemned to death; and even if in all honesty through lack of strength he was unable to render aid, he was at least obliged to bring charges against the brigands and prosecute their transgression of the law; and anyone who failed in this duty according to law was mandatorily sentenced to be flogged with blows and deprived of all food for three days. Again, those who bore false witness against others were forced to suffer whatever punishment would have befallen the accused if it so happened they had been convicted. It was further ordained that every Egyptian had to give the governors a written account of the sources from which he derived a livelihood, and those who lied in these affidavits or followed an illicit occupation were doomed to suffer the penalty of death. It is even said that Solon, after visiting Egypt, introduced this law into Athens.[151]

---

150. The four-step written court proceeding was pretty much as Diodorus describes it, especially in civil cases, although verbal argument was not completely forbidden as he claims; however, it is true that prior to Hellenic influence there were no advocates. There is no evidence of a legal compilation in eight books, but texts of the XVIIIth Dynasty, c. 1550-1307 B.C., mention one in forty scrolls which the "vizier" was obliged to keep before him during public court proceedings. In his sketchy account, Diodorus seems to imply that all cases were tried before the court of thirty; in reality, there were many local courts of justice.

151. Herodotus II.177 gives an identical account of this law and ascribes it to Amasis, 570-526 B.C.   He too says Solon borrowed the law, but this is anachronistic since Solon lived before Amasis. Other classical authors attribute the Athenian version of this law to Draco or Peisistratos.

If anyone purposely were to murder either a free man or a slave, the laws demanded that he too must die. For they wanted, in the first place, to deter all men from evil by the penalties attached to the crimes, not by differences in fortune; and in the second place, to accustom men, through consideration even for the slaves, to avoid all the more doing wrong to free men.

Now the laws did not impose death on parents who killed their children, but decreed instead that they must embrace the corpse and hold it continuously for three days and nights under constant public guard; for the Egyptians considered it unfair to take life away from those who had given life to their children, but rather by a reproof tinged with discomfort and regret to deter others from acts of this kind. But on the other hand, the laws reserved unusual punishments for children who murdered their parents, requiring people convicted of this crime to be burnt alive on a bed of thorns, after having finger-sized pieces of flesh gouged from their bodies with sharpened reeds; for they accounted it men's greatest sin forcibly to take the lives of the parents who had given life to them.

Pregnant women condemned to death were not executed until they had given birth. Many of the Greeks also promulgated this law in the belief that it was altogether unjust for an innocent babe to suffer the same fate as its guilty mother, and unjust to exact retribution from two people for the transgressions of one. In addition to this, since crime is an act of wilful evil, they felt it unfair to visit the same penalty on a child without the faculty of reason. But most importantly, since blame attached to the mother alone, it was thought in no way fitting for the child to be killed, who belonged to the father as well as the mother. Yea, might one consider as equally bad judges both those who spare the murderer, and those who destroy the wholly innocent along with the guilty!

The foregoing, then, are those of the laws about murder which seem to have been the most effective.

78   And of the other laws, that laid down concerning war prescribed not death, but the utmost disgrace, for those who deserted their posts in battle or disobeyed the orders of their commanders; but if later by bravery they chanced to wipe away the infamy, the law restored them to their former dignity. Thus the lawgiver not only made dishonor a more fearful punishment than death, so that he might accustom all men to consider disgrace the greatest of misfortunes, but at the same time he reasoned that, while those put to death can be of no use to the

commonwealth, those who have been shamed will be the source of many benefits because of their desire to regain their places in society. The law further enjoined that those who revealed state secrets to the enemy should have their tongues cut out. As for those who made false weights and measures or counterfeited coins and seals, as well as for government clerks who made false records or deleted anything that had been entered in the public registers, and those who forged contracts, the law commanded both their hands to be struck off in order that, being punished in those parts of the body wherewith they had violated the law, each culprit might endure his irreparable calamity to the day he died, while serving through his own punishment as a warning to discourage others from committing crimes of the same kind.

Their laws touching women were also stringent. They directed the genitals to be cut off any man who raped a free married woman, on the grounds that, by one lawless act, such a person had committed three of the greatest wrongs, to wit: wanton violence, seduction, and the confounding of offspring.   But if anyone committed adultery with consent, the law ordered the man to receive a thousand blows of the rod and the woman's nose to be cut off; for the law found it meet that she who made her face alluring for purpose of illicit lust should suffer disfigurement of the very feature that added most notably to her beauty.

79   They say the law of contracts originated with Bocchoris and stipulated that those who borrow without a written bond may be released from their debt if they but swear an oath that they do not owe the money. The rationale for this was, in the first place, to render oaths of great importance so that men might have a reverent fear of the gods: for since it is evident that people eventually lose faith in the man who has sworn oaths too many times, everyone will deem it of the greatest importance not to have recourse to an oath, lest he lose his credibility. In the second place, the lawgiver assumed that by placing faith entirely in the honor and goodness of men, he would encourage everyone to be of blameless character and thus avoid being held untrustworthy. Besides, he thought it unfair that those who in the first place had been trusted without oath should not later be trusted when they took an oath concerning the very same contracts.

As for those who loaned money under written covenant, he forbade them to exact more in interest than the value of the principal. He also limited the forced repayment of a debt to confiscation of the debtor's property, allowing no circumstance in which the person himself might be seized; for he felt that goods ought to belong to those who had earned them by work or who had received them in gift from someone in authority, but that men's bodies ought to belong to the state, so that the state might claim both in peace and war the public duties owed to it. For it would be absurd if a soldier who had set out in defense of his fatherland should be hauled back before a magistrate and arraigned by his creditor for the money he owed, thus jeopardizing the common security of all to satisfy the cupidity of a private citizen. And it appears that Solon transplanted this law to Athens also, which he styled the Disburdening Ordinance, releasing all citizens from the debts they had contracted on security of their persons.[152] But some commentators not unreasonably find fault with most of the other lawgivers among the Greeks, who forbade tools, ploughshares, or other essential implements to be taken as surety for repayment of a loan, yet allowed the men who use these things to be subject to seizure.

80   The Egyptian law on thievery was also most singular, for it bade those who wished to follow this trade to register themselves with the Prince of Thieves, and openly to convey to him forthwith any stolen articles; while in like manner those who had their property stolen were to notify him of each individual item they had lost, listing the place, the day, and the hour in which the theft had occurred. In this way everything stolen was easily found, and to recover his lost property the owner had only to give the Prince of Thieves a fourth part of its value. For the lawgiver, unable to completely eradicate stealing, devised a way by which payment of a small ransom would redeem anything that had been taken.[153]

Among the Egyptians, the priests marry only one wife, while other men wed as many as they please. For the sake of a large population, they are required to raise every child that is born; for a flourishing population is of the highest importance to the prosperity of the country and its cities. No child is considered a bastard, even one born of a

---

152. In 594 B.C., Solon the poet and intellectual was elected archon at Athens with the express charge of reforming the economic laws. The "Seisachtheia" or Disburdening Ordinance (or Proclamation) was the stunning first act in Solon's social programme. As Diodorus says, it annulled all contracts which pledged the debtor's person as security for a loan, and it also freed all men already enslaved for debt. A subsequent law forbade such practices for the future. It is unlikely that Solon copied the idea from Egypt.

153. There is no evidence to support this tale of the thieves' guild.

slave mother, for the Egyptians suppose that the father is the sole cause of its creation, the mother merely providing nourishment and shelter in her body for the unborn infant.[154] Likewise with trees, they call the ones bearing fruits males, and the ones without fruit females, in direct contradiction to the usage of the Greeks.

They raise their offspring without expense in a very carefree manner that defies belief. For they feed them a potage boiled up from any ingredients that are cheap and abundant, or give them papyrus stems roasted in the fire, or the roots and stalks of marsh plants, some raw, some boiled, and some baked. Also, since the balmy climate allows most of the children to be raised barefoot and naked, parents reckon that it costs no more than twenty drachmas to rear a child to the age of puberty. These are the main reasons why Egypt has such a large population, and through this in turn supports the construction of numerous public works.

81 The priests teach their sons two systems of letters, both the kind termed "sacred" and the kind suitable to the more commonplace type of learning.[155] They also carry geometry and arithmetic to the highest perfection.[156] For every year the river alters the countryside in divers

---

154. Relatively little is known of Egyptian marriage laws and mores. Polygamy seems to have been accepted, but not widely practiced, and indeed throughout most of Egyptian history monogamy was the norm and the ideal. Concubinage seems to have been common, however, and rich men or nobles are sometimes known to have had harems. The legitimacy of children born of a slave mother and a free father contrasted starkly with the usual Greek custom, which held such offspring to be slaves. By Diodorus' day, the Greek usage was beginning to prevail after centuries of Hellenic political and cultural domination. Exposure of unwanted infants was also foreign to Egypt, but it too was introduced by the Greeks.

155. There were actually three major kinds of Egyptian writing in Diodorus' day, not two. Hieroglyphic or "sacred picture" writing is the oldest, and the kind most familiar from thousands of monumental and religious inscriptions. Hieratic was a cursive form of this used for secular purposes. It developed later, but never totally displaced hieroglyphics for use in public inscriptions (the latest example of which dates from A.D. 394). Demotic, the common writing, developed after 700 B.C. and was in general use from about 600 B.C. It represented the existing language of the day, whereas hieroglyphics perpetuated the archaic language of the Middle Kingdom a thousand years earlier. See plate 25.

156. Geometry in this context has the literal meaning of "earth measurement" or surveying. Actually, Egyptian mathematics was quite rudimentary compared to

ways, which furnishes grounds for all sorts of disputes over the boundaries of adjacent fields; and these disagreements are not easily settled unless a geometer can skillfully establish the truth on the basis of his experience. Now arithmetic is useful to them in the management of the household as well as being the foundation for geometry, and it is also of no small service to students of astrology. For if ever a nation took an interest in the observation of the stars and their positions and movements, it is the Egyptians, who preserve extensive records about each star from unbelievably ancient days, having taken great pains from time immemorial concerning such matters; and they most zealously note the motions, periods, and stations of the planets, and the natal influence for good or evil that each exerts on living beings. The astrologers often successfully predict the events fated to befall a man during his life, and they frequently foretell the failure of crops or, conversely, an abundance of yield, as well as plagues on men and cattle. And from long ages of close observation they know in advance of earthquakes and floods and the time when comets will appear, and all the events of which, to common men, it seems impossible to have knowledge. Furthermore, they claim that the Chaldeans of Babylon, who originally were colonists from Egypt, owe their fame in the science of astrology to the knowledge they learned from the priests of Egypt.[157]

But most of the other Egyptians learn the elements of the various occupations in their childhood from their fathers or kinsmen, even as we have told before; they are taught but a smattering of letters, and not everyone at that, but mainly those practicing the crafts. Nor is it customary among them to learn wrestling and music; for they believe

---

the brilliant heights attained in the Greek world. Diodorus obviously knew too little of the subject to judge, or he may only be accepting uncritically a source from centuries earlier, before the flowering of Greek science.

157. There is no evidence that astronomy or astrology in Mesopotamia was an offshoot of Egyptian culture. Astronomy originated about the same time in both areas, but developed much more fully in Babylonia than in Egypt. Egyptian astronomy was more empirical than theoretical, and its chief contribution to civilization was the calendar (see note 102, above). Astrology seems to have been introduced into Egypt from Mesopotamia about 525 B.C. But predicting a man's fate from his day of birth was a longstanding Egyptian practice. See note 56, above. Diodorus covers Babylonian astrology in detail in Book II, chapters 29-31: see *The Antiquities of Asia: A Translation with Notes of Book II of the Library of History of Diodorus Siculus*, by Edwin Murphy; Transaction Publications, 1989.

that young men will never attain bodily health from daily exercise in the wrestling schools, but only a fleeting and quite precarious strength; while music they judge to be not only useless, but even harmful, since it renders effeminate the spirits of its listeners.

82 For preventing illness they subject their bodies to fasts, purgatives, and emetics, sometimes daily and sometimes every third or fourth day. For they contend that most of the food which the body digests is superfluous and causes ill health. Therefore the above-mentioned regimen of treatment, by removing the cause of disease, promotes most effectively the good health of the body. During military campaigns and journeys in the country, all Egyptians receive medical care without payment from their own funds. For doctors obtain their salaries out of the public treasury, and they dispense their treatments according to written rules which were composed by many eminent physicians of ancient times. Now if they are unable to save a patient's life despite having read and followed the directions of the holy book, they are never blamed or punished; but, if they have done anything contrary to the written instructions, they stand trial for their lives.[158] For the lawgiver felt that few remedies would be superior to those sanctioned by long usage and prescribed by the best medical practitioners.[159]

---

158. Herodotus II.77 agrees with Diodorus on the hygienic value the Egyptians placed on diet, purgatives, and emetics. Egyptian medical texts abound in prescriptions for purges, enemas, and emetics. Aristotle, however, is the only other writer who alludes to the penalty for not following the written medical lore: "Even an Egyptian doctor is allowed to depart from his text-book instructions if the patient is not well after four days; if he does so earlier it is at his own risk." (*Politics* III.15).

159. The famous Edwin Smith Surgical Papyrus, copied in the seventeenth century B.C. from a text of the third millenium B.C., may be a precursor of the type of physicians' handbook mentioned by Diodorus. Free of the usual mixture of magic and incantations found in early Egyptian medical papyri, it systematically presents forty-eight cases involving wounds and injuries to different parts of the body. Significantly, thirteen of the wounds are termed "not to be treated," i.e., fatal. This terminology may reflect a prudent regard for the penalties, if any, for unsuccessful treatment.
Case number six from the Edwin Smith Surgical Papyrus is a good example of the pragmatic directions that an Egyptian doctor might find useful:
. . . If you examine a man with a gaping wound in his head, penetrating to the bone, smashing his skull, and rending open the brain of his skull, you

83   The whole question of Egypt's sacred animals naturally seems bizarre to many people, and thus warrants some investigation. For the Egyptians are fanatically addicted to the worship of certain animals, the dead as well as the living, such as cats, ichneumons, and dogs, as well as hawks and the bird they call the ibis; not to mention wolves and crocodiles, and several other creatures of this kind. We shall try to explain the reasons for this homage after first telling a little about the animals themselves.

In the first place, for each species of venerated animal they have consecrated a tract of land which produces a revenue sufficient to feed and care for its members. Besides this, the Egyptians make vows to various gods on behalf of children who have been delivered from serious maladies, and in fulfillment of these vows they shave off their hair and, weighing it against gold or silver, give that amount in money to the caretakers of the above-mentioned animals.[160]

The caretakers for the hawks cut meat into tidbits; then, summoning the birds with a sharp cry, they toss each morsel up to them as they fly by, until they catch it. For the cats and ichneumons, they crumble pieces of bread into milk and with coaxing sounds set it before them; or, they feed them raw Nile fish cut up into pieces. In like manner they provide food suitable to each of the other kinds of animals. And they

---

should feel the wound with your fingers. Should you find that smash which is in his skull to be like those corrugations which form in molten copper, and something throbbing therein, fluttering under your fingers like the weak place in an infant's crown before it becomes whole . . . and the patient discharges blood from both his nostrils and suffers from stiffness in his neck, [this is] an ailment not to be treated. [But] you should anoint the wound with grease. You shall not bind it; you shall not apply two strips upon it until you know he has reached a decisive stage.

"Smashing his skull and rending open the brain of his skull" means that the smash is large, opening to the interior of his skull, to the membrane enveloping his brain, so that it breaks open the fluid in the interior of his head. "Those corrugations which form in molten copper" means copper which the coppersmith pours off before it is forced into the mold, because of something foreign upon it like wrinkles. It is said: "It is like ripples of pus." (Paraphrased from J.H. Breasted, *The Edwin Smith Surgical Papyrus*, the University of Chicago Press, 1930.)

160. Herodotus II.65 gives the same account, adding (as Diodorus implies) that the guardians used the money to buy food for their charges. Diodorus may have taken much of his chapters on animal worship, in abbreviated form, from Herodotus, whose work it closely resembles (II.65-76).

neither shrink from performing this obligatory service nor are they ashamed for the public to see them doing it. On the contrary, being thus engaged in the most important homage to the gods, they adopt a solemn air and go about the cities and country wearing distinctive emblems of their office. So it is evident from afar that they have charge of the animal worship, and those they meet bow down before them in respect.

Whenever any of these animals dies, they wrap its carcass in fine linen; and beating their breasts in lamentation, they take it to be embalmed. There they treat the body with oil of cedar and sweet-smelling substances that can preserve it for a long time, then they bury it in a consecrated grave. (See plate 26.) Anyone who intentionally kills one of these animals is put to death. But should someone kill a cat or an ibis, whether purposely or accidentally, his doom in either case is sealed; for the people rush to the spot and dispose of the offender in fearful measure, sometimes without a hearing.[161] And through fear of these consequences, anyone who sees one of these animals that has died draws afar back and cries out with horror, bewailing the deceased and calling to witness that he had found it already dead. And so deeply has superstitious awe of these creatures sunk into the minds of the populace, and so unalterably disposed by temperament is every man to respect them, that when a certain Roman chanced to kill a cat, a mob quickly assembled at his house, and neither the officials sent by the king to intercede for him, nor even the widespread fear of Rome, was able to save the man from being massacred, notwithstanding his act had been inadvertent. This happened even though, at the time, Ptolemy the king had not as yet been designated "Friend" by the Romans, and when the people, sparing no pains to appease the delegation from Italy, in their anxiety were straining themselves to give no cause for complaint or for war. And we relate this incident not from hearsay; for we saw it happen during the time we spent in Egypt.[162]

---

161. Herodotus II.65 says it was the hawk and ibis whose accidental killing was always punishable by death.

162. This event must have taken place in late 60 or early 59 B.C., the first year of the 180th Olympiad. This was the Olympiad during which Diodorus was, by his repeated statements, a visitor in Egypt. Ptolemy Auletes finally obtained the long-sought appellation "Friend of the Romans" later in the year 59 B.C.

84   But if many people find what we have said thus far to be incredible and rather like fiction, the wonders yet to be told will seem far more marvelous still. For at one time, when the Egyptians were oppressed by famine, it is said that many of them devoured one another out of hunger; but as a general rule no one was accused of having attacked the holy animals. Again, if a dog be found dead in any house, all the inhabitants shave their entire bodies and go into mourning; and stranger still, if wine or grain or any of the necessities of life chance to be lying about the domicile where one of these little beings has died, they will no longer attempt to use them in any way. And if they happen to be on campaign in some other country, they buy cats and hawks and bring them back to Egypt, doing this sometimes even when supplies for the journey are running out.

Now, as for the circumstances surrounding the Apis bull of Memphis or the Mnevis bull of Heliopolis, or the facts about the he-goat at Mendes, the crocodile in Lake Moeris, the lion living in the city called Leontopolis, and many other creatures of this kind, though the details are easy enough to relate, they will scarcely be believed by any who have not witnessed them.[163]   For these hallowed beings pass their lives in consecrated enclosures, where many prominent men attend on them, serving them the most sumptuous foods; they constantly offer them the finest wheaten flour, or groats boiled in milk, besides all manner of sweetmeats mixed with honey, as well as boiled or roasted flesh of goose; and they catch many birds and throw them to the carnivorous animals, and in general they take great pains to provide the dearest fare. They are ever treating their charges to warm baths, anointing them with the most luxurious unguents, burning all sorts of fragrant incense before them, and providing them with the most lavish bedding and with goodly ornaments. They are very solicitous that their beasts may obtain sexual gratification as nature demands; besides this, for each of the animals they keep the most handsome females of the same species, which they call its concubines, and these too they attend with the greatest care and expense. And whenever any one of these divine animals dies, they lament its passing in the same way as those who have lost a beloved child; and they bury it not merely to the best of their ability, but at an expense far exceeding the value of their property. For example, after

---

163. For the Apis bull, see following notes. The "he-goat" of Mendes was really a ram. The lion god of Leontopolis was Ruty or Ruru-ti. For the crocodile god, see note 178 below.

the death of Alexander, and just after Ptolemy son of Lagus had taken control of Egypt, the Apis of Memphis happened to die of old age; whereupon the man who had charge of it spent for the funeral every bit of the great wealth he had accumulated, and in addition he borrowed fifty talents of silver from Ptolemy. And even in our own day, some of the caretakers of these animals have expended no less than a hundred talents on their obsequies.

85   We must add to what has been said above an account of the circumstances surrounding the sacred bull called Apis. For whenever one has died and has been buried in splendor, the priests concerned with these matters seek out a young bull whose bodily markings are similar to those of its predecessor. When they find it, the people put away their mourning, and the priests whose duty it is conduct the bull calf first to Nilopolis, where they keep it forty days; then they put it aboard a state barge with a gilded stall and convey it as a deity to the temple of Hephaestos in Memphis. And during the said forty days, only women may look upon it, and these stand before it and pull up their clothes to reveal the generative parts of their bodies. But at all other times it is absolutely forbidden for women to enter the presence of this divinity.[164]

Now some explain the reason for the sanctity of this bull by claiming that at death the soul of Osiris migrated to one of these animals and continues to do so until this day, at each of his manifestations passing into a younger bull.[165]   But others assert that, after Typhon had

---

164. Diodorus seems to be reliable in his description of the journey of the new Apis to Memphis. The exposure of the women's genitals betrays the ancient fertility aspects of the deity. The dead Apis was given a splendid funeral, borne on a bier and accompanied by priests dressed in fawnskin, carrying "Bacchic" wands, and shouting ecstatically; at least this is the account given two centuries later by Plutarch (*On Isis and Osiris* 35). The new Apis was reputedly the offspring of a cow impregnated by a moonbeam (*Ibid.* 43) and recognizable by various marks (twenty-nine according to Aelian, *H.A.* XI.10). Herodotus, Pliny, Eusebius, Aelian, Manetho, Strabo, Arnobius, and other classical authors describe the Apis, one of the most famous tourist attractions of ancient Egypt. It was generally black, with a white blaze on its forehead, a shining spot on its horns, the outline of a vulture on its back, etc. See plate 27. When the right animal was found "the Egyptians cry 'We have found him! Rejoice!'" (Juvenal, *Satires* VIII.28).

165. In *The Golden Bough*, Sir James George Frazer points out that belief in the transmigration of Osiris' soul to successive generations of the Apis bull probably derives from the widespread ancient concept of the necessary

murdered Osiris, Isis collected all the fragments of his body and put them in a wooden bull draped with fine linen; and that also because of this the city of Busiris received its name. They also tell many other stories about the Apis, but we know it would be tiresome to relate each one of them singly and in detail.[166]

86   Everything the Egyptians do in their veneration of the sacred animals is strange and unbelievable, and this presents great difficulties to anyone investigating its causes.[167]   Their priests hold certain secret doctrines concerning these matters, which we explained earlier in our discussion of their gods. But most of the Egyptians allege one of the following three explanations, the first of which is wholly fabulous and quite in keeping with old-fashioned simplicity of beliefs: for they say

---

regeneration of an incarnate god of fertility (which Osiris once was) into a younger and stronger body unimpaired by age. Some authorities indicate that the Apis was not permitted to die of old age, and was drowned at age twenty-five, thus adding credence to the theory that the power of the god depended on the undiminished vitality of its corporeal manifestation.

166. Apis (Egyptian *Hap*) was originally a symbol of fertility, an incarnation of Ptah-Seker-Osiris, the god of the Memphis necropolis and the local form of Osiris. The cult is of great antiquity, with references dating to the Ist and IInd dynasties; but the great flowering of its popularity started with Psammetichos I and his successors, from which time the Apis tombs became large, elaborate, and costly. Although sometimes identified with the Greek god Epaphus (son of Zeus by Io; see note 48, above), Apis was usually considered "the living soul of Osiris" by the Greek commentators. Diodorus' apparent *non sequiter* about the etymology of Busiris probably implies that the Apis bull was revered because it contained the soul of Osiris, just as the wooden bull contained his body. The tale is farfetched, even for Diodorus. In reality, Busiris was the Greek corruption of the Egyptian *Pr-Wsir* (*Per-Asar*), meaning House of Osiris, and surviving in the modern town named Abusir in the Delta.

167. Egyptian animal worship reaches back into remote antiquity. Its exact origins and development are obscure, but judging from the frequency of animal burials and other evidence, it seems to have gathered increasing popularity from New Kingdom times and to have reached fanatic proportions only in the Saïte and Ptolemaic eras. What probably started as animistic totemism and fetishism seems to have gradually acquired aspects of zoolatry and later of anthropomorphism (e.g., gods with half-human, half-animal forms). Three kinds of sacred animal can be distinguished: those which personify some deity and renew his life; those of lesser sanctity which serve as fetish to a person, group, or locality; and the generality of a species which shares the sanctity of a real or ideal individual of the species.

that the first gods who existed were few in number and oppressed by the multitudes and by the lawlessness of earthborn men;[168] but that they escaped this savagery and cruelty by adopting the forms of various animals. Later, however, when they had come to be masters of the universe, they showed their gratitude to the agents of their earlier deliverance by sanctifying those species of animals which they had imitated, teaching men how to care luxuriously for the living and perform funeral rites for the dead. The second reason they offer is that the Egyptians of old, through lack of discipline in their army, were defeated in many battles by the neighboring peoples, until they conceived the idea of carrying ensigns before the divisions of their host. Therefore, they continue, the leaders fashioned images of the animals which they have now come to worship, and bore them elevated upon javelins; and in this way every soldier was able to recognize his own unit in the line of battle (see plate 9a). And since the good order resulting from these images contributed in large measure to their victories, they began to believe that the animals themselves were the cause of their safety. Therefore, since men wished to show gratitude to them, they made it a custom never to slay the creatures which they had represented by images in those times, but rather to adore them and render unto them the care and honor mentioned above.

87   The third explanation they put forth concerning this question is the service that each of the animals provides for the benefit of mankind and the life of the community. For the cow bears laborers[169] and plows the yielding earth. The sheep drops lambs twice a year, and its wool provides clothing both decorative and protective, while its milk and cheese supply foods as pleasant as they are bountiful. The dog is useful both for hunting and for guarding; wherefore they depict the god whom they call Anubis with the head of a dog, to show that he was one of the bodyguards of Isis and Osiris. And some say that the dogs which guided Isis in her search for Osiris not only protected her from wild beasts and from the people she encountered, but also, being sympathetic to her plight, joined with howling in her search. It is for this reason that dogs lead the solemn procession during the Isis Festival, since those

---

168. i.e., the giants.

169. i.e., beasts of burden.

who established the custom thus commemorate the ancient kindness of this animal.[170]

Now the feline is useful against the deadly biting asps and other venomous snakes. The ichneumon, after searching out the brood of the crocodile, crushes the eggs that it finds. And it performs this deed with diligence and enthusiasm, though it derives no benefit for itself therefrom. If the ichneumon did not behave in this way, the great swarms of reptiles hatching out would make the river unapproachable.[171] But the ichneumons also kill the crocodiles themselves in an extraordinary manner which is quite hard to believe: for they hide in the mud at the time when these monsters are sleeping on the shore, and when they yawn, down they leap through their mouths and descend into the interior of their bodies; then quickly gnawing through their bellies, they escape unscathed, and this causes the immediate death of their victims.

As for birds, the ibis is useful against snakes, locusts, and caterpillars, and the hawk against scorpions, horned serpents,[172] and the smaller animals of noxious bite which kill such great numbers of men. Some contend that the hawk was venerated because the soothsayers used them as birds of omen to prophesy the future for the Egyptians. But certain people say instead that in the days of old a hawk brought to the priests of Thebes a book encircled by a band of purple, in which was written the divine services and honors due the gods, and that this is the reason why the sacred scribes wear on their heads a purple cord and a hawk's feather. But the Thebans revere the eagle too, because they think this animal is noble and worthy of Zeus.

88   They have deified the he-goat as well, just as Priapus, they say, was also glorified among the Greeks, on account of his generative

---

170. Anubis was originally a jackal god, but the Greeks interpreted his jackal-headed symbol as representing a dog. Anubis in early myth was the fourth son of Re', but was drawn into the Osirian cycle as the son of Typhon (Seth) and Nephthys, who was adopted by Isis and became her guardian. There was a separate dog cult, centering at Cynopolis (see note 181).

171. See above, chapter 35 and note 76. See also plate 5.

172. The horned serpent is the Cerastes, a deadly viper several feet long; the female sports a hornlike growth over each eye.

organ;[173] for the goat is very lewd with respect to copulation, and the part of his body which is responsible for generation is fittingly honored as the prime cause of the procreation of animals. And as a rule, not only the Egyptians, but many other nations as well have venerated the genital organ in their mystic rites as the agent of animal genesis. The priests of Egypt, who inherit the sacerdotal office from their fathers, are initiated into the mysteries of this god first of all. Furthermore, it is said that both the Pans and Satyrs are honored among men for the same reason as Priapus; and therefore most statues of them which men dedicate in the temples show the penis erect and resembling a goat's in shape, for tradition has it that this animal is the most proficient at copulation; and therefore through the appearance of these statues men render thanks for the abundance of their own children.

Now the sacred bulls, and I am speaking both of Apis and Mnevis, are honored as gods.[174] Osiris ordained it so, partly because of their usefulness in agriculture, but also partly because the drudgery of these brutes transmits to future generations for all time the fame of those gods who discovered the fruits of the earth. But red bulls were given up to be sacrificed because of the notion that red was the color of Typhon, who plotted against Osiris and whom Isis punished for the murder of her husband. They further allege that in earlier days the kings were wont to sacrifice men of Typhon's color at the tomb of Osiris. Now, few Egyptians are found to be red, although most foreigners are;[175] and

---

173. The Greeks sometimes identified the fertility god Min with their phallic god Priapus, son of Aphrodite and Dionysus (or Adonis in some traditions). Min too is portrayed as ithyphallic, and occasionally with a goat's head, but Diodorus here seems to confuse Min with the ram (or goat) of Mendes (see note 163, above).

174. The Mnevis Bull was regarded as the incarnation of the sun god Re'-Atum, worshipped at Heliopolis. Its honors were similar to those of the Apis (see note 166, above). The Buchis bull of Hermonthis, the white bull of Chemmis, and the black bull of Ka-kam also had cults resembling those of Apis and Mnevis, but were less famous.

175. The exact sense of this passage is debatable. Diodorus clearly refers to Typhon as having red skin, or complexion ($\chi\rho\acute{\omega}\mu\alpha\tau\iota$). But speaking of the human sacrifice of "red" men, he uses only the term   , which can also mean red-haired. Plutarch, presumably following Manetho the Egyptian, says Typhon was red-haired and fair-skinned (*On Isis and Osiris* 30). Color, skin, and nature are related words in the Egyptian language, so some confusion among the Greeks is understandable. As for human sacrifice, there is some evidence that it

through this circumstance the legend about Busiris slaying foreigners gained credence among the Greeks; not that the king was called Busiris, but the tomb of Osiris bore this name in the language of the natives.[176]

Wolves, they explain, are revered because they are quite similar in nature to dogs, for the two species differ little in form, and propagate with each other by sexual intercourse. But the Egyptians also propound an alternative, mythical rationale for the worship of this animal: for long ago, they say, as Isis and her son Horus were preparing to fight against Typhon, Osiris ascended from Hades, in the outward guise of a wolf, as an ally to his wife and son. Whereupon Typhon having been destroyed, the victors established the cult of this animal, after whose appearance the victory ensued. However, some others claim that when the Ethiopians came down against Egypt, many packs of wolves came together and drove the invaders out of the land, beyond the city named Elephantine; and that as a result the nome was called Lycopolite and the above-mentioned wolves obtained veneration.[177]

89   But it still remains for us to discuss the deification of the crocodile, concerning which most people are quite unable to explain how it came to be lawful to honor the most ferocious of man-eating beasts as though they were gods. However, they point out that their country is protected not by the river alone, but even far more so by the crocodiles that live in it; since raiders from both Arabia and Libya are afraid to swim across the Nile for fear of the many savage reptiles. But this could never be the case if these animals were to be hunted down and eradicated with dragnets. But there is yet another story told concerning these fearsome brutes. For some relate how one of the primitive kings, Menas by name, was pursued by his own hunting dogs and fled for safety to the lake called Moeris, where he was miraculously taken up by

---

existed in Egypt at least as late as the XVIIIth Dynasty, c. 1550-1307 B.C., and a few Egyptian texts confirm a preference for red-haired men as victims.

176. For Busiris, see notes 94 and 166 above.

177. Diodorus is our sole source for Osiris appearing in the guise of a wolf, and for the silly tale of the wolfen army. Lycopolite or City of Wolves (Egyptian Zawty, modern Asyut) was the center of the local cult of Wepwawet, the "wolf" god sometimes depicted as companion to Osiris. But this city was capital of the thirteenth Upper Egyptian nome, more than two hundred and fifty miles north of Elephantine. There were no true wolves in Egypt, but wild dogs were called wolves; indeed, Herodotus II.67 describes them as "not much bigger than foxes."

a crocodile and carried away to the other side. Wishing to show thanks
to the animal for his deliverance, he founded a city near this spot and
named it after the crocodiles. He also instructed the inhabitants of the
place to venerate these creatures as gods, and he bestowed the lake on
them for their support.[178] Here also he built his tomb, raising a four-
sided pyramid nearby, and he constructed the Labyrinth, which many
admire.[179]

They also tell of many other Egyptian customs, but it would be
tedious to write of every one. However, they have adopted these
customs because of their advantages in daily life, and this is apparent to
all from the fact that there are many among them who refrain from
certain types of food. For although there is great abundance in Egypt,
some abstain altogether from lentils, some from beans,[180] and some from
cheeses or onions or various other foods, to emphasize that men must
learn to deny themselves useful things, and that if everyone partook of
every food, there would not be enough of the things they consume. But
some people give a different reason for this custom, claiming that, in the
days of the ancient kings, when the people frequently conspired together

---

178. Most Egyptians viewed Sobek or Sebek as a crocodile god. He was
worshipped at various places throughout the land, but especially in the Faiyum,
where he was supposedly incarnate in one of the reptiles (mentioned in chapter 84
above). But the crocodile was viewed as a dangerous pest in many parts of Egypt
and killed for that reason. It was also hunted for sport, for food, and for religious
reasons. See note 75, above, and plate 4.

179. For the Labyrinth, see notes 119 and 132, above. The Menas mentioned
here bears the same name that Diodorus attributed to Egypt's first mortal king, but
here he is said to be the builder of the Labyrinth, which was ascribed to king
Mendes or Marrus in chapter 61, on the shores of lake Moeris, named after
another, earlier king. Diodorus is hopelessly confusing on the point. Probably
Mendes, Marrus, Moeris, and the present Menas are garbled versions of the same
tradition, but distinguishable from the famous Menas of chapters 43 and 45 above
(see note 90), and the Mneves of chapter 94, below.

180. Herodotus II.37 says none of the Egyptians ever ate beans, and that the
priests would not even look at them, considering them unclean. Abstinence from
or ritual use of beans was common among many Indo-European cultures as well,
and various reasons are adduced; the Pythagoreans abhorred them because of their
resemblance to human testicles; the early Romans thought they caused unchastity,
and the Flamen Dialis might not touch them or even speak of them; some even
thought that the souls of the dead dwelt in beans. The Orphic and Eleusinian
traditions also discouraged bean eating. Until modern times, some Beduin tribes
still regarded bean eating with extreme disgust.

and revolted against their sovereigns, a certain king who excelled in wisdom divided the country into a great number of districts and taught the inhabitants of each one to worship a certain animal, or not to eat of a certain food; thus with each locality respecting its own fetishes but scorning those of the others, the people of Egypt as a whole would never be able to unite. And this is evident from the result: for all the neighboring districts are at variance with each other, taking offense at mutual slights to their respective cults.[181]

90   But certain people also give an explanation such as the following for Egyptian animal worship: that when, in the beginning, men came together out of their savage state, they at first fought with and preyed upon one another, and the more powerful invariably prevailed over the weaker. But eventually those without strength learned from experience to combine forces, and they devised for themselves an ensign from one of the animals which later came to be sacrosanct. Then those who were in fear would always rally round this standard, and their assemblage was quite formidable to any who tried to attack it. But since the others did the same thing, the people resolved themselves into organized bands, and the animal which brought about the security of each group obtained godlike adoration for having occasioned the greatest of benefits. For this reason down to the present time the different sects of the Egyptians give honor among themselves to the animals they had worshipped in the beginning.[182]

And they say the Egyptians in general are more gratefully disposed than the rest of mankind for every benefit, holding that repayment of kindness to one's benefactors is of the greatest help in life: for it is evident that everyone will be eager to do kindness most especially to those whom they perceive will most graciously appreciate the favors. And it is apparently for this same reason that the Egyptians worship

---

181. Plutarch, *On Isis and Osiris* 72, gives a similar explanation for the origin of animal worship, but he too neglects to name the "crafty king" who perpetrated the custom.   He continues: "In my day the people of Oxyrhynchus caught a dog, sacrificed it, and ate it as sacrificial meat, because the folk of Cynopolis had eaten of the fish called oxyrhynchus. As a result, they fought a battle and caused one another great harm." Juvenal, *Satires* XV, gives a lively account of a religious blood feud occurring earlier, in 127 A.D., between the citizens of Dendera and those of Ombi.

182. The use of animal figures as tribal standards in predynastic and early dynastic times is well attested. See plate 9a.

their kings and honor them as real gods, assuming on one hand that they could never have attained absolute authority without some kind of divine favor, and on the other hand believing that those who are most willing and most able to show kindness share the attributes of divine nature.

If perhaps we have written too much about the sacred animals, at least we have elucidated some of the most wondrous customs among the Egyptians.

91   Yet any who hear about Egyptian usages with respect to the dead have a no less ample reason to marvel at the peculiar nature of their ways. For when any of them chance to die, their friends and relatives wander the town until the body is buried, heaping dust on their heads and mourning. Indeed, they partake not of the bath, nor of wine, nor of any food worth mentioning, nor do they wear any bright-colored garments.

Now, there are three gradations of burial: the most expensive, the middling, and the humblest, whereof it is said they spend for the first kind a talent of silver, and for the second twenty minae; but for the last they say there is very little in the way of expense. In any case, those who treat the bodies are artisans who learn this traditional skill from their families. They present to the relatives of the deceased a price list showing each of the items of expenditure for a funeral and inquire what degree of treatment they wish for the body. And after mutually agreeing on every detail, they take possession of the corpse and commit it to those who have been appointed to the customary service.

First of all, once the body has been stretched out upon the ground, the person called the scribe traces on its left side how long the incision must be. Next the slitter, as he is called, cuts the flesh as the law commands using the Ethiopian stone, then immediately flees at a run while those present pursue him hurling stones and curses, as if diverting the defilement to his head; for they consider anyone odious who offers violence to the body of a fellow citizen or disfigures it or, in general, does it any harm.[183]

---

183. The "slitter" was probably considered ritually taboo because of the wound he inflicted on the corpse. He fled in symbolic guilt. Compare the similar procedure at the Athenian sacrifice known as the *Bouphonia*, or "murder of the ox," where the butchers fled immediately upon felling the ox and slitting its throat. The use of a stone knife, flint or obsidian to judge by the many examples from Egyptian graves, was undoubtedly a conservative throwback to Neolithic times; the use of stone rather than metal knives for ritual ceremonies (such as

Those called embalmers, on the other hand, are held worthy of all honor and respect; they associate with the priests, and since they are not considered to be unclean, they are able to enter the temples without hindrance. Now when these embalmers have foregathered for the treatment of the body, which has been slit open, one of them plunges his hand through the incision in the cadaver, into the chest cavity, and extracts everything except the kidneys and the heart.[184]   Another cleanses all of the organs, washing them in palm oil and incense. And in general, they purify the entire body with care, first with oil of cedar and certain other concoctions for more than thirty days, then with myrrh and cinnamon and those substances which not only can preserve it for a long time, but which also impart a pleasant odor.

After they have treated the corpse in this fashion, they return it to the family of the deceased, with every part of the body so freshly preserved that even the hairs on the eyelids and eyebrows remain intact, while the whole appearance of the body is unaltered and the cast of the features is recognizable; and for this reason many of the Egyptians maintain the bodies of their ancestors in costly household shrines and gaze in person at those who died many generations before their own birth. Seeing thus their stature and proportions as well as their characteristic features of appearance, they experience the strange sensation of conjuring men from beyond the grave, just as if they had lived with those on whom they look.[185]

---

circumcision) is not uncommon in many cultures throughout the world. As Diodorus correctly observed, the incision was almost invariably made on the left side (in the abdomen).

184. We do not know why the kidneys were not removed along with the other organs, but many Egyptian mummies do retain them in place. The heart was purposely left *in situ* because it was regarded as the essence of being. The liver, lungs, stomach, and intestines were separately preserved and for many centuries were deposited in the tomb, near the corpse, in separate vessels called "canopic jars" by modern archaeologists. By the time of Diodorus, however, it was more common to wrap the treated organs between the mummy's legs.

185. It is unclear what Diodorus means by his description of the lifelike corpses kept on display for the edification of survivors and descendants. Mummies were wrapped in linen or papyrus and encased in wooden coffins and/or stone sarcophagi. (The word "mummy," by the way, derives from Arabic *mumia*, meaning bitumen, which was used in the embalming process; "sarcophagus" is Greek for "devourer of flesh," a rather graphic metaphor.) Diodorus apparently describes only the most expensive of the three grades of embalming. Herodotus II.86 is the only other author, Greek or Egyptian, who

92   Now, when the body is about to be interred, the family proclaims the day of burial both to the judges and to the relatives and friends of the departed one, and they announce that so-and-so — saying the name of the deceased — is about to "cross over the lake." At the appointed time, when forty-two judges have arrived and taken their seats upon a hemicycle built on the side of the lake, the "baris" is launched.[186]   This barge has previously been prepared by those who have this responsibility, and it is piloted by the boatman whom the Egyptians, in their own language, call "Charon."[187]   And thus it is that Orpheus, so they say, after voyaging to Egypt and witnessing this ceremony, wove the myths about Hades, part of which he copied and part of which he invented on his own account, and the particulars of which we will describe a little later.[188]   In any event, after the baris has been launched into the lake, but before the coffin containing the corpse has been placed aboard, the law allows anyone who so desires to bring accusations against the decedent.   Therefore, should someone come forward to accuse him and can prove he has lived an evil life, the judges declare this verdict to all and deny the body the customary

---

gives a detailed account of the process, differing slightly from Diodorus (for instance, he correctly describes the removal of the brain through the nasal opening); he presents a somewhat fuller treatment than Diodorus, and he also briefly covers the two less expensive methods (II.87 and II.88). In fact, scientific study of mummies reveals that the process varied greatly over the course of time. The earliest attempts are from predynastic times. The art reached its highest perfection at the end of the New Kingdom, c. 1100 B.C., followed by a decline which tended to stress the exterior appearance (wrappings, painted coffins, masks, etc.) at the expense of effective preservation techniques. By late Ptolemaic times mummy portraits executed in colored wax were, in the best examples, amazingly lifelike. See plate 28.

186. Diodorus may be describing as a real funeral custom the forty-two mythical "assessors," before whom (according to the Egyptian *Book of the Dead*) a dead soul must pass. It is uncertain what Diodorus means by hemicycle in this context. Herodotus II.96 describes the baris as the common trading vessel on the Nile, made of thorn wood with one mast and one rudder. Wood of the thorn tree, *Mimosa nilotica,* is still used for boat building in Egypt. The word baris seems to be a Hellenicism for the Egyptian word *bari.*

187. The implication is that the Charon of Greek myth, who ferried dead souls across the river Styx, was derived from this Egyptian original, but no real evidence exists for this.

188. See chapter 96, below.

burial; however, should it appear that the prosecution was undertaken unjustly, the accuser is severely punished. But when no accuser appears before the tribunal, or if one comes forward but is found to have borne false witness, the kinfolk put away their mourning and sing the praises of the dead man. Unlike the Greeks, they make no mention of his ancestry, since they consider everyone in Egypt to be equally noble. But after recounting his training and education from childhood, they relate his piety and moral worth, his self-control, and the other virtues he acquired in his adult life, and they call upon the gods below to receive him hospitably as a fellow citizen in the abodes of the just.[189] The crowd shouts its assent and extols the glory of the deceased as one about to spend eternity in Hades among the righteous. Those families having private tombs lay the body in the niche assigned to it, but those who possess no tomb add a new closet to their own houses and prop the coffins upright against the stoutest wall. And the ones who are prohibited from burial because of accusations, or according to the pledges on a loan, they also cause to be interred in their own dwellings; but of these, sometimes the sons of their sons later become rich and acquit them of their bond or of the accusations against them; at which time they are deemed worthy of splendid funerals.

93   Among the Egyptians, there is a serious preoccupation with visible ostentation in the honors shown to parents or ancestors who have gone to their eternal home. They have also a custom of tendering the bodies of their deceased parents as security for loans; but the deepest disgrace attends one who fails to discharge the debt, and at death he himself is denied a funeral.[190] And well might one admire the sages who instituted these customs, because they attempted to instill virtue and excellence of character among men in all possible ways, not only by means of communion among the living, but also through the burial and care of the dead. For the Greeks have handed down their concerns for these qualities by means of contrived myths and discredited legends about the reward of the just and the punishment of the wicked; and therefore indeed, not only are such stories by themselves an

---

189. There is no evidence for the kind of posthumous trial which Diodorus describes (which resembles the trial of the royal corpses already recounted in chapter 72, above).

190. Herodotus II.136 also mentions the mortgaging of corpses, as does Lucian.

insufficiently strong inducement in steering men to live aright, but on the contrary, they are ridiculed by the vulgar and meet with considerable contempt. Among the Egyptians, however, the punishments of the wicked and the rewards of the good are not mythological ideas, but visible facts, and both sorts of people are reminded of their responsibilities every day; and in this way is wrought the greatest and most profitable reformation of man's character. Thus I believe one should count as the most excellent laws, not those by means of which men will become the most wealthy, but those by which they will become most wholesome in character and most perfect in citizenship.

94   But we must also make mention of the lawgivers who arose in Egypt and who ordained such strange and marvelous customs. For in primitive Egypt, after life had become settled (which according to myth took place in the era of gods and heroes), they say that the first person who convinced the people to use written laws was Mneves,[191] a man both lofty in spirit and the most altruistic in his way of life of any lawgiver in memory. He claimed that Hermes had given these laws to him as a source of many substantial benefits; and this, they say, is just what Minos of Crete did among the Greeks and Lycurgos among the Lacedaemonians, the former asserting that he had received his revelations from Zeus, the latter from Apollo. And it is a tradition as well among most other nations that this kind of inspiration was the case, being the cause of many blessings to those who believed. Among the Arians, they record, Zathraustes pretended that the Good Spirit gave him the laws;[192] and among those called the Getae, who aspire to immortality, Zalmoxis in like manner credited the familiar Hestia with the revelation;[193] and among the Judaeans, Moyses attributed them to the

---

191. Mneves is probably a variant of the name Menas, first mortal king of Egypt. See chapters 43 and 45 above, and note 179. In chapter 14, however, Diodorus says Isis Thesmophorus gave the Egyptians their first laws.

192. Zathraustes is Diodorus' name for Zoroaster and, although this form is found nowhere else in classical literature, it is much closer to the old Iranian Zarathustra than the more common spelling. The Good Spirit is undoubtedly a reference to Ormuzd, god of light. Zoroastrianism was founded in the sixth century B.C. Once a major world religion, it is practiced by only a few people today.

193. The Getae were a Thracian tribe and Zalmoxis (or Salmoxis, or according to Herodotus, Gebeleizis) was their prophet; by some accounts he was their god. His doctrine of man's immortality was the point which most impressed the

God called by the name of Iao.[194] For all of them believed either that their intent was wonderfully and thoroughly divine if the result would be of benefit to the mass of men, or else they knew that the common people would obey more readily if they were faced with the majesty and might of the beings said to have devised the laws.

A second lawgiver, say the Egyptians, was Sasychis, a man surpassing in wisdom. He is said to have added new laws to the existing ones, and to have provided most scrupulously for the observances due the honor of the gods. He is said to have invented geometry and instructed the Egyptians in the contemplation and precise observation of the stars.

They relate that the third lawgiver was King Sesoösis, who not only performed more famous feats of war than any other king of Egypt, but also framed laws governing the warrior caste and regulated every aspect of affairs pertaining to military operations. A fourth lawgiver, they continue, was King Bocchoris, a wise man who excelled in guile. This sage promulgated all the regulations concerning the kings and carefully perfected those dealing with contracts; and also, he was so sagacious in deciding cases that many of his judgments are remembered until our own day because of their excellence. But they say he was utterly lacking in bodily vigor and was the most covetously inclined of all their kings.[195]

95 The next to apply himself to the laws, they say, was King Amasis. They record that he gave form to all the statutes concerning the nomarchs and to the fundamental laws for the government of Egypt as a whole. Tradition has it that he was of superior intelligence, as well as kind and just in character; wherefore the Egyptians invested him with the sovereignty, even though he was not of royal blood. Furthermore, they tell that the Eleans, in preparation for the Olympic games, sent ambassadors to him to inquire how the contests might be conducted most fairly. He replied: "If none of the Eleans competes." And to

---

Greeks; one of their traditions, rejected by Herodotus IV.94-95, made him the pupil of Pythagoras, with whose teachings the Greeks detected certain similarities. Hestia was the mild, ever-virgin goddess of the family hearth; her association with the Thracian Zalmoxis is peculiar. Diodorus does not explain it.

194. The reference here, of course, is to Moses and Yahweh (Jehova, or Yehu).

195. The identification of Sasychis is uncertain. For Sesoösis, see above, chapters 53 through 58. Bocchoris is mentioned above in chapters 45, 65, and 79.

Polycrates, the despot of the Samians, who after concluding friendship with Amasis was violently abusing both his own citizens and the foreigners putting into Samos, it is said that Amasis first sent ambassadors to exhort him to moderation. But when he heeded not this advice, Amasis wrote him a letter dissolving their friendship and hospitality, inasmuch as he did not wish himself to be presently plunged into grief. For he correctly foretold that an evil plight impended for one who governed by tyranny in this way. Thus they say Amasis was admired among the Greeks both for his goodness, and because the prediction he made to Polycrates quickly came to pass.[196]

It is reported that Darius, the father of Xerxes, was the sixth person to have attended to the laws of the Egyptians; for he deplored the improprieties which Cambyses, who ruled before him, had inflicted on the temples in Egypt, and he therefore aspired to a good and pious life. Indeed, he is said to have been instructed by the priests of Egypt and to have known both their theology and the affairs written in their sacred books. And having learned from these books of the magnanimity of the ancient kings and of their benevolence toward their subjects, he emulated their plan of life and obtained so much prestige therefrom, that he alone of all the kings was addressed by the Egyptians as a god while living, and after he died was honored in the same way as those who in days of old had ruled Egypt in strict accord with the law.[197]

They say, then, that the common law was brought about by the men described above, and that it acquired a widespread fame among other nations. But in later times, they say, after the Macedonians had

---

196. For Amasis, see above, chapter 68. The Olympic games were hosted by the Eleans, whose impartiality was not above suspicion; the sage advice which Diodorus credits to Amasis, is attributed by Herodotus II.160 to the council of King Psammis (Psammetichos II, 595-589 B.C.). Polycrates of Samos lived in the sixth century B.C., when his hundred-ship navy dominated Ionia and the Aegean Sea. If he had an alliance with Amasis, it was over by 525 B.C., when he sent ships to aid Cambyses in his invasion of Egypt, Amasis having died in the previous year. Polycrates was betrayed and executed by Oroestes, Persian satrap of Sardis, in 522 B.C. See Herodotus III.120-125 and Thucydides I.13.

197. Cambyses (reigned 525-522 B.C.) was disliked by the Egyptians (at least by the priestly class) for his alleged disrespect of the native religion. Herodotus III.16 and III.27ff. portrays him as a madman who, among other acts of outrage, killed the Apis bull and burned the corpse of Amasis. Darius, on the other hand, 521-486 B.C., was remembered with fondness. He ordered the Egyptian laws to be written in the common demotic script (see note 155, above) and even had them translated into Aramaic.

conquered Egypt and destroyed at last the rule of native kings, many of the laws that seemed so good were altered.

96 But now, having thoroughly reviewed these lawgivers, we must recount the number of those who, celebrated among the Greeks for intelligence and learning, ventured to Egypt in olden times, that they might partake of the customs and sample the teaching there. For the priests of the Egyptians cite from the records in their holy books, that in former times they were visited by Orpheus and Musaeus, Melampos and Daedalos, besides the poet Homer, Lycurgos the Spartan, Solon the Athenian, and Plato the philosopher. Pythagoras of Samos and the mathematician Eudoxos, as well as Democritos of Abdera and Oenopides of Chios, also came there.

Now as evidence of these visitors, the priests sometimes point out statues, sometimes places or buildings having the same name as one of them; they also offer proof based on the knowledge each one acquired, since they have established that all the concepts for which these men were noted among the Greeks were transplanted out of Egypt. Orpheus, for example, brought away from there the greatest part of his mystical rites, besides the orgiastic revels that were a feature of his wanderings, and his fables about the souls in Hades. For the ritual of Dionysus is the same as that of Osiris,[198] and the rite of Demeter is very similar to that of Isis, differing only in name. And Orpheus introduced the notions of the punishment of the wicked in Hades, the Fields of the Just, and the other ideas he impressed upon the masses, from his own recollection of the funeral ceremonies in Egypt. Hermes, for example, the Conductor of Souls, according to the ancient Egyptian custom, leads the body of the Apis up to a certain point and hands it over to the one wearing the mask of Cerberus. And after Orpheus had made this known among the Greeks, Homer, in conformity with the idea, inserted this in his poem:

---

198. Diodorus gives, in chapter 23 above, one version of the introduction of the rites and revels of Dionysus (equated with Osiris) into Greece by Orpheus (see note 46). In the more usual tradition, Orpheus opposed Dionysus' invasion of Thrace and was therefore murdered at his instigation. Some scholars claim Dionysus and Orpheus were originally identical; others hold that they were originally separate but that syncretism eventually made them almost indistinguishable. But nearly all agree that the cult of Dionysus entered Greece not from Egypt, but (probably) from Thrace.

Cyllenian Hermes, wand in hand, summoned the souls of the
suitors.[199]

[*Odyssey* 24.1-2]

And then again he later says:

They passed along by Ocean's streams
   and next the Cliffs of White,
Beside the gates of Helios
   and past the Land of Dreams,
And straightaway they came unto
   the meads of asphodel,
Where shades of men, from toil released,
   forever after dwell.

[*Odyssey* 24.11-14]

Now he calls the river "Ocean" because the Egyptians, in their own
language, refer to the Nile as Oceanus. The "gates of Helios" is his
name for the city of the Heliopolitans, and what he calls "the meads,"
that is, the mythical abode of the dead, is the place near the lake known
as Acherousia, not far from Memphis, and which is surrounded by the
finest meadows of marsh, lotus, and reed.[200] And accordingly, the dead

---

199. In Greek myth, one of the important functions of Hermes, the messenger
of the gods, was to guide the souls of the dead into the underworld; his wand is
the herald's staff, which also functioned as a magic baton by means of which he
opened or closed the eyes of mortal men. He left the dead souls on the banks of
the river Styx, to be ferried across by Charon if they paid the fare (see above,
chapter 92 and note 187). The ferocious three-headed dog Cerberus guarded the
further shore of Styx. The correlation with Egyptian myth, if there is one, would
be the god Thoth, who hands the dead souls over to the jackal-headed deity
Anubis.

200. It is difficult to see how Diodorus connects this passage of the *Odyssey*,
which describes the descent of the suitors' souls from Ithaca to Hades, with the
various places of Egypt. Nowhere in his surviving works does Homer refer to the
Nile as Oceanus, although Diodorus twice above (chapters 12 and 19) declares
that this was the early Egyptian name for the river. The meadows of asphodel
refer to the dwelling place of the dead, a cheerless place where shades roam
without hope or purpose. The word asphodel probably derives from the concept
of "the valley of what is not reduced to ashes" — i.e., the soul — on the funeral
pyre. Asphodel came to be the name of a liliaceous plant with pale bluish
flowers, which was planted about the graves of the deceased, and whose edible
roots and seeds were offered to their ghosts. Asphodel grows wild in Egypt.

were spoken of as dwelling in this locality because it contains the greatest number and the most imposing of the Egyptians' tombs. The dead are ferried across both the river and the Lake of Acherousia,[201] and their bodies are interred in the burial chambers located there.

And the other myths of the Greeks concerning Hades also reflect customs that exist even today in Egypt: for the boat which ferries the bodies is called the baris, and the passenger's fee is given to the ferryman, who in the indigenous language is called Charon. They say also that the sanctuary of Gloomy Hecate is near these places, as well as the portals of Cocytos and Lethe, which are banded with fittings of bronze. There are also other gates, of Truth, and near them stands a headless statue of Justice.[202]

97   There are in addition many other ceremonies, now elevated to the realm of mythology, which continue to subsist among the Egyptians, still preserved in name as well as in active observance. For instance, in the city of Acanthos, a hundred and twenty stades from Memphis and across the Nile on the Libyan side, there is a large perforated jar to which three hundred and sixty priests carry water from the Nile day

---

201. Acherousia was a name given by the Greeks to a number of lakes or swamps which at various times were considered a sort of boundary between Hades and the world of men. Eventually, as geographical knowledge expanded, and as even the remoter lakes Acherousia were obviously found to be unconnected with the underworld, the whole concept passed into myth and Acherousia was thought of as being actually in Hades. Besides the Lake Acherousia mentioned by Diodorus, there were counterparts in Epirus (thought to be the archetype), the Argolid, Bithynia, and Campania.

202. See above, chapters 92 and 96 and notes 186, 187, and 199, for the baris and Charon. Gloomy, or Dark, Hecate was in the time of Diodorus a goddess of the infernal regions, powerful in black magic. Earlier, however, she seems to have been a more comprehensive deity of earth, sea, and heaven, probably Thracian in origin. Cocytos ("wailing") and Lethe ("oblivion") were two of the rivers of Hades, tributaries of Styx. Phylarchus, a Greek historian of the late second century B.C., claimed that Memphis had two bronze gates bearing these names, which were opened for the burial of the Apis bull. Diodorus strives to prove that many of the Greeks' mythical details of Hades were merely borrowings of existing Egyptian burial customs and ceremonies. But it is more likely that the Greeks of Egypt, observing indigenous practices, equated them with familiar episodes from their own mythology.

after day.[203]   And nearby, one can clearly see the basis for the story of Ocnos dramatized at a certain high festival, where, as one man plaits a long strand of rope, many others behind his back unravel the fibers he has woven. They claim also that Melampos transferred out of Egypt those ceremonies of Dionysus which are customarily practiced among the Greeks;[204] as also the myths related about Kronos, the tale of the war with the Titans, and in general all the accounts concerning affairs of the gods. Also Daedalos, they say, reconstructed in Crete the tangled paths of the Egyptian Labyrinth, which exists down to the present time and which was built many years prior to the reign of Minos (constructed by Mendes, as some relate; but by King Marrus according to others).[205]

Then again, Egypt's antique statues are identical in form to those later wrought by Daedalos amongst the Greeks. And Daedalos erected the breathtaking propylon of Hephaestos in Memphis; for which, having been much admired, he was awarded a wooden statue of himself, made by his own hands, in the same temple. Eventually, being deemed worthy of great glory because of his ingenuity, and having made many discoveries, he was raised to godlike honors. Indeed, the inhabitants of Egypt to this day still venerate a temple of Daedalos on one of the islets near Memphis.

But for Homer's presence in Egypt the priests offer proofs of another sort, referring especially to the potion which Helen gave Telemachos, in the hall of Menelaus, to make him forget his besetting woes. For the poet was seemingly well acquainted with the nepenthic drug, which banishes care, and which he records that Helen obtained in Egyptian

---

203. Diodorus here assumes in his readers the knowledge that the fifty daughters of Danaus (who fled from Egypt to become king of Argos) were condemned in the afterlife to the labor of trying to carry water forever in perforated jars, for the crime of murdering their husbands, the fifty sons of Egyptus. Thus via the perforated jar Diodorus attributes another Greek myth to an Egyptian custom.

204. Ocnos, the Greek personification of indolence, was condemned in Hades to the endless task of weaving a rope which was eaten by an unseen ass as quickly as it was woven. Melampos was the oldest and most famous of the legendary seers. Diodorus here seems to follow Herodotus II.49 in giving Melampos credit for introducing the Dionysiac rites to Greece, contradicting his earlier assertions, in chapters 23 and 96, that it was Orpheus.

205. For the Labyrinth, see chapter 61 and note 119, above.

Thebes from Polydamna, the wife of Thon.[206] Now although they say that in olden times only the women of Diospolis possessed the secret of this remedy for anger and grief, they claim as well that the women of Thebes exercise this power to the present day; for Thebes is none other than Dios Polis, or the City of Zeus.

Likewise, by ancient tradition among the inhabitants of Egypt, Aphrodite is called The Golden, and a plain near the city called Momemphis is named the Field of Golden Aphrodite.[207] Homer also is said to have imported from Egypt the mythical accounts about the marriage of Zeus and Hera, inferring their nuptial alliance from the solemn festival in which the priests escort both of their shrines to a hilltop strewn with flowers of every kind. In like manner, the story of Zeus' journey to Ethiopia has its origin in Egypt: for every year the Egyptians convey the shrine of Zeus across the river to Libya, and after a certain number of days they bring it back, as if the god is returning from Ethiopia.[208]

98   And Lycurgos also, as well as Solon and Plato, are reported to have inserted many of the Egyptian customs into their own codes of law, while Pythagoras, they say, learned from the Egyptians the doctrine of divine wisdom, the theorems of geometry, the theory of numbers, and in addition, the transmigration of the soul into every living being.[209] The Egyptians are also of the opinion that Democritos lived among them for five years and learned many of the secrets of astrology. Oenopides was in like manner a disciple of the priests and astrologers and learned

---

206. See *Odyssey* 4.220-28. Nepenthic means "banishing pain and sorrow" and was sometimes also used as an epithet of Apollo. The drug was probably opium or hashish.

207. "Golden" is Homer's constant epithet for Aphrodite.

208. The point Diodorus tries to make is that Homer modeled the events in his poems after religious customs he observed in Egypt. This, of course, is nonsense. But the classical reader would know that Diodorus alludes to the embraces of Zeus and Hera in a bower on Mount Ida (*Iliad*, book 14) and Zeus' twelve day sojourn in Ethiopia (*Iliad*, book 1). Perhaps one of the Egyptian customs Diodorus has in mind is the annual Feast of the Nile, in which the bark of Ammon was ferried across from Karnak to the "Libyan" shore to visit the temple of Mentuhotpe II.

209. Transmigration of the soul was not a belief of the Egyptians. Pythagoras indeed taught this doctrine, but we do not know from whence he derived it.

many things, especially that the sun's orbit is an oblique course and traces a retrograde path opposite to that of the other stars.[210]   In somewhat the same way Eudoxos studied astronomy among them and attained an eminent reputation by transmitting much useful knowledge to the Greeks.

Now Telecles and Theodoros, the sons of Rhoecos, who were the most renowned of the ancient sculptors, are also reputed to have spent time with the Egyptians. They carved the wooden statue of Pythian Apollo for the Samians, of which it is reported that half of the image was fabricated by Telecles in Samos, and the other half was completed by his brother Theodoros at Ephesus. But when the parts were brought together, they dovetailed with each other so well that the entire work seemed to have been accomplished by one man. Now this way of working is never practiced by the Greeks, but it is the rule with the Egyptians, for among them the proportions of the statues are not determined by their appearance to the eye, as among the Greeks; rather, as soon as they have laid out the stones and have allocated them among the craftsmen preparatory to beginning work, at this point they determine all the relative proportions, from the smallest to the largest, by dividing the scale of the complete body into twenty-one and a quarter units, whereby they derive the entire symmetry of the image. Therefore, when the artisans have agreed among themselves about the dimensions of the statue, they go their separate ways and execute the components of the project so precisely that their singular method of operation excites amazement. Thus, in conformity with this ingenuity of the Egyptians, the wooden statue in Samos is cleft in two and the figure divided down the middle from the crown of the head to the genitals, each side being identical to the other. For the most part, they say, it resembles the statues of the Egyptians, in that its hands are held straight and the legs are parted in stride.[211]

---

210. Oenopides of Chios, a Greek scientist of the fifth century B.C., was reputed a Pythagorean. It is unlikely that his discovery of the obliquity of the ecliptic, and of the sun's retrograde progression relative to the fixed stars, was in any way attributable to Egyptian influence. See note 157, above.

211. Theodoros was the son of Telecles, not his brother, and grandson of Rhoecos of Samos, the "founder" of Greek sculpture. The family was renowned for its mastery of and improvements in various other arts, notably architecture. They flourished c. 640-560 B.C. They probably owed something of their technique to Egyptian influence, especially the reformed Saïte cannon of art which divided the human figure by twenty-one horizontal grids from sole of foot to root of nose:

However, enough has been said of the subjects related about Egypt and deemed worthy of mention; and, in accord with our professed intention at the beginning of the book, in the following volume we will explain the affairs and myths of other nations in due order, writing first of the deeds done by the Assyrians in Asia.

---

the quarter unit was presumably the remaining height to the crown or the hairline. See plate 29. But Diodorus is anything but clear in his brief layman's discussion of sculptural technique, and his tale of the Egyptian artisans and their Greek imitators assembling colossi from separately worked elements is doubtful. It is a subject Diodorus was not competent to discuss.

Appendix I: Proper Names

This appendix includes all significant proper names (people and places) mentioned in the text and notes, except those mentioned only once and explained adequately in the text or notes, and those about which nothing is known beyond what Diodorus tells us.

Abdera   Greek coastal town in Thrace, opposite the island of Thasos.

Abu Simbel   An Egyptian temple site, from the reign of Ramesses II, near the southern border of modern Egypt (now covered by Lake Nasser).

Abydos   Egyptian town about fifty miles northwest of Thebes.

Acanthos   A city of Egypt, possibly at the site of later Dashour, about 120 stades south of Memphis.

Acarnania   District in northwestern Greece, opposite the island of Ithaca.

Achaia   District in Greece on the north coast of the Peloponnese.

Acheloüs   River in Greece forming the eastern boundary of Acarnania.

Acherousia, Lake   Mythical lake in or near Hades.

Actisanes   According to Diodorus, an Ethiopian king who wrested the throne of Egypt from Amasis, an imaginary early king.

Aegean Sea   The sea between Greece and Asia Minor.

Agatharchides of Cnidos   Greek geographer and historian of the second century B.C., who lived in Egypt and wrote works on Europe, Asia, the Erythraean Sea, and the Troglodytes.

Agyrium   City in the interior of Sicily; the birthplace of Diodorus. Its modern name is San Filippo d'Argiro.

Alexander the Great   Youthful king of Macedonia, who conquered most of the known world in a dozen years; captured Egypt without resistance in 332 B.C.

129

Alexandria   Capital of Egypt under the Ptolemies, this seaport on the western edge of the Delta was for centuries a major cultural and commercial center, one of the greatest cities in the world.

Amasis   (1) Egyptian king, ruling 570-526 B.C.   (2) An imaginary king of the same name, reigning much earlier (according to Diodorus).

Ammon (Amun, or Amon)   Chief god of Egyptian Thebes; acquired great significance during Middle Kingdom; sometimes identified with the son god Re' (Ammon-Re') and with the Greek god Zeus (Zeus-Ammon).

Anaxagoras   Athenian philosopher (originally from Ionia) of the fifth century B.C.

Antaeus   Legendary giant, king of Libya and son of Ge and Poseidon, whom Heracles slew in a wrestling match.   Diodorus also says Antaeus was a governor under Osiris, but this may not be the same person.

Antaeus, Village   Also known as Antaeopolis, the modern Qaw el-Kebir, on the Nile about thirty miles southeast of Asyut.

Antigonus   One of Alexander the Great's successors, founder of Antigonid dynasty in Asia.

Anubis   Jackal-headed (or dog-headed) Egyptian god; aided Isis in her search for Osiris' body.

Aphrodite   Greek goddess of love.

Apollinopolis (Magna)   Egyptian city about seventy miles south of Thebes; modern Edfu. (Apollinopolis Parva was a different town, just north of Thebes, and now called Qus.)

Apollo   Later Greek god of the sun; also god of music, poetry, philosophy, medicine, and mathematics.   His oracle at Delphi was the most famous in the Greek world.   He was often equated with the Egyptian god Horus (= Horapollo).

Apollodorus the Athenian   Philosopher and historian of the second century B.C., who wrote a *Chronology* covering the years 1184-119 B.C.

Apries   Egyptian king, ruling from 589-570 B.C.

Arabia   To Diodorus, Arabia encompassed not only the peninsula still bearing the name today, but the desert parts of Sinai, Palestine, Syria, Jordan, and Iraq west of the Euphrates River, as well as the desert east of the Nile in what is today part of Egypt.

Arabia Felix   Or Arabia the Fortunate, comprising the greatest part of the Arabian peninsula, but especially the fertile area of Yemen in the southwest corner.   The other divisions recognized by the ancients were Arabia Petraea (the Stoney) around Sinai; and Arabia Deserta (the Uninhabited), which includes the Syrian desert and el-Hijaz.

Arabia, Gulf of   The modern Gulf of Suez.

Arcadia   District of Greece in the central Peloponnese.

Archimedes of Syracuse   Famous Greek philosopher, mathematician, and engineer, c. 287-212 B.C.

Argolid   The territory surrounding Argos.

Argos   Famous Greek city in the northeastern Peloponnese.

el-Arish   Site on the Mediterranean coast of the Sinai peninsula, the Rhinocolura of Diodorus.

Aristotle   Celebrated Greek philosopher and polymath, 384-322 B.C., who was the pupil of Plato, tutor of Alexander the Great, and founder of the Peripatetic school of philosophy.

Arsinoë   One of the several towns of the same name in Egypt. This one, mentioned by Diodorus, was near the head of the Gulf of Suez.

Asia   (1) One of the three continents recognized by the Greeks, corresponding roughly with our own conception; however, Diodorus and some other classical authors considered the Nile valley, not the Red Sea and Isthmus of Suez, to be the dividing line between Libya (= Africa) and Asia.   (2) Western Anatolia (Turkey), our "Asia Minor."

Assyria   District in what is now northern Iraq, along the upper Tigris river.

Atbara, River   A major tributary of the Nile, running mostly through eastern Sudan.

Athena   Virgin daughter of Zeus; goddess of wisdom, war, and the sky.

Athens   The most prominent metropolis in Greece, and chief city of Attica.

Attica   The peninsula in east-central Greece, of which Athens was the metropolis.

Babylon   (1) Mesopotamian Babylon; famous city on the river Euphrates, erroneously said by Diodorus to have been founded by Belus as an Egyptian colony.   (2) Egyptian Babylon; site of an ancient fortress at what is now Old Cairo, or el-Fustat.

Babylonia   A district of southern Mesopotamia centering on the city of Babylon.

Bactria   Region in central Asia, approximately centered around northern Afghanistan.

Barcê (or Barca)   Greek city in Libya, west of Cyrenê and about twelve miles from the coast.

Belus   Son of Poseidon; father of Egyptus and Danaus; erroneously believed to be the founder of Babylon.

Bithynia   Region of Asia Minor (modern Turkey) on the southwest shores of the Black Sea.

Bitter Lakes   A chain of natural lakes in the southern part of the isthmus of Suez.

Bocchoris (the Wise)   A king of Egypt in the XXIVth Dynasty, c. 717-712 B.C.

Boeotia   A district in central Greece northwest of Attica. Its chief city was Thebes.

Bubastis   Egyptian town in the eastern Nile Delta; the modern Tell Basta.

Busiris   (1) Kinsman of Osiris. (2) Legendary king of Egypt, who slew all foreigners entering his land. (3) An Egyptian city in the center of the Delta, one of several places now known as Abusir.

Cadmus   Legendary founder of Boeotian Thebes; father of Semelê.

Cadmus of Miletus   The earliest Greek historian; some say the earliest writer of Greek prose; lived in the sixth century B.C.

Caesar, Gaius Julius   Famous Roman general, conqueror of Gaul. His sole rule, after the subsequent Roman civil war, laid the basis for the Roman Empire and destroyed forever the ancient republic. Contemporary with Diodorus Siculus.

Camarina   Greek city on the south coast of Sicily.

Cambyses   Persian king who conquered Egypt in 525 B.C. and was said to have ruled harshly.

Campania   Region on the coast of Italy around Naples.

Candia   Alternate name for Crete.

Caria   A district on the southwest coast of modern Turkey, opposite the island of Rhodes.

Cataracts   Sections along the Nile where rapids or falls occur.

Caucasus Mountains   The wild and rugged mountain range which stretches from the Black Sea to the Caspian Sea.

Cecrops   Legendary first king of Attica, half man and half serpent. Diodorus' claim that he was Egyptian represents a late addition to the legend.

Cenchris (Cenchreae)   One of the two ports of Corinth, on the Saronic Gulf.

Cephisus, River   River in Greece flowing through Phocis and Boeotia.

Cerberus   Three-headed ferocious dog of Greek myth, which guarded the entrance to Hades.
Charon   The mythical Greek ferryman who transported dead souls across the river Styx to Hades.
Chemmis   According to Diodorus, the Egyptian king who erected the Great Pyramid at Giza. Also see Chemmo.
Chemmo (or Chemmis)   City on the Nile, about one hundred miles downstream from the Thebaid; called Panopolis by the Greeks, today's Akhmim.
Chios   Large island off the western coast of Asia Minor.
Cisalpine Gaul   Area of northern Italy between the Alps and the Apennines.
Cnidos   Greek coastal city in Caria, not far from Rhodes.
Coele-Syria   Properly speaking, this appellation (meaning "hollow Syria") signified only the Beka'a Valley in what is now Lebanon, but sometimes it was used in an extended sense to designate the entire eastern littoral of the Mediterranean and adjacent inland areas, such as Palestine.
Colchis   A land at the eastern extremity of the Black Sea, south of the Caucasus range.
Cophen, River   A tributary of the Indus, probably identical with the modern river Kabul.
Crete   Large Mediterranean island south of the Aegean Sea.
Ctesias of Cnidos   Greek historian of the fourth century B.C., whose twenty-three book history of Persia was well known in antiquity but apparently quite untrustworthy by modern standards.
Cyclades Islands   Archipelago southeast of Attica, including the islands of Andros, Paros, Naxos, Delos, and many others.
Cynopolis   Ancient Egyptian town on the west bank of the Nile, about 150 miles south of Memphis.
Cyprus   Large island in the eastern Mediterranean.
Cyrenê   Important Greek city in Libya, about five hundred miles west of the Nile Delta and eight miles from the sea. Its modern name is Shahat.

Daedalos   A mythical Greek craftsman, famous for building the Cretan Labyrinth and for escaping Crete by flying on artificial wings. Diodorus claims he visited Egypt.
Danaus   Son of Belus; twin brother of Egyptus. Became king of Argos after fleeing Egypt.

Daphnae   The modern Tell Dafana in the eastern Nile Delta near the Suez canal.

Darius   Persian king, reigning 521-486 B.C., whose empire included Egypt.

Delta   The fertile and cultivated area between the branching arms of the lower Nile, in northern Egypt. The name derives from its topographic resemblance to the Greek letter Delta (Δ).

Demeter   Greek goddess of grain and of the seasons. Her cult at Eleusis was the most renowned religious observance of the Greeks. Said to be equivalent to the Egyptian goddess Isis.

Democritos of Abdera   Early Greek philosopher, mathematician, and scientist, c. 460-370 B.C.

Dendera (Dendara)   Egyptian town about thirty miles north of Thebes.

Derr (or el-Derr)   Egyptian site about one hundred miles southwest of Elephantine; now covered by Lake Nasser.

Dionysus   Son of Zeus by Semelê, daughter of Cadmus; usually credited with the discovery of wine. Identified by Diodorus with the Egyptian god Osiris.

Diospolis   Alternate name for Egyptian Thebes; the name means "city of Zeus."

Draco   Author of first written code of laws at Athens, c. 621 B.C.

Ecbatana   Ancient capital of Media; now called Hamadan, in modern Iran.

Edfu   Modern name for Appollinopolis, about fifty miles north of Elephantine.

Egypt   To Diodorus, Egypt consisted of little more than the cultivated areas of the Nile valley, the Delta, and the coastal regions. The desert to the east was part of Arabia, and that to the west was part of Libya. The southern boundary of Egypt, in Diodorus' day, was Philae at the first cataract.

Egypt, Lower   The Nile Delta and adjacent areas, including Memphis.

Egypt, Upper   The Nile valley from Memphis to Elephantine.

Egyptian Sea   The area of the eastern Mediterranean off the coast of Egypt.

Egyptus   Said by Diodorus to be an early Egyptian king, after whom the country received its name.

Eileithyia   Greek goddess of childbirth (sometimes spelled Eileithuia).

Elephantine   Egyptian city on an island of the same name, near modern Aswan; the traditional southernmost town of Egypt proper.

Eleusis City in Attica, famous as the site of the mysteries of Demeter and Persephone.

Ephesus Greek seaport on the coast of Lydia.

Ephorus of Cumae Greek historian of the fourth century B.C. He was the first to attempt a systematic universal history, but his accuracy was criticized by many ancient authors.

Epirus Coastal area of northwestern Greece, north of Acarnania.

Erectheus Early king of Athens. Said to have conquered Eumolpos and the Eleusinians. Diodorus claims he was of Egyptian birth and introduced the mysteries of Demeter to Greece.

Erythraean Sea The "Red Sea," by which the Greeks denoted not only the modern gulf of that name, but the Indian Ocean and Persian Gulf as well.

Esna Egyptian city about seventy miles north of Elephantine; its Greek name was Latopolis.

Ethiopia In ancient times, this name designated the territory south of Egypt on both sides of the Nile, in what is today Nubia (southern Egypt, and Sudan). In an extended sense, the term sometimes referred as well to all of sub-Saharan Africa.

Eudoxos of Cnidos Greek astronomer and geometer, c. 366 B.C.

Eumolpos (1) War leader (some say king) of Eleusis at the time of the Athenian conquest. (2) Little known early Greek poet.

Euphrates, River One of the two rivers enclosing Mesopotamia. The Euphrates rises in Armenia and flows generally southeast to join the Tigris before reaching the Persian Gulf.

Euripides Athenian playwright of the fifth century B.C.

Europe One of the three continents recognized by the Greeks, corresponding roughly with our own conception. The river Tanaïs (= Don) was the boundary north of the Black Sea between Europe and Asia.

Faiyum Fertile depression west of the Nile and a little south of Cairo, reclaimed from the Birket Qarun, or Lake Moeris.

Fields of the Just A mythical place in Hades where the souls of the righteous dwell in peace.

el-Fustat Old Cairo, site of the Egyptian Babylon.

Ganges, River Large river flowing southeast through northern India to the Bay of Bengal.

Ge Greek goddess; personification of "mother" earth.

Giza Site of the Great Pyramid, just southwest of modern Cairo.

Hades   The underworld in Greek myth, dwelling place of dead souls.

Hawara Channel   Channel by which Nile waters enter the Faiyum.

Hecataeus of Abdera   Greek historian of early third century B.C., on whose *Aigyptiaka* Diodorus heavily relied in his own account of Egypt.

Hecataeus of Miletus   Greek writer of later sixth century B.C., who wrote a book of world travels and another on history and genealogy.

Hecate   In later Greek myth, the goddess of infernal powers and black magic; called Gloomy, Dark, or Black Hecate.

Helen   Wife of Menelaus, king of Sparta. Her abduction was the cause of the Trojan War.

Heliopolis   Greek name for the important Egyptian city of Unu, in the southern Delta at the present site of Tell Hisn. It was a city of learning, sacred to the Sun.

Helios   (1) Early Greek god of the sun. (2) Alternate name for Heliopolis.

Hellanicus of Mitylene   Prolific Greek writer of fifth century B.C., chiefly of mythological, genealogical, and chronological works.

Hellespont   The straits now called the Dardanelles which connect the Aegean Sea with the Sea of Marmara, between Europe and Asia.

Hephaestos   Greek god of the forge; sometimes equated with the Egyptian god Ptah.

Hera   Wife of Zeus.

Heracles (Hercules)   (1) Greek hero of many adventures. Gained immortality after performing twelve labors for King Eurystheus of Tiryns. (2) Kinsman of Osiris.

Hermes   The messenger of the gods; the god of wisdom; the conductor of souls to Hades; patron of herdsmen and thieves.

Herodotus of Halicarnassus   Born about 485 B.C. This widely traveled Greek author's history of the Persian wars has earned him the epithet "Father of History." Diodorus followed him in some parts of his own work on Egypt.

Hesiod   One of the earliest Greek poets; from Boeotia.

Hestia   Greek goddess of the domestic hearth.

Homer   "The poet." Author of the *Iliad* and the *Odyssey*.

Horus   Egyptian god, son of Isis and Osiris, who avenged his father's murder by Typhon. Sometimes equated with the Greek god Apollo.

Hydaspes, River   The northernmost of the five great tributaries of the Indus; it is now known as the Jhelum.

Iao   Diodorus' rendition of the Hebrew name for God.

Ida, Mount   A large mountain range in Phrygia.

Ilium   Alternate name for Troy.

India   This term applied roughly to the area of modern Pakistan and India, but it also connoted, in a nebulous way, all of southern Asia with which the Greeks were familiar.

Indus, River   Large river flowing southwest through modern Pakistan into the Indian Ocean.

Io   Mother of Epaphus, by Zeus. Sometimes equated with the Egyptian goddess Isis.

Ionia   The coastal area, including offshore islands, of Greek settlement in western Asia Minor, between the rivers Meander and Hermus; Ionia lay just north of Caria.

Iopê   Joppa or Jaffa; a seaport in Palestine, south of the modern Israeli city of Tel-Aviv.

Isis   Egyptian goddess, wife and sister of Osiris; her cult was popular in Diodorus' day.

Ister, River   The Danube

Italy   In the time of Diodorus, this name did not apply to the whole peninsula, but excluded Cisalpine Gaul (q.v.).

Ithaca   Island off the western coast of Greece; home of Odysseus.

Josephus   Jewish historian of the first century A.D.

Juvenal   Roman satirist of the first century A.D.

Kadesh (Qadesh)   An ancient Hittite city on the upper Orontes River in Syria; the site is now known as Tell Neby Mend.

Karnak   Modern Egyptian name for part of the ancient metropolis of Thebes.

Kronos   Ruler of the universe in Greek myth, and the father of Zeus, who dethroned him to become king of gods and men.

Lacedaemon   An alternate name for the territory of Sparta, in the southwestern Peloponnese.

Leontopolis   A former town in the central Nile Delta, at the site of the present Tell el-Muqdam (not to be confused with another Leontopolis near Memphis, at Tell el-Yahudiya).

Levant   A general designation for the eastern Mediterranean area.

Libya   (1) Daughter of Io; mother of Belus by Poseidon. The Greeks named after her the continent of Libya. (2) One of the three continents recognized by the Greeks, now called Africa. Diodorus and others considered the Nile Valley the dividing line between Libya and Asia.

el-Lisht   A pyramid site west of the Nile about twenty-five miles south of Giza.

Lower Egypt   See Egypt, Lower.

Luxor   Modern Egyptian city on the site of ancient Thebes.

Lycopolite Nome   The thirteenth Upper Egyptian nome, about 200 miles upstream from Memphis. Diodorus seems to believe it was much further south.

Lycurgos   (1) Ancient lawgiver of the Spartans. (2) Legendary king of Thrace who opposed Dionysus.

Macedon   According to Diodorus, a son of Osiris; Macedonia was said to have been named for him.

Macedonia   District in what is now northern Greece, west of Thrace. It was the birthplace of Alexander the Great.

Maeotic Lake   Gulf in the northeast of the Black Sea, now known as the Sea of Azov.

Manetho   Egyptian priest of the third century B.C., whose invaluable account of Egyptian history (written in Greek) survives only in fragments.

Maria (or Marea)   Diodorus calls this a village, but it was probably the vanished Egyptian city of Mareia in the western Delta, south of Alexandria on the eastern shore of Lake Mareotis (modern Lake Mariut).

Maron   Agricultural expert in Osiris' army.

Marrus   See Mendes.

Matris   Little known Greek writer of an encomium on Heracles.

Meander, River   Winding stream in southwestern Asia Minor, forming the boundary between Lydia and Caria.

Melampos   In Greek myth, the first person to have the gift of prophecy and to practice as a physician. By some accounts, it was he who introduced the rites of Dionysus into Greece.

Memphis   Prominent Egyptian city at the southern point of the Nile Delta; it was sometimes the capital of Egypt.

Menas   (1) Legendary first mortal king of Egypt. (2) A later king whom Diodorus says founded Crocodilopolis and built the Labyrinth.

Mendes   (1) According to Diodorus, a king of Egypt who built the Egyptian Labyrinth. (2) An ancient town of the central Nile Delta, at the site of the present Tell el-Rub'a.

Menelaus   Legendary ancient king of Sparta whose wife, Helen, became the cause of the Trojan War.

Menestheus   Son of Petes; the first demagogue at Athens, and opponent of Theseus. Led the Athenian contingent in the Trojan War.

Meroë   (1) Chief city of the "island" of Meroë. (2) "Island" of Meroë: not a true island, but the territory semi-encompassed by the confluence of the Nile and the river Atbara, in what is now eastern Sudan. To Diodorus, this was the heartland of Ethiopia. (3) The mother of Cambyses, according to Diodorus.

Mesopotamia   The land between the rivers Tigris and Euphrates in what is now Iraq.

Minos   Legendary king of Crete, for whom Daedalos built the Labyrinth.

Mneves   Variant of Menas. See Menas (1).

Moeris   King of Egypt who, according to Diodorus, excavated the lake named after himself, now called the Faiyum.

Moeris, Lake   Formerly occupying most of the Faiyum, this body of water (the modern Birket Qarun) is now much reduced in size due to land reclamation.

Momemphis   A strong city of ancient Egypt in the northwestern Delta, southeast of Alexandria.

Moyses   Diodorus' rendition of Moses, who led the Hebrews out of Egypt.

Musaeus   Semi-mythical poet of early Greece, sometimes reputed to be the son of Orpheus, and often connected with the mysteries of Demeter at Eleusis.

Napata   The original Nubian capital of the early XXVth (Nubian) Dynasty, located at the modern Gebel Barkal, below the Fourth Cataract in northern Sudan.

Naucratis   A Greek trading town in the western Nile Delta, granted to the Greeks by king Amasis.

Necho I   A king of Egypt in the XXVIth Dynasty; reigned 672-664 B.C.

Necho II   A king of Egypt in the XXVIth Dynasty; reigned 610-595 B.C.

Nile, River   The longest river in the world, flowing north from central Africa to the Mediterranean.

Nilopolis   Former island town in the Nile not far from the Faiyum.

Nineveh   An ancient capital of Assyria, on the Tigris River opposite today's Mosul.

Nubia   A general name for the Nile valley and adjacent lands south of Egypt proper, from Elephantine to Meroë. Diodorus refers to this region as Ethiopia, however.

Nysa   (1) City said to be the birthplace of Dionysus; variously located by different authors, but said by Diodorus to be in Arabia. (2) Indian Nysa; a city supposedly founded by Dionysus and named after his birthplace.

Oceanus, Oceanê, or Ocean   Extremely ancient deity, said by Homer to be the source of men and of gods. Also, god of the river Ocean which encompasses the world in mythical geography and spawns all seas and rivers. Supposedly an early name for the Nile, or the "wet" element in general among the Egyptians.

Odysseus (Ulysses)   Wily Greek hero from Ithaca who wandered ten years in his return home from the Trojan war. Chief character of Homer's *Odyssey*.

Oenopides of Chios   Early Greek astronomer and mathematician, probably of the fifth century B.C.

Orontes, River   The modern Nahr el-'Asi in northwestern Syria.

Orpheus   Legendary poet and musician whose playing caused the trees to dance. Various myths connect him with the cult of Dionysus. Diodorus says he introduced the cult to Greece.

Osiris   Mythical god-king of Egypt, a world-conquering hero whose worship was popular in Diodorus' day.

Osymandias   A king of Egypt, probably Ramesses II, c. 1290-1224 B.C., and builder of the famed Ramesseum at Thebes.

Oxyrhynchus   The present day town of el-Bahnasa, west of the Nile about forty miles south of the Faiyum.

Pan   Goat-legged god of rural Arcadia. Renowned for his love of sport and fun. Invented the "pan pipes."

Panopolis   See Chemmo.

Paraetonium   Coastal city about two hundred miles west of Alexandria, Egypt. It's modern name is Mersa Matruh.

Peisistratos (or Pisistratos)   Athenian tyrant of the sixth century B.C., at whose instigation the poems of Homer were first committed to writing.

Pelusium   A strong Egyptian fortress town at the easternmost mouth of the Nile; the site is now called Tell el-Farama, which, due to shifts

in the Nile's course and to the silting of the coastline, is now miles
from the sea and even further from the river.

Persepolis   City of Persia (modern Iran) which was once the capital of
the Persian empire.

Perseus   Argive hero and son of Zeus, who slew the serpent-haired
gorgon Medusa and rescued Andromeda from the sea beast; became
king of Tiryns and founder of Mycenae.

Petes   Father of Menestheus and grandson of Erechtheus.

Pharos   Small island off the coast of Egypt at Alexandria, the site of a
famous lighthouse.

Philae   Island in the Nile near Elephantine.

Philip of Macedon   King of Macedonia (died in 336 B.C.) and father of
Alexander the Great.

Phocis   District in Greece northwest of Boeotia.

Phoenicia or Phoenicê   The coastal area of Lebanon, especially the
cities of Sidon, Tyre, Byblos, and Berytus (Beirut). The people were
noted traders and mariners.

Phrygia   A district in northwest Asia Minor.

Phthia   A district in southeastern Thessaly.

Plato   Famous Athenian philosopher, a follower of Socrates and
founder of the Academy; died in 347 B.C.

Pliny (the Elder)   C. Plinius Secundus, prominent Roman author
whose encyclopaedic *Natural History* still survives. He died in the
eruption of Mount Vesuvius in A.D. 79.

Plutarch   Greek biographer and philosopher of the first century A.D.

Pluto   Euphemistic name ("giver of wealth") for Hades, god of the
underworld.

"The Poet"   Homer.

Polycrates of Samos   Tyrant of the island of Samos in the late sixth
century B.C.

Pontus   The Black Sea.

Poseidon   Greek god of the sea, brother of Zeus.

Priapus   Greek god of fruitfulness and fertility; an ithyphallic deity.

Prometheus   A Titan who incurred the wrath of Zeus by teaching men
to make fire. The father of Deucalion.

Psammetichos I (of Saïs)   A king of Egypt in the XXVIth Dynasty,
reigning from 664-610 B.C. He reunified Egypt and was the first
king to employ Greek mercenaries.

Ptah   In the Egyptian pantheon, Ptah was originally a creator god,
patron of artisans. The Greeks sometimes identified him with their
deity Hephaestos.

Ptolemy I son of Lagus   One of Alexander the Great's successors, founder of the Ptolemaic dynasty in Egypt in 304 B.C.

Ptolemy II Philadelphos   King of Egypt, 285-246 B.C., son of Ptolemy I son of Lagus.

Ptolemy III Euergetes   King of Egypt, 246-221 B.C.

Ptolemy XII Auletes ("The New Dionysus")   King of Egypt, 80-58 and 55-51 B.C.   More or less purchased the title "Friend of the Romans" in 59 B.C.   Diodorus visited Egypt during his reign.

Pythagoras of Samos   Influential Greek philosopher of the sixth century B.C., whose teachings mixed asceticism, mysticism, and mathematics.

Pythoness of Delphi   Holy woman who spoke Apollo's oracles.

Red Sea   See Erythraean Sea.

Rhea   Wife and sister of Kronos.

Rhinocolura (Rhinocorura)   The modern el-Arish on the northeast coast of Egypt, about seventy miles east of Pelusium.

Rome   The city in west-central Italy which, in Diodorus' day, was the dominant power in the Mediterranean region.

Sabaco   Shabaka the Numidian, first king of the XXVth Dynasty in Egypt, ruling c. 712-698 B.C.

Saïs   City in the western Nile Delta, the modern Sa el-Hagar.

Samos   Greek island off the coast of Ionia, opposite Ephesus. Its capital was also named Samos.

Scythia   A general name for the vast Eurasian land mass north of the Black Sea and the Caucasus range.

Selenê   Greek moon goddess, later identified with Artemis, and sister of Helios.

Seleucus   One of Alexander the Great's successors, founder of the Seleucid dynasty in Asia.

Semelê   Daughter of Cadmus; mother of Dionysus by Zeus.

Semiramis   Legendary queen of Assyria.

Seneca   Roman statesman and philosopher; tutor and advisor to the emperor Nero, at whose order he died in A.D. 65.

Serapis   Egyptian deity combining elements of Osiris and Apis; Serapis was declared the state god by Ptolemy I, but his cult spread widely and was more popular in Greece and Rome than in Egypt.

Serbonis, Lake   Center of a swampy area to the east of the Nile Delta.

Sesoösis (or Sesostris)   Legendary world-conquering early king of Egypt (usually called Sesostris).

Set (or Seth)   See Typhon.

Shabaka   See Sabaco.

Sicily   The large island southwest of Italy. Diodorus was born there. In his day Rome ruled the island with its large Greek population.

Sidon   Important mercantile city of Phoenicia, south of Beirut.

Sinai Peninsula   The territory between the Nile Delta and Palestine, bounded on the south by the gulfs of Aqaba and Suez.

Sirius   God of the dog-star, whose rising inaugurated the Athenian new year.

Solon   Lawgiver of the Athenians and reformer of their constitution in 594 B.C. He was also a respected poet.

Sparta   Xenophobic and militaristic Greek city-state, for centuries the leading power in the Peloponnese; also known as Lacedaemon.

Strabo   Greek geographer, c. 58 B.C.-A.D. 24.

Syene   City on the site of modern Aswan, near the first cataract of the Nile in southern Egypt.

Syracuse   Originally a Greek colony, this was long the most important city in Sicily.

Syria   In a restricted sense, this name was applied to the fertile lands north and northeast of Palestine. In an extended sense, it encompassed the non-desert parts of what we now call Israel, Lebanon, northern Syria, and northwestern Iraq, i.e., the areas north and northwest of Arabia (q.v.).

Syrtis, Gulf of   (1) Syrtis Major: the modern Gulf of Sidra off the coast of Libya. This was the region where the Nasamonians once dwelt. (2) Syrtis Minor: the modern Gulf of Gabes, off the eastern coast of Tunisia.

Susa   Winter residence of the Persian kings, now called Shush, in modern Iran.

Tanaïs, River   The modern Don, in Russia, flowing into the Black Sea.

Tartarus   Alternate name for Hades.

Telemachos   Son of Odysseus.

Tethys   Wife of Oceanus.

Thales   Early Ionic philosopher and sage, c. 636-546 B.C.

Thebaid   The area just around Egyptian Thebes, although Diodorus seems sometimes to include much of southern Egypt within the extended meaning of the term.

Thebes   (1) Egyptian Thebes: one of the major cities of ancient Egypt, in the southern part of the country at the site of modern Luxor. It was often the capital city. (2) Boeotian Thebes: the metropolis of the central Grecian district known as Boeotia. Said to have been founded by Cadmus.

Theophrastus   Greek philosopher, the student and successor of Aristotle, whose philosophy he further developed. He died c. 287 B.C.

Theopompos of Chios   Greek historian, born c. 378 B.C., whose work survives only in fragments.

Thessaly   Area on the eastern Greek mainland south of Macedonia.

Thrace   An area including the modern districts of European Turkey, southern Bulgaria, and northeastern Greece, and sometimes including also the lands extending as far north as the river Danube.

Thucydides   Athenian historian, c. 457-401 B.C., whose *Peloponnesian War* is one of the classics of world literature.

Triptolemus   Agricultural expert in Osiris' army, according to Diodorus. In Greek myth, he was the bringer of the gift of agriculture from Demeter to mankind.

Triton, River   A brook in Boeotia.

Tritonis, Lake   A lake in Libya, variously placed by different ancient writers from Cyrenaica to Mauretania, but probably to be identified with one of the salt lakes of modern Tunisia.

Troy (Ilium)   (1) The famous city in northwestern Asia Minor, scene of the Trojan war, c. 1180 B.C. It is at the site of modern Hissarlik in Turkey. (2) A town in ancient Egypt a little south of Giza; possibly the modern Tura.

Typhon   Egyptian god who murdered Osiris, his brother, in an attempt to usurp his rule. Also known as Seth or Set.

Uchoreus   According to Diodorus, Uchoreus, the eighth descendant of Osymandias, was the Egyptian king who founded Memphis. His father was also named Uchoreus.

Upper Egypt   See Egypt, Upper.

Vitruvius   Roman engineer of the first century B.C., whose book on architecture gives valuable insights into ancient building practices and theories.

Xenophon   Prominent Athenian writer and historian, c. 430-369 B.C.

Xerxes   King of Persia, 486-466 B.C.   Invaded Greece in 480 B.C., but was defeated at Salamis.

Zalmoxis   Thracian cult figure.

Zeus   Chief god of the Greek pantheon.

Appendix II: Terminology

Aramaic   An ancient Semitic language of southwestern Asia, adopted as a *lingua franca* by many peoples, including the Jews, in the centuries before the Christian era.

Areopagites (The Areopagus)   The Athenian Council of Elders, whose name derives from one of their meeting places, the Hill of Ares, and having some political powers as well as judicial competence in cases of homicide and arson.

Barbarian   The term merely connoted "non-Greek," without any necessary implication of savagery or lack of civilization.

Book of the Dead   An Egyptian collection of magical formulae and advice for the benefit of the dead; its purpose was to guide and protect them in their journey to the next world.

Celts   A powerful people whose various branches inhabited much of central and western Europe in Diodorus' day, especially Britain, France, northern Italy, and parts of Germany. These were the fierce "Gauls" whom Caesar conquered, and whose Gaelic-speaking descendants still are found in parts of Ireland, Scotland, Wales, and Brittany.

Chaldeans   To Diodorus, the term signified the Babylonian priests reputedly skilled in magic, astronomy, divination, and astrology.

Colossi (singular Colossus)   Larger-than-life statues depicting humans.

Coptic   Language of the Copts, the pre-Arab descendants of the ancient Egyptians.

Cubit   The theoretical distance from the elbow to the tip of the middle finger. The actual value varied over time and place, but was usually close to eighteen inches.

147

Dorians   One of the major divisions of the ancient Greek people; the Dorians conquered the earlier Mycenaean civilization in the Peloponnese and ruled there from about 1100 B.C.

Drachma   Greek unit of value, equal by weight to one hundredth of a mina, or sixty-seven grains of silver (approximately .154 ounces).

Elders of the Lacedaemonians   The aristocratic Council of Elders at Sparta, known as the Gerousia, consisting of thirty members elected for life and exercising elements of political, legislative, and judicial power.

Equinox   The point in spring or fall when day and night are of equal length. In the modern calendar, the equinox occurs approximately March 21 and September 23.

Eumolpidae   The descendants of Eumolpos, and the hereditary priests of Demeter at Eleusis.

Eupatridae   The ancient Athenian nobility.

Fathom   The length of the outstretched arms, or approximately six feet (*orgyia* in Greek).

Finger   The width of a finger, about 2/3 of an inch, used as a measure of length.

Flamen Dialis   One of the principal priests of the Roman state religion.

Foot   The Greek foot was approximately 12.15 inches.

Giants (Gigantes)   Monstrous offspring of Ge and the blood of Uranus.

Hellenic   Adjective essentially synonymous with "Greek."

Hellenistic   Of or relating to Greek culture in the context of its widespread influence after the conquests of Alexander the Great.

Hittites   An ancient race of Asia Minor whose empire, finally destroyed about 1200 B.C., was in frequent conflict with the expanding Egyptian empire in northern Syria at that time.

Hyksos   A non-Egyptian people, probably from Asia Minor, who conquered most of Egypt about 1640 B.C. and, constituting the XVth and XVIth dynasties, was not finally driven out until approximately 1532 B.C.

Ithyphallic   Of or relating to phallic worship.

Middle Kingdom   The period in Egyptian history from c. 2040-1640 B.C., comprising the XIth to the XIVth dynasties.

Mina   A Greek measure of value equal to 100 drachmae; as a weight, 1/60 of a talent (approximately 15.4 ounces).

Minotaur   The mythical half man, half bull monster inhabiting the Cretan Labyrinth.

Muses   The nine maiden goddesses of Greek myth, daughters of Zeus, whose special concern was poetry, music, and the other arts.

New Kingdom   The period in Egyptian history from c. 1550-1070 B.C., comprising the XVIIIth, XIXth, and XXth dynasties.

Nomarch   Governor of a nome in Egypt.

Nome   Administrative subdivision of Egypt.

Old Kingdom   The period in Egyptian history from c. 2575-2134 B.C., comprising the IVth to the VIIIth dynasties.

Olympiad   The four-year, sequentially numbered period between successive Olympic games, used as a chronological reference by the Greeks.

Palm   A measure of length, about three or four inches; the theoretical width of a man's palm.

Pans   Beings of Greek mythology derived from the Arcadian god Pan, and somewhat akin to Satyrs in their goat-like features and love of sensual pleasure. Pans frequented primarily rural, pastoral settings.

Phalanx   Greek and Macedonian infantry formation consisting of massed spearmen; this was the primary combat unit of Hellenic military science.

Plethron (plural Plethra)   One sixth of a stade, or approximately 101 English feet.

Predynastic Era   The period prior to the unification of Upper and Lower Egypt under the Ist dynasty in c. 2920 B.C.

Ptolemaic Period   Period of Macedonian rule by the house of Ptolemy in Egypt, from 304 to 30 B.C.

Pyramid texts   Early mortuary literature of Egypt, usually engraved in the passages of pyramid tombs for the benefit of the dead.

Schoinos (plural schoinoi)   An Egyptian land measurement varying from thirty to one hundred and twenty stades, or three and one-half to fourteen miles (often spelled schoenus, schoeni in English).

Saïte Era   The period of the XXVIth dynasty of Egypt, which ruled from Saïs in the Delta from 664-525 B.C.

Satrap   Ruler of a province in the Persian empire.

Satyrs   Mythical half-human beings with goat-like characteristics who were connected with the revels of Dionysus. They were fond of wine and all other sensual pleasures.

Seven Works of Wonder   The seven wonders of the world, which included the Great Pyramid, the hanging gardens of Babylon, the Mausoleum, etc.

Solstice   The day in mid-summer (or mid-winter) when the sun seemingly "stands still" before reversing its daily ascent from (or descent toward) the equator. The solstice occurs approximately June 22 and December 22 in the modern calendar.

Stade   Also called the stadium, it was the ordinary Greek measure of distance, usually equal to 606 and two-thirds English feet, but subject to variation in different eras and countries.

Talent   A measure of weight; the Attic talent was the equivalent of approximately 57.85 lbs. (English).

Titans   In Greek myth, these were the children of Uranus, the sky god, and Ge, the earth goddess. One of their number, Kronos, dethroned his father Uranus, only to be dethroned in turn by his own offspring Zeus.

Trogodytes   Diodorus vaguely uses this term to designate certain tribes in the interior of Ethiopia (q.v.). Although most Greek writers imaginatively added a letter to make the word "troglodytes," meaning cave dwellers, Diodorus seems to follow an earlier pronunciation of unknown signification.

Wadi   Arabic term for stream bed or valley, especially one which is dry for long periods.

Appendix III: Chronology

Readers unfamiliar with ancient Egyptian chronology will find the account given in Book I of the *Library of History* confusing. Not only is Diodorus wrong in many chronological aspects, but he does not present his material in a straightforward, organized manner. He also leaves gaps in his history for which he gives no information, covering intervals of centuries with phrases such as "many generations later . . . ." Add to this the controversies of Egyptian chronology as debated by modern Egyptologists, and it is inevitable that a nonspecialist will find it difficult to reconcile Diodorus' account with the actual historical record.

This appendix provides a general outline of Diodorus' chronology and compares it, to the extent possible, with one widely accepted timeline of Egyptian history. No attempt is made to give a detailed overview of Egyptian chronology, but only to relate the sequence and approximate dates of Diodorus' kings to those of their real-life counterparts and to the periods and dynasties into which researchers divide Egyptian history.

Despite his confused presentation and his ignorance (in common with all people of that age) about the real ancient history of Egypt, Diodorus is more internally consistent than he appears at first glance. From Menas, the first mortal ruler of Egypt, up to the Persian conquest, Diodorus tries to give a connected history based on the reigns and deeds of prominent kings. Since according to Diodorus this period lasted almost 5,000 years, the two dozen kings mentioned by name give only the barest outline of the purported chronology. From about 800 B.C., Diodorus has the correct sequence of kings, but his dates are increasingly distorted as he goes further back in time: for instance, he places Amasis about 50 years too late, and Bocchoris about 80 years too early. Diodorus had a fairly accurate idea of Egyptian history after 525

B.C., which was well known to writers of the day. But Book I is not concerned with recent history, which is reserved for later books, and Diodorus makes only incidental references to events after the Persian conquest.

For events and personages earlier than Bocchoris, Diodorus is hopelessly lost. He places the IVth Dynasty pyramid builders just prior to Bocchoris, over 1,500 years too late, although even here he has the sequence of kings correct. Everything else, however, is legend. Osymandias, Sesoösis, Cetes, and Busiris can be located at least approximately on Diodorus' timeline, but they are shadowy figures who cannot be linked with certainty to real kings of Egypt.

CHRONOLOGY OF EGYPTIAN HISTORY ACCORDING TO BOOK I OF DIODORUS SICULUS

(See note at end of table)

Years B.C.	Diodorus' Chronology	Actual Chronology	Period
(23,000–5,000)	The reigns of gods and heroes: Helios, Hephaestos, Kronos, Zeus, Osiris, Isis and Horus.		
5,000	Menas, c. 5,000 B.C. (52)		
4,000	Busiris I, c. 4,000 B.C. (7) Busiris II, c. 3,800 B.C.		
3,000	(?)	Na'rmer	LATE PREDYNASTIC PERIOD
2,900 2,800 2,700 2,600	Osymandias (= Ramesses II?) (6)	Menes ('Aha) Khufu (= Chemmis)	EARLY DYNASTIC PERIOD 2920–2575 B.C. Dynasties I to III

Years B.C.	Diodorus' Chronology	Actual Chronology	Period
2,500	Uchoreus I Uchoreus II Egyptus	Kephren (= Cephren) Menkaure' (= Mycerinos)	OLD KINGDOM 2575–2134 B.C. Dynasties IV to VIII
2,400 2,300 2,200	(11)		
2,100	Moeris		(intermediate period)
2,000	(6) ... Sesoosis I (= Senwosret I?)	Amenemhet I, Senwosret I	MIDDLE KINGDOM 2040–1640 B.C. Dynasties XI to XIV
1,900 1,800 1,700	Sesoosis II		
1,600	(?)		(intermediate period)
1,500 1,400	Amasis I Actisanes Mendes, or Marrus (5)	Tuthmosis II	NEW KINGDOM 1550–1070 B.C. Dynasties XVIII to XX
1,300		Tut'ankhamun	
1,200	Cetes, or Proteus Remphis	Ramesses II	

1,100			
1,000	(7)		
900	Chemmis (= Khufu)		
	Cephren (= Kephren)		
	Mycerinos (= Menkaure')		
	Tnephachthos (= Tefnakhte)		
800	Bocchoris the Wise	Tefnakhte (= Tnephachthos)	
750		Bocchoris	
700	(?)	Shabaka (= Sabaco)	
		Necho I	
650	Sabaco (= Shabaka)	Psammetichos I (of Saïs)	
	The Twelve Kings		
600	Psammetichos I of Saïs	Necho II	
	(3)	Apries	
550	Apries	Amasis	LATE PERIOD
	Amasis II	Cambyses	712–332 B.C.
500	Cambyses	Darius I	Dynasties XXV to XXX
	Darius I	Xerxes I	
450	Xerxes I		
400			
350			

(intermediate period)

Years B.C.	Diodorus' Chronology	Actual Chronology	Period
	Alexander the Great	Alexander the Great	
300	Ptolemy I Son of Lagus	Ptolemy I Son of Lagus	
	Ptolemy II Philadelphos	Ptolemy II Philadelphos	
250			MACEDONIAN PERIOD 332–30 B.C.
200	Ptolemy III Euergetes	Ptolemy III Euergetes	
150			
100			
50	Ptolemy XII Auletes	Ptolemy XII Auletes	

NOTE: The numbers in parentheses refer to generations which Diodorus says intervened between various kings. Only for the fifty-two generation interval after Menas does Diodorus give a number of years, 1040, but from this we can infer that he thought of a generation as equal to about twenty years. A question mark in parentheses (?) indicates an interval for which Diodorus does not give an actual number of generations but expresses himself in terms such as "many generations later...."

Although the sequence of kings from Osymandias to Sesoösis II is fairly precise, spanning about 600 years, it is hard to place the whole sequence in the timeline because it is both preceded and followed by indeterminate intervals. Sesoösis has been located on the chart according to the fairly common assumption that he reflects the exploits of kings of the early XIIth Dynasty.

Select Bibliography

The bibliography includes most of the books consulted in the preparation of the footnotes and appendices. In the interest of brevity, however, it includes only a few of the more important journal and periodical articles.

Ancient Sources

Aelian, *Varia Historia*, edited by Rudolph Herscher. Lipsiae: Teubner, 1866.

(Agatharchides). Included in *The Periplus of the Erythraean Sea*, translated by G. W. B. Huntingford. London: Hakluyt Society, 1976.

(Anaxagoras). Included in *Early Greek Philosophy*, translated by Jonathan Barnes. London: Penguin Books, 1987.

Apollodorus. *Gods and Heroes of the Greeks: The "Library" of Apollodorus*, translated by Michael Simpson. Amherst: University of Massachusetts Press, 1976.

Apuleius. *The Golden Ass*, translated by William Adlington. London: The Navarre Society, 1924.

Aristophanes. *The Wasps*, translated by Douglas Parker. New York: New American Library (Mentor), 1962.

Aristotle. *History of Animals*, translated by Richard Cresswell. Bohn's Classical Library, 1862.

Aristotle. *The Works of Aristotle*, edited by David Ross. Oxford: The Clarendon Press, 1930.

Arrian. *Anabasis of Alexander* and *Indica*, translated by James Chinnock. London: George Bell and Sons, 1893.

Arrian. *The Campaigns of Alexander*, translated by Aubrey de Selincourt. Revised edition. Bungay, Suffolk: Penguin Books, 1971.

The Bible.

Censorinus. *De Die Natale*, translated by William Maude. New York: The Cambridge Encyclopedia Company, 1900.
Cicero. *The Treatises of M. T. Cicero on the Nature of the Gods, on Divination, etc.*, translated by C. D. Yonge. Bohn's Libraries. London: George Bell and Sons, 1892.
Cicero. *Tusculan Disputations*, translated by Andrew P. Peabody. Boston: Little, Brown, and Company, 1886.
Cicero. *Tusculan Disputations*, translated by C. D. Yonge. New York: Harper and Brothers, Publishers, 1877.
Curtius, Quintus. *History of Alexander*, translated by John C. Rolfe. The Loeb Classical Library. Cambridge, Massachusetts: Harvard University Press, 1971.

Diodorus Siculus. *The Antiquities of Asia: A Translation with Notes of Book II of the "Library of History" of Diodorus Siculus*, translated by Edwin Murphy. New Brunswick, New Jersey: Transaction Publishers, 1989.
Diodori Siculi. *Bibliothecae Historicae Quae Supersunt*, Greek text edited and translated into Latin by L. Dindorf. Paris: Didot, 1842-1844.
Diodorus Siculus. *The Historical Library of Diodorus the Sicilian*, translated by G. Booth. London: 1700.
Diodorus Siculus. *The History of Diodorus Siculus*, translated by Henry Cogan. London, 1653.
Diodorus Siculus. *The Library of History*, translated by C. H. Oldfather *et al.* Loeb Classical Library, 12 volumes. Cambridge, Massachusetts: Harvard University Press, 1933-1967.

Eusebius. *Chronicorum*, edited by Alfred Schoene. Second edition. Dublin: Weidmann, 1967.

Heliodorus. *Aethiopica*, translated by Thomas Underdowne. Revised and edited by F. A. Wright. London: George Routledge and Sons, Ltd., n.d.
Herodotus. *Histories*, translated by G. Rawlinson. Revised and annotated by A. W. Lawrence. London: The Nonesuch Press, 1935.
Herodotus. *The Histories*, translated by Aubrey de Selincourt. Bungay, Suffolk: Penguin Books, 1965.

Hesiod: The Poems and Fragments, translated by A. W. Mair. Oxford: The Clarendon Press, 1908.

Hippocrates. Translated by W. H. S. Jones. Loeb Classical Library. Cambridge, Massachusetts: Harvard University Press, 1923.

Homer. *The Homeric Hymns*, translated by Thelma Sargent. New York: W. W. Norton and Company, 1973.

Homer. *The Iliad*, translated by Alexander Pope. New York: The Heritage Press, 1943.

Homer. *The Odessey*, translated by E. V. Rieu. Ayelsbury: Penguin Books, 1946.

Josephus. *The Jewish War*, translated by G. A. Williamson. Aylesbury: Penguin Books, 1959.

Josephus. *The Works of Josephus*, translated by William Whiston. Reprint. Philadelphia: David McKay, Publisher, 1899.

Juvenal. *The Sixteen Satires*, translated by Peter Green. Baltimore: Penguin Books, 1967.

Lucian of Samosata. *Works*, translated by H. W. and F. G. Fowler. Oxford: The Clarendon Press, 1905.

Lucretius. *On the Nature of the Universe*. Harmondsworth, Middlesex: Penguin Books, 1977.

Periplus of the Erythaean Sea, translated by G. W. B. Huntingford. London: Hakluyt Society, 1976.

The Periplus of the Erythraean Sea, translated by Wilfred H. Schoff. New York: Longmans, Green, and Company, 1912.

Philo of Alexandria. *De Animalibus*, translated and edited by Abraham Terian. Chico, California: Scholars Press, 1981.

Photius. *Bibliothèque*, texte et traduit par René Henry. Paris: Société d'Editione "Les Belles Lettres," 1959.

Pliny. *Natural History*, translated by H. Rackham. Loeb Classical Library. Cambridge, Massachusetts: Harvard University Press, 1962.

Plutarch. *Lives of the Noble Grecians and Romans*, translated by Thomas North. New York: Limited Editions Club, 1941.

Plutarch. *On Isis and Osiris*, translated by Frank Cole Babbitt (volume V, *Plutarch's "Moralia"*). The Loeb Classical Library. Cambridge, Massachusetts: Harvard University Press, 1969.

(Seneca). *Physical Science in the Time of Nero: Being a Translation of the "Quaestiones Naturales" of Seneca*, translated by John Clark. London: Macmillan and Company, Limited, 1910.
Strabo. *The Geography*, translated by H. C. Hamilton and W. Falconer. Bohn's Libraries. London: George Bell and Sons, 1913.

Theophrastus. *Enquiry Into Plants*, translated by Arthur Hort. Loeb Classical Library. Cambridge, Massachusetts: Harvard University Press, n.d.

Vitruvius. *The Ten Books on Architecture*, translated by Morris Hickey Morgan. Reprint. New York: Dover Publications, 1960.

Modern Sources

Adcock, F. E. *The Greek and Macedonian Art of War*. Berkeley, California: The University of California Press, 1957.
Africa, Thomas J. "Herodotus and Diodorus on Egypt," *Journal of Near Eastern Studies*, v. XXII, October 1963; pp. 254-258.
Aharoni, Yohanan and Avi-Yonah, Michael. *The MacMillan Bible Atlas*. New York: MacMillan Publishing Company, Inc., 1968.
Andrews, Carol. *Egyptian Mummies*. London: The British Museum, 1984.
Angus, S. *The Mystery Religions*, reprint. New York: Dover Publications, Inc., 1975.

Baines, John and Malek, Jaromir. *Atlas of Ancient Egypt*. New York: Facts On File Publications, 1980.
Barker, William P. *Everyone in the Bible*. Old Tappan, New Jersey: Fleming H. Revell Company, 1966.
Bevan, Edwyn R. *The House of Ptolemy: A History of Hellenistic Egypt Under the Ptolemaic Dynasty*. Reprint. Chicago: Ares Publishers, Inc., 1985.
Bowder, Diana, editor. *Who Was Who in the Greek World*. Oxford: Phaidon Press, 1982.
Bowder, Diana, editor. *Who Was Who in the Roman World*. Oxford: Phaidon Press, 1980.
Bowman, Alan K. *Egypt After the Pharaohs*. Berkeley, California: University of California Press, 1986.

Breasted, James Henry. *The Edwin Smith Surgical Papyrus.* California: University of California Press, 1930.

Breasted, James Henry. *Egypt: A Journey Through the Land of the Pharaohs: With the Stereographs of Underwood and Underwood.* Abridged reprint. New York: Camera/Graphics Press, Ltd., 1979.

Breasted, James Henry. *A History of Egypt.* Second edition. New York: Charles Scribner's Sons, 1912.

Budge, E. A. Wallis. *Egyptian Language: Easy Lessons in Egyptian Hieroglyphics.* Reprint. New York: Dover Publications, Inc., 1983.

Budge, E. A. Wallis. *From Fetish to God in Ancient Egypt.* Reprint. New York: Dover Publications, Inc., 1988.

Bunbury, E. H. *A History of Ancient Geography.* Second edition. New York: Dover Publications, 1959.

Burton, Anne. *Diodorus Siculus: Book I, A Commentary.* Leiden: E. J. Brill, 1972.

Bury, J. B. *A History of Greece.* Revised edition. New York: The Modern Library, 1913.

Butler, Alfred J. *The Arab Conquest of Egypt and the Last Thirty Years of the Roman Dominion.* Oxford: The Clarendon Press, 1902.

deCamp, L. Sprague. *The Ancient Engineers.* New York: Doubleday and Company, 1960.

Carpenter, Rhys. *Beyond the Pillars of Heracles.* New York: Delacorte Press, 1966.

Casson, Lionel. *Ancient Egypt.* New York: Time-Life Books, 1965.

Cimmino, Franco. *Ramesses II, il Grande.* Milan: Rusconi, 1984.

Clagett, Marshall. *Greek Science in Antiquity.* New York: Collier Books, 1955.

Cory, Isaac Preston. *Ancient Fragments.* Reprint of 1832 edition. Minneapolis: Wizard's Bookshelf, 1975.

Cumont, Franz. *Astrology and Religion Among the Greeks and Romans.* New York: G. P. Putnam's Sons, 1912.

David, Rosalie. *The Egyptian Kingdoms.* Oxford: Elsevier/Phaidon, 1975.

Davies, Nigel. *Human Sacrifice in History and Today.* New York: Dorset Press, 1981.

Dilke, O. A. W. *Mathematics and Measurement.* London: British Museum Publications, Ltd., 1987.

Drews, Robert. "Diodorus and His Sources," *American Journal of Philology,* v. LXXXIII, October 1962; pp. 383-392.

Drews, Robert. *The Historiographical Objectives and Procedures of Diodorus Siculus*, dissertation. Baltimore: The Johns Hopkins University, 1960.

Ebers, A. *L'Egypte du Caire à Philae.* Paris, 1881.
Encyclopaedia Britannica, 1957 edition.
Encyclopaedia Universalis. *The World Atlas of Archaeology.* English Edition. New York: Portland House, 1988.
Encyclopaedia Universalis. *The World Atlas of Architecture.* English Edition. New York: Portland House, 1988.
Everyman's Library. *Atlas of Ancient and Classical Geography.* London: J. M. Dent and Sons, Ltd., 1948.

Fairservice, Walter A. *The Ancient Kingdoms of the Nile.* New York: The New American Library (Mentor), 1962.
France, Commission Des Monuments D'Egypt. *Description De L'Egypte.*
Frazer, James George. *The Golden Bough: A Study in Magic and Religion.* One volume abridged edition. New York: The Macmillan Company, 1963.
Freed, Rita. *Ramesses the Great.* Memphis, Tennessee: City of Memphis, 1988.

Gager, John G. *Moses in Greco-Roman Paganism.* Nashville, Tennessee: Abingdon Press, 1972.
Gordon, Cyrus H. *Forgotten Scripts: Their Ongoing Discovery and Decipherment.* Revised and enlarged edition. New York: Dorset Press, 1987.
Graves, Robert. *The Greek Myths.* Baltimore: Penguin Books, 1955.
Graves, Robert. *The White Goddess.* Amended and enlarged edition. New York: Farrar, Straus and Giroux, 1966.
Green, Roger Lancelyn. *Tales of Ancient Egypt.* Harmondsworth, Middlesex: Penguin Books, 1967.
Griffiths, J. G. "Diodorus Siculus I.22.4f." *The Classical Review,* v. XXIII (n.s.), March 1973; p. 9.
Griffiths, J. G. "Diodorus Siculus I.47.3." *The Classical Review,* v. LXII, December, 1946; pp. 114ff.
Griffiths, J. G. "Shelly's *Ozymandias* and Diodorus Siculus." *The Modern Language Review,* v. XLII, January, 1948; pp. 80-84.

Grollenberg, L. H. *Atlas of the Bible*, translated and edited by Joyce M. H. Reid and H. H. Rowley. London: Thomas Nelson and Sons, Ltd., 1956.

Hamlyn, Paul, editor. *Egyptian Mythology*. New York: Tudor Publishing Company, 1965.

Hobson, Christine. *The World of the Pharaohs*. New York: Thames and Hudson, 1987.

James, Thomas Garnet Henry. *The Archaeology of Ancient Egypt*. New York: Henry Z. Walck, 1972.

Keller, Werner. *The Bible As History*, translated by William Neil. London: Hodden and Stoughton, 1969.

Kinder, Herman and Hilgemann, Werner. *The Anchor Atlas of World History*, translated by Ernest A. Menze. Garden City, New York: Anchor Press/Doubleday, 1974.

Kravitz, David. *Who's Who in Greek and Roman Mythology*. New York: Clarkson N. Potter, Inc., Publisher, 1975.

Lamy, Lucie. *Egyptian Mysteries*. New York: Crossroad, 1981.

Lane, Mary Ellen. *Guide to the Antiquities of the Fayyum*. Cairo: The American University in Cairo Press, 1985.

Leeder, S. H. *Modern Sons of the Pharaohs*. London: Stodder and Houghton, 1918.

Lempriere, J. *Classical Dictionary*. Revised edition by F. A. Wright. Reprint. London: Bracken Books, 1984.

Levi, Peter. *Atlas of the Greek World*. New York: Facts On File Publications, 1980.

Liddell, Henry George and Scott, Robert. *A Greek-English Lexicon*. New, revised edition. Oxford: The Clarendon Press, 1940.

Lurker, Manfred. *The Gods and Symbols of Ancient Egypt: An Illustrated Dictionary*. New York: Thames and Hudson, 1980.

Manniche, Lisa. *An Ancient Egyptian Herbal*. London: The British Museum, 1989.

Mantinband, James H. *Dictionary of Greek Literature*. Paterson, New Jersey: Littlefield, Adams, and Company, 1963.

Mantinband, James H. *Dictionary of Latin Literature*. Paterson, New Jersey, 1964.

Mertz, Barbara. *Temples, Tombs, and Hieroglyphs: A Popular History of Ancient Egypt.* New York: Dodd, Meade and Company, 1978.
Michalowski, Kazimierz. *Karnak.* Munich: Anton Schroll and Company, 1970.
Murnane, William J. *The Penguin Guide to Ancient Egypt.* Harmondsworth, Middlesex: Penguin Books, 1983.

Newberry, Percy. *Beni Hasan, Part I.* London: Egypt Exploration Society, Archaeological Survey of Egypt (Memoir #13), 1893.

Oates, Joan. *Babylon.* Revised edition. London: Thames and Hudson, 1986.
Otto, Walter F. *Dionysus: Myth and Cult.* Reprint. Dallas: Spring Publications, 1981.

Parr, J. "Shelley's *Ozymandias* Again," *The Modern Language Review,* v. XLVI, July 1951; pp. 441-442.
Pearson, Lionel. *The Lost Histories of Alexander the Great.* New York: The American Philological Association, 1960.
Petrie, W. M. Flinders. *Hawara, Biahmu, and Arsinoë.* London: Trubner and Company, 1889.
Petrie, W. M. Flinders. *The Labyrinth, Gerzeh, and Mazghuneh.* London: School of Archaeology in Egypt, University College (London), 1912.
Pritchard, James B., editor. *The Ancient Near East: An Anthology of Texts and Pictures.* Princeton: Princeton University Press, 1958.

Quibell, J. E. *The Ramesseum.* London: Bernard Quaritch, 1898.

Le Ramesseum. Cairo: Centre de Documentation et d'etudes sur l'ancienne Egypte, 1973.
Rhymer, Joseph. *Atlas of the Biblical World.* New York: Greenwich House, 1982.
Robatham, D. M. "Diodorus Siculus in the Italian Renaissance," *Classical Philology,* v. XXVII, January 1932; pp. 84ff.
Rogerson, John. *Atlas of the Bible.* New York: Facts On File Publications, 1985.

Samuel, Rinna. *The Negev and Sinai.* Jerusalem: Weidenfeld and Nicolson, 1973.

Scott, J. A. "Diodorus and Homer," *Classical Journal*, v. XXII, April 1927; pp. 540-541.

Scott, Joseph and Scott, Lenore. *Egyptian Hieroglyphics for Everyone.* New York: Funk and Wagnalls, 1968.

Seligman, Kurt. *The History of Magic.* New York: Pantheon Books, 1948.

Service des Antiquitiés De L'Egypte. *Catalogue Générale des Antiquitiés Égyptiennes du Musée du Caire.* Die Demotischen Papyrus, Text. Cairo: 1908.

Seton-Williams, Veronica. *Egypt (Blue Guide to Egypt).* New York: W. W. Norton, 1983.

Shinnie, P. L. *Meroe.* New York: F. A. Praeger, 1967.

Smith, William, editor. *Dictionary of Greek and Roman Biography and Mythology.* Boston: Charles C. Little, and James Brown, 1849.

Smith, William, editor. *Dictionary of Greek and Roman Geography.* Boston: Little, Brown, and Company, 1854.

Smith, William. *Smaller Classical Dictionary.* Reprint. New York: E. P. Dutton, 1958.

Smith, W. Stevenson. *The Art and Architecture of Ancient Egypt.* Corrected edition. Harmondsworth, Middlesex: Penguin Books, 1965.

Spruner Von Merz, Karl. *Atlas Antiquus.* Second edition. Gotha: Justus Perthes, 1855.

Thayer, Joseph Henry, editor and translator. *A Greek-English Lexicon of the New Testament.* Corrected edition. New York: American Book Company, 1889.

Thompson, Dorothy J. *Memphis Under the Ptolemies.* Princeton, New Jersey: Princeton University Press, 1988.

Thomson, J. Oliver. *Everyman's Classical Atlas.* London: J. M. Dent and Sons, Ltd., 1963.

Thorndike, Lynn. *A History of Magic and Experimental Science.* Second printing, with corrections. New York: The MacMillan Company, 1929.

Tomlinson, R. A. E. *Argos and the Argolid: From the End of the Bronze Age to the Roman Occupation.* Ithaca, NY: Cornell University Press, 1972.

Tozer, H. F. *A History of Ancient Geography.* Second edition. New York: Biblo and Tannen, 1971.

Van der Heyden, A. M. and Scullard, H. H., editors. *Atlas of the Classical World*. London: Thomas Nelson and Sons, Ltd., 1967.

Varille, Alexandre, *Karnak*. Cairo: L'Institut Française d'Archéology Orientale, 1943.

Vlastos, G. "On the Prehistory in Diodorus," *American Journal of Philology*, v. LXVII, January 1946; pp. 51-59.

University of Chicago, Oriental Institute. *Medinet Habu VI: The Temple Proper, Part II*. Chicago: University of Chicago Press, 1963.

Webster's Geographical Dictionary. Springfield, Massachusetts: G. and C. Merriam Company, Publishers, 1969.

Weigall, E. P. *A Guide to the Antiquities of Upper Egypt from Abydos to the Sudan*. London: Methuen and Company, Ltd., 1910/1913.

West, John Anthony. *The Traveler's Key to Ancient Egypt: A Guide to the Sacred Places of Ancient Egypt*. New York: Alfred A. Knopf, 1985.

White, Jon E. Manchip. *Egypt and the Holy Land in Historic Photographs: 77 Views by Francis Frith*. New York: Dover Publications, Inc., 1980.

Wood, Roger. *Egypt in Color*. London: Readers' Union/Thames and Hudson, 1965.

Index

Topics are indexed by **chapter numbers** and then by **footnote numbers**, in that order. (For added clarity, footnote references are preceded by *n* or *nn* and are set in *italic type*.)

The index covers all significant proper names used in the text and footnotes, and also all important concepts, subjects, and ideas.

167

Semelê 23, *n46*
Semiramis 56
Seneca *n118, n131*
Senmut *n45*
Senwosret I, king *n96, n106, n116*; kiosk of *n108*
Senwosret III, king *n106*
Serapis 25
Serbonis lake 30
Serpent, horned 87, *n172*
Sesoösis I, king 53-59, *n71, n106, n114*; brother of 57; companions of 53, 54, 56; conquests of 53-55, 57, 58, *n106*; death of 58; father of 53; laws of 94; plot against 57; statue of, at Memphis 58, *n115*; stelae of 55; treatment of foreign kings 58; wife and sons of 57, 58, *n114*; works of 55-57, *nn111-114*
Sesoösis II, king 58-60, *n116*
Sesoöstris *see* Sesoösis
Seth *n27, n170*
Seven wonders of the world, or Seven works of wonder 63
Sextus Empiricus, *Outline of Pyrrhonic Philosophy n11*
Shabaka *see* Sabaco, king
Sheep 36, 87, *n78*
Shelley, Percy Bysshe, *Ozymandias n99*
Ships, shipbuilding 55, *n186*; ceremonial barks 57, 85, 92, 96 *n113, n208*
Shu *n27, n47*
Sicily 4, 34, *n6*
Sidon *n109*
Silver 33
Sinai peninsula *n118*
Sirius, star 19, *n102*
Slaves, slavery 77, 80, *n140, n149, n154*
the Slitter, in embalming ceremoney 91, *n183*
Snakes 87
Sobek *n178*
Solon the Athenian 69, 77, 79, 96, 98, *n151, n152*
Sopdet, or Sothis, star 19, *n102*
Speech *see* language

Spontaneous generation of life 7, 10, 40, *n11*
Stoic philosophers *n10*
Stone knives, ritual use of 91, *n183*
Story of Sinuhe n112
Strabo *n71, n110, n118, n119, n132, n136, n164*
Styx, river *n187, n199, n202*
Sudan *n67*
Sukhumi, Gruzinskaya S.S.R. *n109*
Sun 11, 26, 38, 50, 98, *n17, n20, n210*
Susa 46
Swine 35, *n78*
Syene 47, *n116*
Syncretism *n19, n49, n198*
Syria 28, 57, 60, 67, *n100*
Syrtis *n82*

Taboos *n141, n145*; dietary 89, *n180*; ritual guilt 91, *n183*
Taharqa, king *n92*
Tahpanhes *n134*
Tanaïs, river 55, *n109*
Tartars *n131*
Tartarus *n53*
Tauromenium *n6*
Tefenet *n27*
Telecles 98, *n211*
Telemachos 97
Tell Dafana *n134*
Thales 38
Thebaid, Egyptian 15, 22, 27, *n56*
Thebes, Boeotian 23, *n46*
Thebes, Egyptian 23, 45-50, 57, 65, 75, 87, 97, *n67, n94, n96, n97, n103, n113*; etymology *n29*; founded by Busiris 15, 45-46, *n29, n94*; founded by Osiris 15, *n29, n46*; mortuary temples of 46-49, *n95, nn97-101*
Thieves' guild 80, *n153*
Theocratic monarchies *n141*
Theodoros 98, *n211*
Theogony (Hesiod) *n38*
Theophrastus, *History of Plants n40, n74, n89*
Theopompus 37

Plate 1. The temple of Isis on the island of Philae, at the first cataract of the Nile. Photo by Francis Frith, 1856. Philae is now submerged beneath the waters of the Aswan High Dam, but the major temples, most of which existed in Diodorus' day, have been reconstructed nearby. *Library of Congress*

Plate 2.   An Egyptian raising water with the Archimedes' screw, which Diodorus calls the *cochlea*, or snail shell. Photo c. 1930.

Library of Congress: The Matson Collection

Plate 3. The papyrus plant.
Library of Congress: The Matson Collection

Plate 4. The fearsome Nile crocodile, photographed by Francis Frith about 1856 at the first cataract. Note the "closely packed rocks sticking up like peaks"—Diodorus I.30. *Library of Congress*

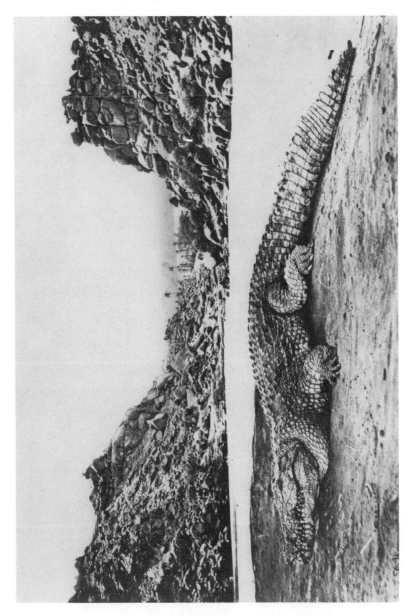

Plate 5. Statuette of the Egyptian ichneumon, or mongoose. *Courtesy of the Trustees of the British Museum*

Plate 6a. Hunting a hippopotamus with harpoon and line, as described by Diodorus. Scene from an Old Kingdom tomb. *Courtesy of Lincoln Press*

Plate 6b. Egyptian farmers driving sheep across sown fields to trample in the seed. Scene from an Old Kingdom tomb. *Courtesy of Lincoln Press*

Plate 7. The Nilometer at Philae, about 1930.
Library of Congress: The Matson Collection

Plate 8. The River Niger in Mali, 1978. Herodotus considered this to be the upper Nile, a theory rejected by Diodorus. *Courtesy of William Jegl*

Plate 9a. Slate palette, c. 2950 B.C. (obverse), showing king Na'rmer at upper left following his army. Note the animal images held aloft as standards, as described by Diodorus. The original is in the British Museum.
Courtesy of Lincoln Press

Plate 9b. Slate palette, c. 2950 B.C. (reverse), showing Na'rmer, one of the late predynastic kings, smiting his enemies.
Courtesy of Lincoln Press

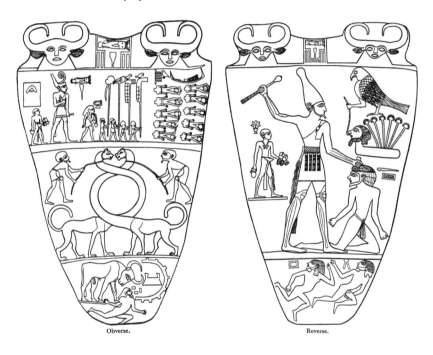

Obverse.   Reverse.

Plate 10a. Interior of the Great Hypostyle Hall in the temple of Ammon-Re' at Thebes (Karnak). Photo by Francis Frith, about 1856.
Library of Congress

Plate 10b. Plan of the temple of Ammon-Re', Thebes (Karnak).
Courtesy of Lincoln Press

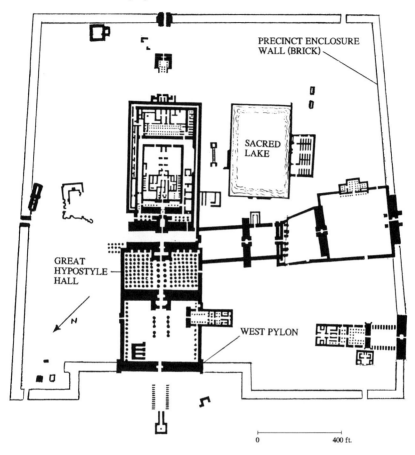

PRECINCT ENCLOSURE
WALL (BRICK)

SACRED
LAKE

GREAT
HYPOSTYLE
HALL

N

WEST PYLON

0   400 ft.

Plate 11. The vicinity of Egyptian Thebes, showing principal temple complexes.
Courtesy of Lincoln Press

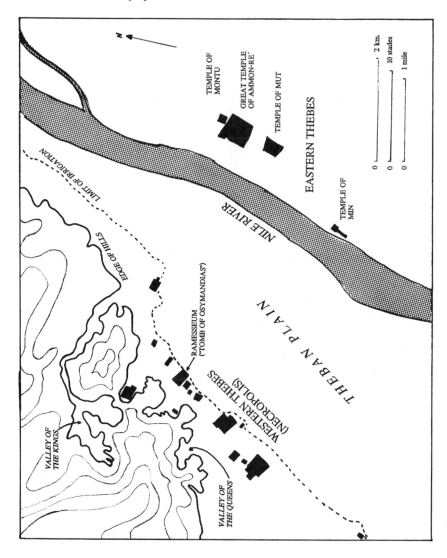

Plate 12.   Typical Egyptian temple pylon. Most temples such as the Ramesseum incorporated one or more such pylons. *Courtesy of John Bennet*

Plate 13. Plan of the Ramesseum at Thebes, which Diodorus calls the funerary temple of Osymandias. *Courtesy of Lincoln Press.*

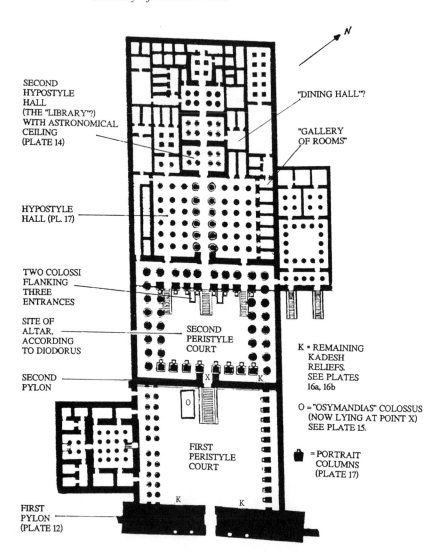

SECOND HYPOSTYLE HALL (THE "LIBRARY"?) WITH ASTRONOMICAL CEILING (PLATE 14)

"DINING HALL"?

"GALLERY OF ROOMS"

HYPOSTYLE HALL (PL. 17)

TWO COLOSSI FLANKING THREE ENTRANCES

SITE OF ALTAR, ACCORDING TO DIODORUS

SECOND PERISTYLE COURT

SECOND PYLON

K = REMAINING KADESH RELIEFS. SEE PLATES 16a, 16b

O = "OSYMANDIAS" COLOSSUS (NOW LYING AT POINT X) SEE PLATE 15.

FIRST PERISTYLE COURT

= PORTRAIT COLUMNS (PLATE 17)

FIRST PYLON (PLATE 12)

N

0   120 FT

Plate 14.   The astronomical ceiling in the second hypostyle hall of the Ramesseum, Thebes.
Courtesy of the Oriental Institute of the University of Chicago: Medinet Habu, Epigraphic Survey VI, *plate 478*

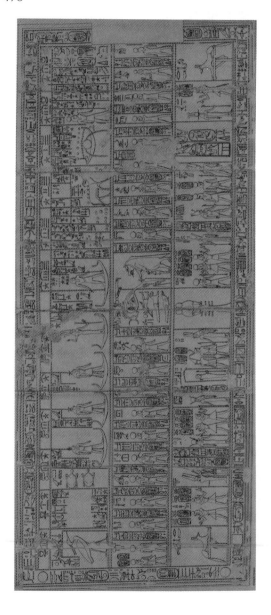

Plate 15. Fallen colossus of Ramesses II in the Ramesseum at Thebes. It originally stood fifty-seven feet high. This statue inspired Shelley's famous poem *Ozymandias*, based on the Osymandias legend preserved by Diodorus. Photo by Francis Frith, 1856.
Library of Congress

Plate 16a. Battle relief from the Ramesseum, Thebes. Ramesses II charges from the left; routed Hittites struggle to cross the Orontes River, which surrounds the city of Kadesh on the right. The lion mentioned by Diodorus appears to be a chariot ornament.
Courtesy of Lincoln Press

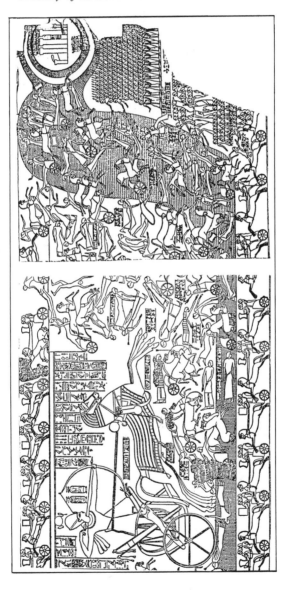

Plate 16b. A relief from the Ramesseum, Thebes. Scribes tally the number of slain Hittites by counting heaps of their severed hands, while bound captives are led away. *Courtesy of Lincoln Press*

Plate 17. Remains of the first hypostyle hall in the Ramesseum, Thebes, viewed from the east. Note the Osiriform columns and one of the entrance stair ramps.
Courtesy of John Bennet

Plate 18. The Faiyum and Birket Quarun, which Diodorus calls Lake Moeris.
Courtesy of Lincoln Press.

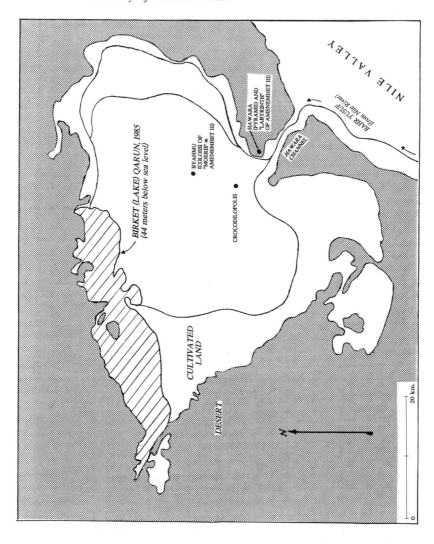

Plate 19. Portrait statue of king Senwosret III, 1878–1841 B.C., whose conquests may have contributed to the legend of Sesostris (Sesoösis). The original is in the Egyptian Museum, Cairo.
Courtesy of the Trustees of the British Museum

Plate 20. Plan of the Roman fortress of Babylon, built on the site
of earlier Egyptian fortifications.
Courtesy of Lincoln Press

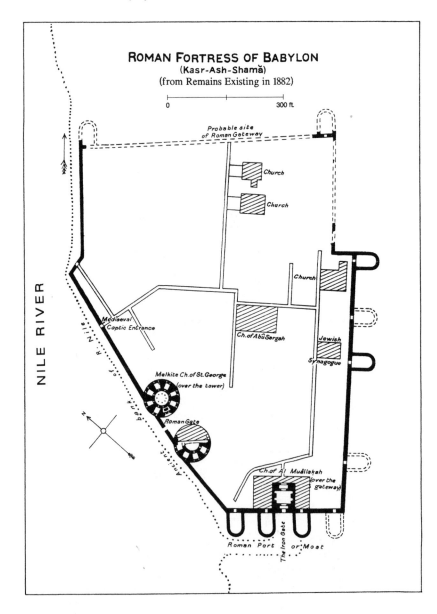

ROMAN FORTRESS OF BABYLON
(Kasr-Ash-Shamä)
(from Remains Existing in 1882)

Plate 21.   Colossus of Ramesses II from the temple of Ptah (Hephaestos) at Memphis. This may be the statue of Sesoösis
mentioned by Diodorus at I.57.
Library of Congress: The Matson Collection

Plate 22.   Obelisk of Senwosret I at Heliopolis, one of the pair that
Diodorus attributes to Sesoösis II (see I.59).
Library of Congress: The Matson Collection

Plate 23.   The Pyramids of Giza. Left to right: Menkaure' (which Diodorus calls Mycerinos), Khafre' (Chabryes), and Khufu (Chemmis). Note remains of the outer limestone casing at top of center pyramid. Photo by Francis Frith, 1856. *Library of Congress*

Plate 24. Egyptian mourners, from the papyrus of Ani.
Courtesy of the Trustees of the British Museum

Plate 25.   Samples of the three types of writing used by the Egyptians of Diodorus' day.
Courtesy of Lincoln Press

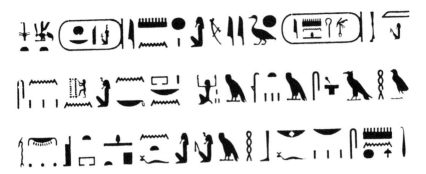

Hieroglyphic

Hieratic

Demotic

Plate 26.   Mummy of a cat.
Courtesy of the Trustees of the British Museum

Plate 27. Statuette of the Apis bull, showing some of its characteristic markings.
Courtesy of the Trustees of the British Museum

Plate 28. Mummy and painted coffin of an Egyptian priestess.
Courtesy of the Trustees of the British Museum

Plate 29. The reformed artistic canon of the Saïte period used 21 horizontal reference grids (21-1/4 according to Diodorus I.28)
Courtesy of Lincoln Press

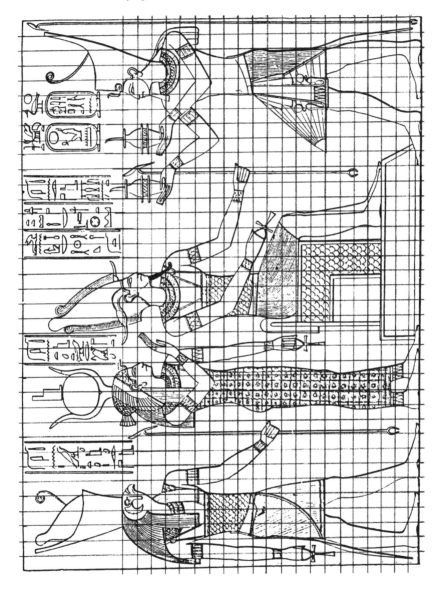